Demographic Change and Inequality in Japan

JAPANESE SOCIETY SERIES
General Editor: Yoshio Sugimoto

Lives of Young Koreans in Japan
Yasunori Fukuoka

Globalization and Social Change in Contemporary Japan
J.S. Eades, Tom Gill and Harumi Befu

Coming Out in Japan: The Story of Satoru and Ryuta
Satoru Ito and Ryuta Yanase

Japan and Its Others:
Globalization, Difference and the Critique of Modernity
John Clammer

Hegemony of Homogeneity: An Anthropological Analysis of Nihonjinron
Harumi Befu

Foreign Migrants in Contemporary Japan
Hiroshi Komai

A Social History of Science and Technology in Contempory Japan, Volume 1
Shigeru Nakayama

Farewell to Nippon: Japanese Lifestyle Migrants in Australia
Machiko Sato

The Peripheral Centre:
Essays on Japanese History and Civilization
Johann P. Arnason

A Genealogy of 'Japanese' Self-images
Eiji Oguma

Class Structure in Contemporary Japan
Kenji Hashimoto

An Ecological View of History
Tadao Umesao

Nationalism and Gender
Chizuko Ueno

Native Anthropology: The Japanese Challenge to Western Academic Hegemony
Takami Kuwayama

Youth Deviance in Japan: Class Reproduction of Non-Conformity
Robert Stuart Yoder

Japanese Companies: Theories and Realities
Masami Nomura and Yoshihiko Kamii

From Salvation to Spirituality: Popular Religious Movements in Modern Japan
Susumu Shimazono

The 'Big Bang' in Japanese Higher Education:
The 2004 Reforms and the Dynamics of Change
J.S. Eades, Roger Goodman and Yumiko Hada

Japanese Politics: An Introduction
Takashi Inoguchi

A Social History of Science and Technology in Contempory Japan, Volume 2
Shigeru Nakayama

Gender and Japanese Management
Kimiko Kimoto

Philosophy of Agricultural Science: A Japanese Perspective
Osamu Soda

A Social History of Science and Technology in Contempory Japan, Volume 3
Shigeru Nakayama and Kunio Goto

Japan's Underclass: Day Laborers and the Homeless
Hideo Aoki

A Social History of Science and Technology in Contemporary Japan, Volume 4
Shigeru Nakayama and Hitoshi Yoshioka

Scams and Sweeteners: A Sociology of Fraud
Masahiro Ogino

Toyota's Assembly Line: A View from the Factory Floor
Ryoji Ihara

Village Life in Modern Japan: An Environmental Perspective
Akira Furukawa

Social Welfare in Japan: Principles and Applications
Kojun Furukawa

Escape from Work: Freelancing Youth and the Challenge to Corporate Japan
Reiko Kosugi

Japan's Whaling: The Politics of Culture in Historical Perspective
Hiroyuki Watanabe

Gender Gymnastics: Performing and Consuming Japan's Takarazuka Revue
Leonie R. Stickland

Poverty and Social Welfare in Japan
Masami Iwata and Akihiko Nishizawa

The Modern Japanese Family: Its Rise and Fall
Chizuko Ueno

Widows of Japan: An Anthropological Perspective
Deborah McDowell Aoki

In Pursuit of the Seikatsusha:
A Genealogy of the Autonomous Citizen in Japan
Masako Amano

Demographic Change and Inequality in Japan
Sawako Shirahase

Social Stratification and Inequality Series

Inequality amid Affluence: Social Stratification in Japan
Junsuke Hara and Kazuo Seiyama

Intentional Social Change: A Rational Choice Theory
Yoshimichi Sato

Constructing Civil Society in Japan: Voices of Environmental Movements
Koichi Hasegawa

Deciphering Stratification and Inequality: Japan and beyond
Yoshimichi Sato

Social Justice in Japan: Concepts, Theories and Paradigms
Ken-ichi Ohbuchi

Gender and Career in Japan
Atsuko Suzuki

Status and Stratification: Cultural Forms in East and Southeast Asia
Mutsuhiko Shima

Globalization, Minorities and Civil Society:
Perspectives from Asian and Western Cities
Koichi Hasegawa and Naoki Yoshihara

Fluidity of Place: Globalization and the Transformation of Urban Space
Naoki Yoshihara

Advanced Social Research Series

A Sociology of Happiness
Kenji Kosaka

Frontiers of Social Research: Japan and beyond
Akira Furukawa

A Quest for Alternative Sociology
Kenji Kosaka and Masahiro Ogino

MODERNITY AND IDENTITY IN ASIA SERIES

Globalization, Culture and Inequality in Asia
Timothy S. Scrase, Todd Miles, Joseph Holden and Scott Baum

Looking for Money:
Capitalism and Modernity in an Orang Asli Village
Alberto Gomes

Governance and Democracy in Asia
Takashi Inoguchi and Matthew Carlson

Liberalism: Its Achievements and Failures
Kazuo Seiyama

Health Inequalities in Japan: An Empirical Study of Older People
Katsunori Kondo

Demographic Change and Inequality in Japan

Edited by

Sawako Shirahase

Trans Pacific Press
Melbourne

First published in Japanese in 2006 by University of Tokyo Press as *Henka suru Shakai no Fubyōdō*.
First published in English in 2011 by
Trans Pacific Press, PO Box 164, Balwyn North, Victoria 3104, Australia
Telephone: +61 (0)3 9859 1112 Fax: +61 (0)3 8611 7989
Email: tpp.mail@gmail.com
Web: http://www.transpacificpress.com

Copyright © Trans Pacific Press 2011

Designed and set by Digital Environs, Melbourne, Australia. www.digitalenvirons.com

Printed by BPA Print Group, Burwood, Victoria, Australia

Distributors

Australia and New Zealand
DA Information Services/Central Book Services
648 Whitehorse Road
Mitcham, Victoria 3132
Australia
Telephone: +61-(0)3-9210-7777
Fax: + 61-(0)3-9210-7788
Email: books@dadirect.com
Web: www.dadirect.com

USA and Canada
International Specialized Book Services (ISBS)
920 NE 58th Avenue, Suite 300
Portland, Oregon 97213-3786
USA
Telephone: 1-800-944-6190
Fax: 1-503-280-8832
Email: orders@isbs.com
Web: http://www.isbs.com

Asia and the Pacific
Kinokuniya Company Ltd.
Head office:
3-7-10 Shimomeguro
Meguro-ku
Tokyo 153-8504
Japan
Telephone: +81-(0)3-6910-0531
Fax: +81-(0)3-6420-1362
Email: bkimp@kinokuniya.co.jp
Web: www.kinokuniya.co.jp
Asia-Pacific office:
Kinokuniya Book Stores of Singapore Pte., Ltd.
391B Orchard Road #13-06/07/08
Ngee Ann City Tower B
Singapore 238874
Telephone: +65-6276-5558
Fax: +65-6276-5570
Email: SSO@kinokuniya.co.jp

All rights reserved. No reproduction of any part of this book may take place without the written permission of Trans Pacific Press.

ISSN   1443–9670 (Japanese Society Series)

ISBN   978-1-920901-63-9

Cover illustration: Three girls clad in Japanese traditional kimono, attending the ceremony of the Coming-of-Age Day, a national holiday held on the second Monday of January for people who turned 20 years old in the course of the previous year. Their demographic future remains increasingly uncertain, with a declining birthrate and increasing lifespan. Photo taken at the Heian Shrine, Kyoto. Courtesy of Noriyuki, PIXTA.

Contents

Figures	viii
Tables	ix
Contributors	xi
Acknowledgments	xiii
Introduction: The Inequalities Hidden in the Low Birthrate/Aging Society *Sawako Shirahase*	1
1 An Explosion of Inequality Consciousness: Changes in Postwar Society and 'Equalization' Strategy *Toshiki Satō*	16
2 Unequal Japan: Implications for Households and Gender *Sawako Shirahase*	46
3 Young, Japanese, and Not in Education, Employment or Training: Japan's Experience with the NEET Phenomenon *Yūji Genda*	76
4 Hidden Educational Inequalities in Postwar Japan: Misconceptions and Reconceptions *Takehiko Kariya*	98
5 Health and Inequality *Hiroshi Ishida*	125
6 Inheritance, Pensions, Childbirth, Childrearing and the Inequalities They Bring: A Case Study of Impact on Net Financial Assets *Katsumi Matsuura*	151
7 The Consequences of Applying Individual Accounting to Social Security: Public Pensions as a Form of Risk-Sharing *Naomi Miyazato*	181
Conclusion: The Changing Structure of Social Inequality in Japan *Sawako Shirahase*	203
Notes	216
Bibliography	224
Index	236

Figures

1.1:	Total number of children born to married women, 1890–1952	31
1.2:	Future/present focus of life objectives, 1973–2003	34
2.1:	Trends in the household structure and ageing population	53
2.2:	Age distribution of household head and trends in gini coefficient by age of household head	57
2.3:	Trend in poverty rates by age of household head	59
2.4:	Trends in the percentage of women in single-person households by age of household head	66
2.5:	The percentage of single-person households by decile by age of household head in 2001	69
3.1:	Non-employed Japanese aged 15–34 by stance	81
3.2:	Chief reasons for not seeking work	83
3.3:	Percentage who desire full-time, permanent employment	85
3.4:	Work preference	86
3.5:	Highest educational attainment	88
3.6:	Japanese aged 15–34 with an annual household income of more than ¥10 million	92
3.7:	Japanese aged 15–34 with an annual household income of less than ¥3 million	93
3.8:	Non-employed Japanese aged 35–49 by stance	96
6.1:	Consumption level differentials between cohorts	166
7.1:	Trends in the elderly population index	189
7.2:	Trends in profitability for high-risk and low-risk investments	192
7.3:	Trends in Japanese life expectancy	194
7.4:	Survival probability by age group for Japanese people born in 2000 and 2050	195
7.5:	Influence on optimal income-replacement rate of declining population growth	197
7.6:	Influence on optimal income-replacement rate of increasing survival probability	197

Tables

2.1:	Trends in household structure by age of household head	54
2.2:	Trend in gini coefficients by household structure and age of household head	61
2.3:	Trends in poverty rates by household structure and age of household head	64
2.4:	Marital status of single-person households by gender and age	67
2.5:	Poverty rates of single-person households by gender and age	68
2.6:	Trends in household structure by gender	71
2.7:	Income disparity between two-parent and single-parent families	71
2.8:	Poverty rates of two-parent and single-parent families	73
3.1:	Definitions of categories of nonemployed young people (aged 15–34)	79
3.2:	Percentage with work experience	91
4.1:	Regression analysis for arithmetic test scores – by elementary school fifth-graders	121
4.2:	Regression analysis for Japanese language test scores – by elementary school fifth-graders	121
5.1:	Descriptive statistics	134
5.2:	Logistic regression predicting chronic health conditions	137
5.3:	Logistic regression predicting visits to doctor's office	137
5.4:	Logistic regression predicting physical discomfort	139
5.5:	Logistic regression predicting activity restriction	139
5.6:	Logistic regression predicting depression	141
5.7a:	Logistic regression predicting self-reported health	142
5.7b:	Logistic regression predicting change in self-reported health	143
5.8:	Logistic regression predicting smoking, drinking, walking and access to medical information	144

5.9: Relationship between health-related activities and health outcomes	146
6.1: Net financial assets in terms of inheritance and pensions	164
6.2a: Descriptive statistics for 1996	170
6.2b: Descriptive statistics for 2002	171
6.3: Estimation results for 1996	172
6.4: Estimation results for 2002	176
7.1: Pros and cons of Defined Benefit (DB) and Defined Contribution (DC) pensions	187
7.2: Mean return and standard deviation for safe and risky assets	193

Contributors

Yuji Genda is Professor of Labor Economics at the Institute of Social Science, University of Tokyo. His recent English publications include: 'Long-term effects of a recession at labor market entry in Japan and the United States,' *Journal of Human Resources* (co-authored, 2010, 45(1)); 'Have jobs and hope gone forever in Japan?,' *Japan in Decline: Fact or Fiction?* (edited by Jain and Williams, 2011, Global Oriental); and 'No place to belong,' *Reimaging Japan: The Quest for a Future that Works* (edited by McKinsey & Company, 2011, VIZ Media).

Hiroshi Ishida is Professor of Sociology at the Institute of Social Science, University of Tokyo. His research interests include comparative social stratification and mobility, school-to-work transition and health inequality. He is the author of *Social Mobility in Contemporary Japan* (1993, Stanford University Press), the co-author of *Schools, Public Employment Offices and the Labor Market in Postwar Japan* (in Japanese, 2000, University of Tokyo Press) and the co-editor of *Social Class in Contemporary Japan* (2009, Routledge). He served as editor-in-chief of *Social Science Japan Journal* (published by Oxford University Press) from 2005 to 2010, and currently directs the Japanese Life Course Panel Survey.

Takehiko Kariya is Professor in the Sociology of Japanese Society, Nissan Institute of Japanese Studies and the Department of Sociology, Oxford University. His research interests include the sociology of education, social stratification, school-to-work transition, educational and social policies and social change in postwar Japan. He is co-editor of *Challenges to Japanese Education: Economics, Reforms, and Human Rights* (2010, Teachers College Press).

Katsumi Matsuura is Professor in the Department of Social Science, University of Hiroshima. His main research interests center on econometrics and finance. He is the co-author of *Micro-Econometrics* (in Japanese, 2009, Toyokeizai Shinposha).

Naomi Miyazato is Associate Professor of Economics at Nihon University. His research interests include social security systems and public finance. His recent publication in English is 'The optimal size of Japan's public pensions: An analysis considering the risks of longevity and volatility of return on assets,' *Japan and the World Economy* (2010, 22(1)).

Toshiki Satō is Professor in the Department of Advanced Social and International Studies, University of Tokyo. He is a comparative and historical sociologist, particularly interested in the modernization of western and non-western countries. His work focuses mainly on the interaction between modern organization and native culture. He is the author of the following books in Japanese: *Modernity, Organization and Capitalism* (1993, Minerva), *Social Inequality in Contemporary Japan* (2000, Chuo-Kouron), *Japanese Tradition and the Cherry Blossom* (2005, Iwanami) and *Meaning and System* (2008, Keisou).

Sawako Shirahase is Professor in the Department of Sociology, University of Tokyo. Her main research interests include social stratification and demographic change with a cross-national perspective and comparative studies of welfare states from the analytical frameworks of gender and generation. She is the author of three books in Japanese: *Unseen Gaps in an Ageing Society: Locating Gender, Generation and Class in Japan* (2005, University of Tokyo Press), *Thinking about Inequalities in Japan: A Comparative Study of Ageing Societies* (2009, University of Tokyo Press) and *Inequalities in Life Courses: Looking for a Mutually Supportive Society* (2010, Iwanami).

Acknowledgments

This volume was originally published in Japanese by the University of Tokyo Press in 2006. I would like to thank the UTP for granting permission to publish this English version. We were fortunate to have Professor Tom Gill translate the volume, aside from the third chapter. We are grateful not only for his excellent translation skills but also for his insightful comments and questions that helped improve the quality of our work. Mr. Waku Miller translated Chapter 3, and we would also like to acknowledge his efforts.

It took some time to publish this work in English. Moreover, expressing our arguments and findings in a way that can be easily understood by readers in foreign nations presented a difficult task. I would like to express gratitude to Professor Yoshio Sugimoto and his editorial team for their strong support in developing the Japanese volume into English and for the final production of the book. I very much appreciate his enthusiasm and support in publishing our work in English. Particular thanks are due to Ms. Miriam Riley who copyedited the volume at the last stage of production with great competence.

I would like to acknowledge the support of the Grant-in-Aid for Scientific Research (S) (grant number 20223004) of the Japan Society for the Promotion of Science. We were able to publish the English volume owing to its financial support.

Last, but not least, I would like to thank my colleagues who contributed chapters to this volume. Our endless debates and arguments stimulated each other's intellectual interests, and I feel fortunate to work with such a highly professional and competent group of scholars.

Sawako Shirahase

Introduction: The Inequalities Hidden in the Low Birthrate/Aging Society
Sawako Shirahase

The low birthrate/aging society and inequality

In recent years Japan has seen an active debate on the theme of economic differentials and social inequality. Since 2005 the debate has noticeably intensified, with more and more books being published on the differential society and special features on the topic in all the media. There was a time when Japan was routinely presented as an 'all middle-class society' (*sōchūryū shakai*), classless and egalitarian (Murakami 1984). In the 1970s, that image combined with international awareness of Japan's phenomenal rate of economic growth to draw the attention of many researchers around the world, who sought to explain the mechanism of Japan's economic miracle. Okouchi et al. (1973) pointed to the advantageous aspects of 'Japanese customs,' Dore (1973) compared Japanese and British industrial practices, Cole (1979) evaluated Japanese and American workers, and Vogel famously came to the conclusion that Japan was 'Number One' among industrial nations (1979). Not only had Japan emerged from the chaos of defeat in war to achieve miraculous levels of economic growth, but had simultaneously succeeded in achieving a high degree of economic equality. The OECD formally described Japan as one of the world's most equal nations (Sawyer 1976). Studies like these tickled the vanity of the small, defeated nation that was Japan.

The 1973 oil shock ushered in a period of lower economic growth, but 10 years later the advent of the bubble economy brought a very different era, in which the people of Japan were 'drunk with wealth.' Expensive brand products sold like hotcakes, high-rise buildings sprang up all over the cities, and Japan basked in her position as a winner in global competition, while glancing at the industrial countries of Europe, which in the mid-1980s were plagued by trade deficits and rising unemployment, especially among the young. But this proved to be but a fleeting moment in history, and the start of the 1990s saw Japan plunged into a period of prolonged economic stagnation.

Unemployment, previously seen as somebody else's problem, began to afflict Japan, with growing numbers of unemployed youths joining the ranks of middle-aged workers affected by *risutora* – meaning 'restructuring,' a word that soon became a polite euphemism for getting the sack. Little by little people started to become aware of unfairness and differentials. In the midst of all this, economist Tachibanaki Toshiaki published his seminal book, *Nihon no Keizai Kakusa* (Japan's economic differentials; 1998), and had a bestseller on his hands. His shocking message, that Japan was now just as unequal as the United States, or even more so, tapped straight into the pent-up sense of unfairness among his readers. A further blow to morale came two years later, when sociologist Toshiki Satō published *Fubyōdō Shakai Nihon* (Japan as an unequal society; 2000), in which he pointed to a high level of inter-generational continuity among higher level white-collar workers that was making it increasingly difficult for newcomers to join that class of society. Satō saw this as the key to explaining the growing differentials in status seen in Japan from the start of the 1990s. Kariya (2001) took the argument into the classroom, suggesting that declining academic ability among school children was serving to widen status differentials.

Yamada (2004) published a book called *Kibō Kakusa Shakai*, or 'The hope differential society.' Not only wealth and status, he argued, but even hope was now being distributed unfairly within Japanese society. This book also found many readers, and *kibō kakusa* (hope differential) became a new buzz word, along with *nikyokubunka* (polarization), *kachigumi-makegumi* (winners and losers), and *make'inu no tōboe* (the distant howling of beaten dogs), the title of a controversial book by Junko Sakai (2003), describing women who had passed the age of thirty without getting married or having children as 'beaten dogs' (*make'inu*). All these terms connoted social division, and Atsushi Miura's frank assertion of the existence of a distinct lower class culture, *Karyū Shakai* (Lower-class society; 2005) became yet another bestseller. Recently, words that used to be taboo (like 'loser,' 'low-class' and 'poor') have started cropping up regularly in daily conversation.

Somewhat in contrast, Seiyama (2003) emphasized 'stratification as narrative,' arguing that status differentials themselves had always been there but were now being accorded far more attention.

His work cast considerable doubt on the argument recently made by other scholars to the effect that status differentials are widening, that status reproduction is strengthening, and that the structure of social status is becoming more rigid. Ishida (2000, 2002) analyzed trends in intergenerational status mobility, focusing on the relationship between family background and achieved status and taking marginal distribution into account. He concluded that no consistent trend could be identified in class differentials since the end of the high economic growth era that might speak to a significant change in the degree of openness and equality of Japanese society, either in a positive or negative direction. Likewise Matsuura (2002) calculated the extent of inequality not only in income but also in consumption and assets, and found no great change in the degree of inequality during the 1990s.

Among the background factors in the sudden increase in awareness of differentials was a pair of alarming demographic trends: a rapid decline in the birthrate, and the aging of the population. Nineteen-ninety brought the '1.57 shock': the news that the birthrate had fallen to 1.57, far below population replacement level, made the government and people acutely aware of the severity of the problem. In 2005, elderly people aged 65 and over accounted for more than 20% of Japan's population. The establishment 10 years later of the long-term care insurance program as a fifth plank of Japan's social insurance system was one of the governmental responses to the rapid aging of the population.

Today, the medical costs associated with aging continue to escalate, along with government outlays on pension payments. Under the 2004 reform of the pension system, the government introduced a macroeconomic sliding scale designed to take account of population changes in adjusting the level of payments, deciding also that from 2017 onward the state pension would be set at 40% of the pensioner's pre-retirement income, down from 50% under the present system. Meanwhile, the number of young people continued to stagnate and the rate of unmarried people continued to rise, until in 2005 the total fertility rate hit its lowest ever level at 1.26.

Ohtake (1994) was one of the first scholars to notice that the aging of society that had set in during the 1980s was tending to widen income differentials. He argued that much of the expansion in differentials from the second half of the 1980s onward was due to population aging, and that the changes in economic fundamentals usually blamed for it were often just an illusion. It suited the government to believe Ohtake, and it became the government position that widening differentials in the general population were caused by the growth of the elderly population, which is known to exhibit wider economic differentials than younger segments of the population. As we entered the 21st century, the debate on widening differentials became ever more intense.

But has Japan really changed that drastically? Has some new kind of inequality emerged that was not there before, turning Japan into a much more unequal place? A look at the empirical data does not show a clear trend toward inequality (Ishida 2000; Seiyama 2000; Shirahase 2005b). Why then is it that people nonetheless nod in assent when told of the dramatic worsening of inequality in Japan, and insist on dividing society into bunches of winners and losers? Is the world really susceptible to such simple analysis?

Despite the popularity of extreme language and the loud arguments, often with names of star debaters attached to them, the world is not, in fact, such a simple place. It is a vague and opaque sort of place. Behind people's willingness to believe all the talk about winners and losers, of the rich getting richer and the poor getting poorer, there lies a more complex, ambiguous world. Amid all the arguments about inequality that seem to run along on parallel lines, what this book sets out to do is to undertake an honest, direct investigation of the many little-understood mechanisms that make the world work the way it does.

Opaqueness amid evident change

The phenomenon of 'the low birthrate coupled with an aging society' (*shōshi-kōreika*) may be broadly read from four different demographic aspects:
1. The trend among young people to postpone marriage (*bankonka*) or not get married at all (*mikonka*).
2. The decline in the number of child(ren) born to married couples.
3. An increase in the proportion of people aged over 65 in the overall population.
4. Increased longevity, as seen in the relative increase in the number of elderly people in the late old-age group, those aged 75 and over.

Now these demographic changes are not just abstract numbers. They bring with them qualitative change in the relations between the people who make up society, and to the various systems governing that society. Yet, although these changes are clear and undeniable, and are inexorably transforming Japanese society, their content remains unclear and indefinable. The aging society is definitely on its way, yet despite all the discussion about it, its implications are surprisingly poorly understood. Confronted with our own very near future, we still do not know what it is going to be like. Confronted by change that is evidently going to emerge, people become extremely anxious, and sometimes overly pessimistic. Yet, if they think they are getting excessively pessimistic, they may rush to the opposite extreme and become rashly optimistic. People's feelings can swing like a wild pendulum. This unsettled feeling is what makes them especially susceptible to extreme and over-simplified messages.

This mode of thought, that impulsively jumps to forced conclusions dividing society into black and white, ignoring all the shades of grey between, is ultimately escapist. People feel strangely convinced by extreme words, and end up accepting the status quo. Why? Because behind the appeal of polarizing arguments lies the ability to evade social problems by seeing them as not directly concerning oneself. Consider the expression 'winners and losers.' Interestingly, the Japanese term, *kachigumi-makegumi*, literally means 'winning team/gang' and 'losing team/gang,' further emphasizing that these are two distinct groups. Presented with the concept of these two extreme categories, most real people feel that they do not belong to either of them. Perversely, however, the very fact that this kind of polarization theory applies to only a small minority of real people is the very key to its popularity. The real world is a little more complex than that, and most people live in a gray zone where they cannot simply be described as winners or losers. This majority group makes no appearance in discussions of economic or cultural polarization. Hence the vital point: for most people the argument over differentials is a drama in which they themselves do not feature.

The first key feature of Japanese demographic change that we have to acknowledge is its speed. Because change is fast, people experience mood swings, becoming excessively pessimistic or excessively optimistic. When seeking to design the society of the future, which changes should we factor in? Because change is so fast, we do not have the time for careful deliberation over questions like that, and so we try to think on our feet, dreaming up ambitious plans for the future while struggling to keep up with the present. Because we are running alongside change, it can be difficult for us to figure out where change is happening and where it is not. In this book, therefore, what we want to do is start from the clear and undeniable quantitative change embodied in the falling birthrate and aging population, and try and see how those quantitative changes relate to qualitative change in Japanese society, starting with a look at structures of inequality in terms of the distributive principle within society.

Differentials and inequality

Inoki (2003) asks the question of why and how income differentials become problematic. If differentials existed as only a simple fact of life, they would not be treated as a social problem and debated so heatedly by economists and sociologists. However, if income differentials are indeed a problem, that is because they are accompanied by related forms of consciousness in people's minds – and here Inoki focuses particularly on 'aspiration' to work (*yaruki*). Differentials become a problem not simply because of the gaps in material wealth that they represent, but more because they are mediated through feelings of socioeconomic superiority/inferiority. This superiority/inferiority of which I speak determines not only positions on that continuous curve representing income levels in a population, but also people's social standing, including such notions as prestige and honor, which derive ultimately from levels of income. It also determines people's material standard of living. Material standard of living, in turn, determines not only quality of life at any particular point in time, but also people's latent ability to deal with future risks, including those of illness, unemployment, and those associated with old age and childbearing/childrearing. This kind of superiority/inferiority and variation in latent coping ability, derived from quantitative differences, gives birth to a more all-encompassing structure of social inequality. One key to understanding inequality as discussed here is the notion that differentials are *unfair*. If one rejects that notion, insisting that socioeconomic differentials are simply the outcomes of differences in ability or effort, then those differentials may seem unavoidable or even just. One may deny the very existence of inequality as a social problem, and morally justify differentials. The current tendency in Japan to view differentials not just as gaps in income but as *inequality* in a broader, more political sense, reflects the existence of a degree of unfairness that cannot be explained away by reference to individual responsibility.

The Japanese terms *fubyōdō* ('inequality') and *kakusa* ('differential') tend to be used more or less interchangeably. There is of course a considerable overlap in definition, but at this point I think we should pause to reflect on the precise meanings of these terms.

The first thing to bear in mind when thinking about differentials is the existence of subjective values that people use to assess the degree of them (Satō 2005). People have values for what they consider to be a desirable level of differential, and they measure inequality and unfairness in terms of the degree to which reality deviates from those ideal values. That degree of deviation connotes a system of ranking, so that the differentials we are talking about here may be called 'ranked differences' – that being the literal meaning of the characters making up the Japanese term, *kakusa*. Differentials imply an ideal base value for difference, for example zero, and indicate the distance between reality and that ideal value. Most people believe that small differentials are preferable, but since the reference line tends to be defined in relative, not absolute, terms, the meaning of differentials will inevitably have an element of vagueness to it.

This raises such fundamental questions as whether the ideal level for differentials really is zero; that is, whether our ultimate goal is a society where everyone is at exactly the same level no matter what they do or achieve. Even if such a society could theoretically exist, most people would probably not view it as desirable. If differences in achievement were not reflected in differences in reward to some extent, society would exhibit another kind of unfairness. If individual achievement is justly appraised, then differentials in income based on that appraisal may also be described as just. But in the case of inequality, individuals are not appraised fairly, and differentials are influenced by unfair elements that have nothing to do with individual ability. That is the point where income differentials become unjust and unfair. The very concept of differentials implies a scale within which the difference between individuals is evaluated. It is when differentials go off that scale that society becomes unequal in a pathological sense. So, although differentials and inequality are closely related terms, the latter connotes a higher level of value judgment than the former. Whether differentials indicate social inequality depends on the degree of justice with which each individual's achievements and ability are evaluated.

In short, the concept of 'differentials' emphasizes experiential, empirically measurable socioeconomic difference. 'Inequality,' by contrast, is a concept that seeks not only to measure difference but also to ascribe social/political norms to it. In the present work, therefore, we will define inequality as differentials with a stronger conceptual framework attached. Inequality is a distributive concept related to the question of how wide the differentials between individuals can be before they become unacceptable in terms of social fairness.

Perceptions of unfairness

Every 10 years since 1955, Japanese researchers – mostly sociologists – have conducted a survey on social status and social mobility. These 'SSM surveys' reveal that many Japanese people feel that their society is afflicted by various kinds of unfairness (SSM 1995 Research Group, 1997). The field with the highest percentage of respondents describing it as 'very unfair' was 'unfairness in educational credentials' (48.6%), followed by 'unfairness in income' (39.0%) and 'unfairness in assets' (36.6%). In contrast, a relatively low 24.2% felt a strong degree of unfairness in 'family background.' These results show that many people sensed unfairness in terms of *outcomes* – income, assets, etc. – while they sensed relatively little unfairness in terms of family status, a variable that precedes and influences income and asset status, and indeed the opportunity to acquire educational credentials. Since no one can decide what family they are born into by their own effort or ability, it is perhaps viewed as a site where the distributive principle does not function.

That brings us back to the number one item on the list of perceived sites of unfairness – education. Income and occupation are *outcome variables* – indicators of social status at a given point in time. Education is principally an *opportunity variable*, helping determine the degree to which one is given the chance to attain high social status. At the same time it is also an outcome variable since one's educational qualifications are another factor contributing to social status. Thus, education is a field with the potential for both outcome inequality and opportunity inequality, and this probably explains why people are particularly sensitive about unfairness in this area. If differentials are the outcome of a fair distributive principle, people do not sense that they are unfair. But underlying people's perceptions of unfairness is a suspicion that the outcomes themselves are based on an unfair distributive principle (Umino 2000; Shirahase 2005). If everyone is given a fair chance, most people will accept differentials in outcomes as something that cannot be helped. But if the chances themselves have not been distributed fairly, people will not be able to accept the emergence of differing outcomes. People sense unfairness behind the outcomes, and that inflames their sense of inequality.

Attitude towards stratification

How are we to understand people's subjective sense of differentials or inequality in terms of the relationship between whole and part? For example, there is no consistent evidence demonstrating that the degree of socioeconomic inequality in Japanese society as a whole clearly and continuously increased during the 1990s (Ishida 2003; Seiyama 2003). However, when people thought about their future, or their children's prospects, they felt pessimistic and hence became more sensitive to present-day inequality. What this disjuncture means is that micro-level individual consciousness does not directly reflect macro-level change. At the same time of course, individual consciousness is by no means independent from macro-level social conditions.

The falling birthrate and aging society are real and inescapable social changes, and they do not bode well for the future. We understand that the great demographic changes stemming from those two phenomena are steadily progressing. But how are we to understand the lifeways of individuals living in the low birthrate/ aging society? 'To live one's whole life without having children'; 'to live much longer after retiring from work'; 'to look after one's elderly parents for many years.' These are the micro-level realities. Bad prospects for the future may be read as provoking unwarranted anxiety about the present, but that negative outlook is based on real concerns: how well is one prepared for a future clouded by uncertainty? A psychological sense of readiness to face the future is intimately connected to the presence of some kind of safety net, in the form of financial and human resources. Thus one's view of the future is not just a matter of subjective attitude: it has a status component backed by actual financial and other resources. Therein lies the meaning in looking at problems of consciousness from the perspective of status and differentials. How aware people are of the structural inequality of the world around them, how they respond to the grim outlook for the aging society – these things are in fact closely related to the individual's position in the here and now. Just as there are stratified differentials in individual and family standing, so too is consciousness stratified. Rather than viewing people's consciousness just as a problem of consciousness, we have to think of it in relation to socioeconomic structure. Consciousness is not merely a flat and simple projection of reality on the individual mind. Society is made up of conscious individuals, and those individuals and their households are bound up in stratified socioeconomic mechanisms.

Quantitative change and qualitative change: The whole and its parts

It crossed the minds of many people observing the quantitative change brought to society by the falling birthrate that perhaps this would mean a smaller number of competitors and hence a bigger share of society's rewards for themselves. In fact, however, though the number of children may decline, and even the population as a whole may reduce, the competition for admission to elite schools has shown no signs of abating, while unemployment has risen in response to economic stagnation. Even the middle-aged and elderly, hitherto the age groups least threatened by unemployment, have found that the risk of sudden dismissal from work also applies to them. 'What is going on? Maybe society really is unequal!' Suddenly, people have a real sense of inequality. But just because the individual's sense of inequality has strengthened, that does not mean that real inequality has suddenly made a dramatic appearance. This is, in no small measure, a kind of illusion brought on by the suddenness of change experienced by the individual.

Another element in the creation of this illusion is confusion between the whole of society and its parts. Since the birthrate hit an all-time historical low of 1.26 in 2006, there has been an outburst of debate on such issues as how to make it easier for people to have children. But in thinking about this we have to carefully distinguish between two different issues: the macro-level fact of the falling birthrate, and the micro-level question of what it actually means to be childless, to cut the links between one generation and the next. When warning of the risks of population decline, we have to ask what sorts of problems it will bring at the level of individuals, families and households.

It is no easy matter to compile an accurate index of inequality. But that is no reason to reject the attempt. What kind of differences do we view as differentials? How far do differentials have to change before we call the change 'big'? How do we define widening differentials; how do we define growing inequality? None of these questions has a single right answer. But that is no bad thing; nor is it a bad thing if people have different views of changes in differentials. Nor do such differences imply that one of the views is wrong. Why not? Because different views very often emerge because people are looking at different aspects of the phenomenon. We may look at the matter in terms of the whole and its parts. The overall degree of income inequality calculated by Gini coefficients may not be consistent with the degree to which people actually feel inequality. In fact, just because no big change in the level of inequality in society as a whole can be seen, that does not necessarily mean that there has been no change in certain aspects or sub-groups of society (Ishida 2002).

Genda (2002) shows that young people and the self-employed are two groups within society that have been placed in a disadvantageous position relative to retirees and people in regular employment. Genda clarifies how the economic fortunes of these two groups have fallen relative to the rest of society. What, then, is the connection between the overall demographic change that is the aging society, and the socioeconomic structure within that societal change? In analyzing that crucial question, we have to distinguish very carefully between overall change affecting the whole of society, and localized change affecting only certain segments of society.

The present volume attempts to meet head-on the difficult challenge of analyzing the fuzzy, hard-to-see differentials concealed within the aging society. It is a matter of great urgency. The aging society is on its way, and it is not well understood. Let us look it straight in the eye and try to understand it. The map of modern society has been wrongly simplified in the heated, highly political debate on the aging society. Let us take another look at that map – a long, cool look. That, in a nutshell, is the shared perception motivating us, the authors of this book. Words like differential and inequality are being bandied around these days as a kind of shorthand for each pundit's personal preoccupations. All the more reason to give these complex issues the careful study they deserve and require.

Outline of the book

This book has eight main chapters. In Chapter 1, Toshiki Satō looks at the debate on inequality that started in the 1990s, characterizing it as 'an explosion of inequality consciousness.' Satō skillfully teases out the connections between the aging society – which signifies change in the population and the family – and widening inequality, which indicates shifts in the structure of resource distribution within society. Reading the falling birthrate as a mark of deficiency in the continuity between parent-child generations, he analyzes it as a mechanism underlying the explosion of inequality consciousness. People with children can at least hope that unfairness in their own lives may be offset by gains enjoyed by their children, whereas people who have no children must settle their personal accounts with society in a single lifetime. This makes them far more sensitive to inequality in their own lives. Satō seeks to tie together the mechanisms that underlie people's instincts.

In Chapter 2, I attempt to relate the key quantitative changes of the falling birthrate and aging society to the social structures of household and gender. Recognizing that quantitative change does not just manifest itself at the level of the individual, I focus on the household as the basic site of everyday life, and seek to theorize structural change in the household from the perspective of economic inequality. From the mid-1980s, the degree of income inequality has been widening. At the same time, single-person households, households consisting only of couples, and single-parent households, have all been increasing. The decline of the 'standard' household with parents and children is closely related to the issue of economic inequality. I seek to find the meaning of people's changing way of life from the standpoint of economic differentials.

One of the leading factors in the falling birthrate is an increase in the number of young people who do not marry. Many youths do not try to get married or to get a steady job. These traits have been intensely discussed in arguments over the new generation of youth, as symbolized in the popular discourse on 'freeters' ('free arbeiters,' people still in part-time jobs or insecure employment after completing their education) and 'NEETs' ('Not in Employment, Education or Training). The former are at least in employment, albeit irregular employment. But the situation of NEETs is less well understood. So in Chapter 3, 'Young, Japanese, and Not in Education, Employment, or Training: Japan's Experience with the NEET Phenomenon', Yūji Genda asks just how many NEETs there are in Japan, and clarifies the problems facing them. Unemployed people who are looking for work feature in labor statistics, but those who are not looking for work, or are not interested in getting employed, are not included in those statistics except as a residual category when all the others have been subtracted from the whole. Genda warns that judgmental accounts of these youths, accusing freeters and NEETs of being too fussy about their choice of occupation, refusing employment that does not suit their own fastidious tastes, or of declining full-time employment because they can still live parasitically with their parents, have become widely accepted although they are not based on an adequate grasp of reality.

In Chapter 4, Takehiko Kariya looks at the postwar Japanese education system, showing how it valorized egalitarianism, sought systematically to root out ability-based elitism, and viewed selective education as a form of discrimination. From a situation where many youths could not afford to go to senior high school because of household poverty, educational opportunities spread rapidly through the population in the 1970s and '80s, to the point where proceeding to senior high school was so embedded in popular culture that it virtually became part of the compulsory education system. However poor a family a child might be born into, if he or she made the effort, a high level of education could be attained. That opened up the path to going up in the world through the power of educational credentials. Now anyone had the chance to be reborn through education. Such, at least, was the message sent out by the authorities as they pursued their program of spreading education to the masses. In fact, however, there never was a truly level playing field for people of every background to compete on equal terms in the pursuit of educational credentials. Kariya argues that the egalitarian avoidance of competition paradoxically led to a 'popularization of meritocracy,' which did not eradicate inequality so much as hiding it away where fewer people would notice it.

Since the establishment of the national health insurance system in 1961, access to healthcare has been guaranteed to all, irrespective of ability to pay. The postwar Japanese healthcare system was designed so that poverty would no longer bar people from medical help and drive them to an early grave. For many years it was almost taboo even to discuss the relationship between health and socio-economic status. But is there really no status stratification at all in people's health? Today, the aging population is the biggest single factor driving up medical costs in Japan. But that does not mean that when people reach the age of 65 they all suddenly become more prone to illness, of course. In Chapter 5, Hiroshi Ishida takes on the issue of inequality in healthcare in an attempt to answer this kind of question within the framework of social stratification theory.

Children cannot choose their parents. Those who are born to wealthy parents and receive a huge inheritance can enjoy a wealthy lifestyle without making any effort of their own. In Chapter 6, Katsumi Matsuura attempts a detailed quantitative analysis of differentials over which people have no control: the starting line from which they commence their lives. Matsuura looks at the micro-level transfer of assets from parent to child through inheritance; the macro-level transfer of assets from the younger generation to the old through the public pension system; and the framework of parent-child continuity at the micro level of childrearing. He argues that breaking up unconditional continuity from parent to child is an important element in reducing inequality between generations.

The aging society means a relatively smaller working generation and a relatively larger one of older retirees, and thereby brings imbalance between generations. This puts pressure on social insurance funding resources, puts an excessive financial burden on the shoulders of the working generation, and thereby saps the vitality of the Japanese economy. Consequently, the man in the street starts to feel the attractions of 'small government' that will reduce his tax burden. Under small government, people are expected to take personal responsibility for coping with the risks of everyday life – of illness, unemployment, aging, etc. In Chapter 7, Naomi Miyazato describes the design of Japan's public pension system and analyzes recent moves in the direction of individual accounting. It is impossible to make the individual personally responsible for the cost of every major life event: having children, bringing them up, losing one's job, falling ill, etc. Miyazato criticizes recent panic-driven moves by the government toward linking pensions more directly to personal contributions as unlikely to improve the welfare of the people.

In Chapter 8, I look over the findings of all the chapters and try to identify the new structures of inequality that have started to appear amid the predictable and evident progress of the aging society. The objective of this book is to see through the smoke of the battle between extreme arguments and seek the true structure of inequality brought by the aging society. I look at a collection of social features that have not been sufficiently discussed in research on inequality in Japan: the meaning of the falling birthrate at the micro level; single-person households; unemployed youths; the postwar education system; health, assets, the social security system and the problem of self-responsibility, etc.

We live in times of rapid change, facing a future that is hard to discern. What is changing, and what remains the same? What is the nature of the inequality hidden in the midst of all the change? I will suggest some answers to these questions in the concluding chapter.

1 An Explosion of Inequality Consciousness: Changes in Postwar Society and 'Equalization' Strategy
Toshiki Satō

What 'widening inequality' really means

We are all too prone to forget the basic fact that society is something that lives in the fourth dimension: time. The same goes for social change.

We tend to find it easy to envision social change in terms of milestones and turning points. To take a familiar example, if you talk to students around twenty years old, you will often hear them say that they 'can't understand the youth of today,' or that 'junior high school kids have totally changed since I graduated from junior high myself.' Interestingly, the lines themselves have not changed at all. Twenty-year-old students have been talking that way at least since I was one of them myself – which was about 20 years ago.

That is not to say that in reality nothing has changed at all. No doubt both children in general and junior high-school kids in particular have changed. The point is that we tend to find it easier to notice change at a particular point in time, such as the moment we finished junior high school and thereby completed our compulsory education. Change is easier to grasp in terms of milestones, or to take the argument a step further, talking about those milestones makes it easier for people to perceive change. We have that habit, we have that mechanism.

'Widening inequality,' the topic of this book, is another case in point. Around the end of the 1990s, widening social inequality, or *fubyōdōka* (literally, 'unequalization'), became a hot topic in Japan. In discussing this phenomenon, I want to first make it clear that the notion that 'society is becoming more unequal' is not quite the same kind of notion as 'junior high school kids have changed.' The latter has been a popular stereotype for decades, but the former is far more recent. It is only in the last 10 years or so that *fubyōdōka* has become a buzz-word. Before that, most people tended to think that Japanese society was marked by relative equality.

This fact may serve as a hint to us that 'unequalization' is a particularly time-specific notion – not that I am denying the possibility that the notion of the youth of today having changed may not itself change with time. However, it is overly simplistic to see unequalization as a sudden drastic change at a particular point in time. Society is not like that. It has the power to resist change and remain consistent. It takes time to change society at its roots. Sometimes change can only be measured over a period of decades – such as changes in occupational continuity from one generation to the next, where the basic unit of time is the age difference between parents and children.

'Unequalization' is closely bound up with changes like this. It is a compound of many different changes, some of them mid-term shifts occurring over several decades, some of them short-term changes taking a single decade or so, and some of them almost instantaneous – by which I mean taking just a few years. The best way to view unequalization is as a gigantic complex of all the above, appearing on the outside as a single mighty transformation.

How the explosion of inequality consciousness occurred

I would argue, then, that what we witnessed in Japan from the late 1990s was not so much an explosion of inequality as one of inequality consciousness.

I do not mean by this that widening inequality was all in the mind. Indeed, society is constructed of people's thoughts and feelings, so that even if widening inequality really *was* all in the mind, it would still be a significant social change. If the general public really did get the impression of widening social inequality with no grounding whatsoever in economic reality, that would indicate that the government had done something to lose the trust of the people – a truly disastrous policy failure, itself deserving of criticism.

People's feelings do not faithfully reflect reality. The ongoing debate on income differentials and trends in intergenerational occupational mobility has shown that if we limit ourselves to reality as measured by statistical data, any change that may have occurred has been marginal enough for some observers to dispute whether it has happened at all. When people speak from their feelings, however, they speak as if change is an established fact, visible to all.

Whether or not this sea-change in feelings has any direct relation to statistical data, it surely has responded to *something* in the real world. I use this expression, 'an explosion of inequality consciousness,' to describe the complex of realities and feelings that has developed around the concept of inequality.

As I read the situation at present, the explosion of inequality consciousness is the product of three kinds of change:

1. Mid-term change measured in units of several decades: the disappearance of the postwar social mechanism.
2. Short-term change measured in units of decades: the recession induced by the bursting of the bubble economy and changes in employment practices caused by globalization.
3. Policy failures: government policies that have had the effect of exacerbating anxieties and distrust regarding widening inequality.

There has already been a considerable amount of research done on item (2), and chapters 3 and 6 of the present volume also address it. Item (3) is also discussed in other chapters, and I will have more to say about it myself, but for now let me simply observe that as I see it items (1) and (2) created an underlying sentiment that was highly sensitive to inequality, and that despite that, or possibly even because of that, the Japanese government pursued policies that might almost have been designed to inflame that sensitivity.

Let me put it in more concrete terms. At a time when people were already becoming increasingly sensitive to inequality of opportunity, the government applied policies in various fields, including economic management, taxation and education, which ignored opportunity inequality or even denied its existence. While the general public grew ever more sensitive to the issue, the government became increasingly insensitive. The net result was an explosive rise in consciousness of inequality.

The enforcement of government policy has a particular date; that is to say we can put a date on its impact. That impact was the final trigger that launched the explosion of inequality consciousness. It turned inequality into a 'turning point': despite its close relationship with items (1) and (2), both of them phenomena stretching over a lengthy time-span, inequality came to be seen as a sudden, dramatic change.

Needless to say, this is just a hypothesis. It will need to be verified by empirical study in the years to come. But if my premise is even partially correct, it means that widening inequality is a product of several different (albeit related) kinds of change. It follows that a combination of different policies will be needed to form a response to the problem. The phenomenon we call 'widening inequality' was not the outcome of a single cause, and it follows that there is no single silver bullet that will put everything to rights. It will require not only policymaking developed over several years, but also determined monitoring over several decades and a response at the level of the fundamental mechanism of society as a whole.

Another phenomenon: The erasure of inequality consciousness

Of the three factors I mentioned above as causing the widening inequality phenomenon, items (2) and (3) will be dealt with in earnest in other chapters, so I would like to take a closer look at item (1) here.

Broadly speaking, item (2) concerns economic mechanisms, while item (1) concerns social mechanisms. Of course the economy and society cannot be separated as neatly as the academic division between economics and sociology might suggest: they are locked in deep interplay. Nonetheless, I do think it makes sense to retain that rough and ready distinction when discussing inequality. The very fact that the two are so closely related in the real world makes it worth separating them as a first-order approximation.

The disappearance of the postwar social mechanism, which I have labeled factor (1), has in turn a number of aspects. For instance, long-term change can in itself create a feeling of inequality that goes beyond ground-level reality. I have called this 'the illusion of decline' (Satō 2003). When a long-term trend toward decreasing inequality comes to an end, that in itself is enough to give people the impression that inequality is increasing. People are particularly prone to such an illusion since inequality of opportunity is something that is supposed in principle to have no place in modern society.

This illusion is itself the long-term product of long-term change, an effect of the kind of changes that have occurred in real life. The content of change in social mechanisms, what exactly has changed – these things are replete with meaning. We may assume that the illusion of decline interplays with these real-life changes to affect the way people feel about things.

Looking at change in the actual content of society, we discover another interesting fact about inequality. As I mentioned earlier, the end of the 1990s saw an explosion in consciousness of inequality in Japan. In other words, people felt that inequality was widening more sharply than it really was; until then most people had thought of Japan as a relatively equal society.

In this previous orthodoxy too, we can discern a disjunction between reality and perception. As Hiroshi Ishida (1993) and Kazuo Seiyama (1994) have pointed out, even in the days when Japan was thought of as an equal society, Japanese levels of intergenerational occupational mobility were low enough to make Japanese society look not particularly equal when compared with those of other industrialized countries such as the UK and Germany. In other words, during the period from the 1970s to the early 1980s Japan felt more equal than it really was. There was, if you like, an 'erasure of inequality consciousness' in those days.

Why did such a thing happen? To a sociologist, this is just as important a puzzle to solve as that of the more recent explosion of inequality consciousness. The first linguistic evidence of the erasure of inequality consciousness can be traced to the early 1970s, when the term *sōchūryū* (general middle class) started to come into vogue. In the Social Stratification and Mobility (SSM) Survey of 1975, we can clearly observe what Tōru Kikkawa calls 'floating status consciousness' (Kikkawa 2006). That lost awareness of inequality appears to have lasted for roughly 30 years, from the late 1960s to the early 1990s.

In that case, we have to consider the possibility that there was some mechanism at work in the society created by postwar Japan that made people feel inequalities of opportunity relatively lightly.

My own view is that along with demographic and macroeconomic factors such as the flow of population from country to city and the structure of an economy increasingly centered on secondary industry and its blue-collar labor force, the emergence of the postwar Japanese family and subsequent changes to its structure are also closely linked to that exaggerated sense of equality. I would argue that the postwar family was a mechanism that worked to lessen feelings of inequality, and that when that postwar family started to break up, the anesthetic effect on people's status awareness started to wear off. Population shifts and economic structural change also played a part, no doubt about that, but the family – a system directly involved with human reproduction – also was a major factor in the growing sense of inequality. Inequality of opportunity is inextricably interlinked with the family, and is therefore particularly likely to be influenced by changes in it.

In that sense, the two great changes observed since the mid-1990s – the shift in family life and population profile seen in the declining birth rate and graying society, and the change in resource acquisition and distribution so keenly studied under the rubric of 'widening inequality' – are intimately related.

The family as a threat to equality of opportunity

The connection between the family and inequality of opportunity is one that may be generally observed, far beyond the case of postwar Japan. As worldwide cases of aristocracies and hereditary status and wealth clearly show, the special connection between family ties and social inequality is at least as old as recorded history and has become particularly significant since the establishment of modern society.

Modern society proclaims equality of opportunity as its fundamental organizing principle – or to be precise, many modern societies have made that proclamation (Satō 1998, 2001). In reality, however, the family has always been an obstacle to attaining that ideal.

The first people to fully experience the depth of that contradiction were the protestant settlers who arrived in America to establish colonies in New England in the 17th century. In the Massachusetts Bay colony, the right of citizenship, embodied in the status of stockholder in the Massachusetts Bay Company and the title of 'freeman,' was conferred only upon adult males who were members of a church recognized by the government of the colony. This important principle became known as the 'New England Way' or the 'Congregational Way' (Morgan 1965 *inter alia*). However, to become a member of the church, one first had to persuade the existing members that one really had 'awoken to the true faith,' by presenting a 'conversion narrative' that the congregation would listen to before passing judgment.[1] This meant that even the children of church members had no guarantee of being admitted to the congregation themselves, which in turn meant that the children of parents with citizenship would not necessarily obtain citizenship themselves.

Now citizenship is the most fundamental status category in modern society: and in the Massachusetts Bay colony, citizenship was not an ascriptive status based on whose offspring you were, but an achieved status to be won through one's own virtue. In this respect, the Massachusetts Bay colony, at least until the third quarter of the 17th century, was the strongest example the world has so far seen of a society that sought to defend the modern social principle of meritocracy.

However, this strict meritocratic principle came into direct conflict with another powerful tenet – that of the continuity of the family. After a number of intense conflicts over the issue of whether or not to grant automatic church membership to the offspring of pastors and other members of the colony's leadership class, a compromise solution known as the Halfway Covenant was adopted. This policy, adopted in 1662, allowed the offspring of church members to obtain partial membership in the church, and thereby citizenship, without demonstrating a conversion experience. In the final quarter of the 17th century, this system gradually became established, but only in the face of determined opposition. For example, the Halfway Covenant was rejected by the First Church in Boston, the colony's oldest church, which led pro-Covenant members to secede in 1669 and found the Third Church in Boston, known today as the Old South Church. The Puritans' fundamental belief, that a person should be judged not on his ancestry but on his own personal achievement, such as whether he had had a true conversion experience, was not to be easily discarded.

Looking at this 17th century conflict in terms of equality of opportunity, we may read it as a dispute over whether or not blood lineage, a factor over which the individual had no control, should play a part in the acquisition of citizenship – a dispute, in short, over lineage-based inequality in the opportunity to acquire citizenship. It was closely related to another issue, that of the inheritance of privately-owned assets. Indeed, the key members of the Third Church in Boston were wealthy merchants and men of property (Peterson 1997). Without the rights of citizenship, the rights of property ownership would not be guaranteed either. That certainly made the Halfway Covenant a matter of particular urgency for members of the wealthy stratum within the colony, but it would be an oversimplification to characterize it as simply a reflection of their economic interests. In those days Puritans believed that Adam was a real person, whose original sin had been inherited by his descendents. It bothered many of them that if one denied *any* continuity through the bloodline, one would inevitably end up denying the doctrine of original sin.

Another major focus of debate was education. Most of the colonists belonged to Puritan sects that rejected the Catholic doctrines of confession, forgiveness and papal indulgence. Instead they insisted that each individual would be judged by God according to the good or evil of the deeds done during his or her lifetime. Their doctrine was the principle of self-responsibility taken to extremes, but it ran up against the problem of how to theorize the discipline and education provided by parents to their children. If one believed that children grew up good or bad according to the influence exerted on them by their parents, one could hardly hope to judge good and evil at the individual level. Clearly if bad parenting set a child on the road to bad deeds, those deeds could not be viewed as the responsibility of the child alone.

Of course one could deny that influence in theological terms, but in that case there would be no reason to maintain the family – that 'secret garden' hidden from broader society – at all. In that case the logical thing would be to construct communal childrearing institutions all over the colonies. While it might be possible to view families as subdivisions of such institutions, there would be no need to recognize any special relationship there.

No reliable records remain, but it seems that in the 16th to 17th centuries, some of the most hard line Protestants, such as Anabaptists and Antinomians, did in fact try to break up the family. In New England, if parents were judged unable to educate their children correctly, legal provisions were in place for the children to be taken away from their parents and brought up until they reached adulthood by a citizen judged more suitable to the task, for whom they would work as a servant (Massachusetts Laws of 1648; Connecticut Laws of 1673). However, the authorities stopped short of denying the family as a whole, and the contradiction between the principle of personal responsibility for moral decisions and the existence of the family system remained unresolved. To borrow Morgan's precise terminology, church and society in 17th century New England were founded on both 'congregational form' and 'domestic origin' (Morgan 1966: 134–136).

One approach that was tried was to include the behavior of children in the good and bad deeds of their parents (Morgan 1966: 91–92). Since the good and bad deeds of children were entered in the ledger of their parents, it would follow that parents had the right and the duty to educate their own children. For the parents this was indeed a way of reconciling self-responsibility with the family system, but for the children it flatly denied the whole principle of self-responsibility. The prevalent way of thinking about these matters is summed up by Morgan as follows:

> God made the "covenant of grace" with a believer and his seed: he promised godly parents that he would save their children as well as themselves. As extended to children, however, the promise was not unconditional, for even a believer's children were born ignorant. The covenant did not give them an absolute claim to salvation, but it did give them a better chance than other children. ... It was important to teach a child good habits, not because they would save him, but because it was unlikely that he would be saved without them. If his education was neglected, his chance of salvation was small, but if education provided a means of grace, there was every hope that God would use the means. (Morgan 1966: 90–91, 95)

Needless to say, this doctrine denies equality of opportunity to achieve salvation. However, it is the inescapable conclusion of any way of thinking that recognizes a definite meaning and effectiveness in family-based education. Present-day US society, which is descended from those Puritans, has yet to resolve this contradiction. It would probably be most accurate to say that the US today lives in denial of it. Hardly anyone outside the small world of historians and historical theologians even knows that the 17th century Puritans experienced such trauma as they grappled with this contradiction. In their ignorance, most people simply believe the myth that 'the Puritans upheld the sanctity of the family.' In truth, being fundamentalists, the 17th century Puritans could hardly avoid being aware of that contradiction. In contrast, in the US today there is virtually no attempt even to reflect upon it. People simply ignore it and believe that 'the family and self-responsibility are both ordained by God.' To me, that speaks to the seriousness of this intellectual conflict. It is precisely because it is so serious that people want to ignore its very existence.

The system we call the family demands continuity of character between its members – for example between parents and children. That destroys the principle of self-responsibility and poses a threat to the principle of equality of opportunity.

How the family makes people forget inequality of opportunity

However, my main argument lies elsewhere: for the family can also be a powerful tool for *realizing* equality of opportunity.

While it is true that the family poses a threat from the outside to the principle of equality of opportunity, that principle itself also contains an extremely awkward internal problem: the fact that inequality of opportunity cannot easily be *measured* with any exactitude. Since the very concept of 'opportunity' includes an element of uncertainty, we have to conclude that there is no certain way of ascertaining how present-day factors such as occupation or income may affect future outcomes.

It follows that in order to accurately measure inequality of opportunity, we have to wait until the game is over and all the outcomes are known – which strictly speaking means waiting until the people we are studying, and all other members of their generation, have died. The trouble there, of course, is that even if we were able to identify some serious inequality, it would be a bit late to do anything about it.

Accurately measuring inequality of opportunity means waiting until the share of wealth possessed by each of the subjects of our study has been clearly established – which means waiting until they are dead, or until for some other reason we can be certain that there will be no further change to the resources in their possession. But waiting that long makes it impossible to correct inequalities of opportunity. That is the paradox at the heart of the principle of opportunity equality.

Conversely, if we wish to correct inequalities of opportunity, we have to intervene at a point when outcomes are not yet fully known. Policymakers must act on the basis of an estimate that 'there is probably some inequality here,' and policies based on such inexact estimates will inevitably attract suspicion of injustice. Indeed, the more significant inequality is – or to put it another way, the more it affects people's life opportunities – the more opposition will be aroused by attempts to correct it. That is because members of society who lose out when new policies are instituted will inevitably feel that something important is being taken from them on the basis of logic that rests on infirm foundations.

Those who preach equality of opportunity will always be taking a risk, and here we find one of the reasons for that. When people call for improvement or correction of society on the basis of this principle, they can easily sound as though they are speaking of something that by its nature cannot be measured, just as if it really *could* be measured. I suppose that all attempts to intervene in the workings of society are attended by uncertainty, but when it comes to correcting inequality of opportunity, the issue is so deeply entwined in every person's life that the policymaker has a particularly heavy responsibility to present evidence of the justness of his cause. In contrast to other spheres of policymaking, such as public works or environmental protection, it is difficult to get away with a fuzzy compromise based on a rough idea of how the public interest might best be served. Solid evidence will be demanded, and when policymakers respond to those demands they must do their best to at least give the impression that they know what they are talking about.[2] Just like their opponents who insist on imposing the principle of self responsibility, those who demand the correction of inequality will always be playing a rough game with logic: treating something that cannot be measured as if it could (Satō 2005).

The Puritans were not troubled about questions of how to measure or correct inequality. For them, God was an infallible observer and recorder, who would judge the deeds of men in this world when they arrived in the next. Society today is different. Nowadays we have to judge the deeds of men in this world while they are still here – which leads to the serious problem of assessment that I have been discussing.

However, if there is someone whose personhood is linked to that of the person who is being judged – someone who can serve as a proxy of the individual or as his avatar or mini-me or 'subself' – then any unfairness caused by the deeds of the individual being judged can be cancelled out by measures affecting the sub-self. In truth it would probably be better to say that the *possibility* emerges of canceling out the deeds of the person being judged; but even so, as a logical grounding to a system, I would argue that this approach has some validity.

In modern society, the notion of the individual as the basic unit of society is so well established that the notion of a sub-self is not widely accepted. However, there is a possible exception to that way of thinking. The special connection between family members, and especially between parents and children, offers a possible compromise solution to the paradox I have been discussing.

Fairness derived from the parent-child bond

Correcting inequalities through measures affecting a person's children rather than the person him/herself: this may seem like an outrageous proposition at first glance, but in fact it is quite a realistic solution.

First of all, since inequalities do not have to be corrected via the original individual, it becomes feasible to measure inequalities after the distribution of resources to that individual has become fairly well established. This will make corrective measures more acceptable to those who have to accept negative economic consequences from them. Secondly, even if inequalities are not corrected directly on the original individual, if they are corrected through the person of his/her proxy, or 'sub-self,' they will carry a degree of legitimacy as measures applied to his/her descendent. In other words, if we accept the notion of a 'sub-self,' we can both measure inequality accurately and take meaningful steps to correct it.

If we treat the parent-child dyad as our unit for redistribution policy, and seek to correct imbalances of opportunity among individuals via their offspring, we can accurately measure the degree of inequality between people and correct it through their (sub-)selves. Admittedly, I do not envisage systems of compensation at the level of the individual, so much as reducing unequal elements in the overall game of status pursuit, thereby turning it into a fairer game. However, since the principle of opportunity equality itself evades precise definition, this imperfect approach to correcting inequality may actually be a solution that matches the nature of the problem quite well. It will never be possible to precisely compute the degree of inequality experienced by an individual. Even after death, we could hardly hope to compile a comprehensive inventory of all the different factors involved in his/her life – a degree of uncertainty would always remain. Rather than getting bogged down in futile debate on just how much influence that uncertainty might have on our calculations, it would be more rational to try to eradicate known sources of inequality in a new game.

Actually, people calling for equality of opportunity have always tended to show a mysteriously powerful orientation to the future, though it is hard to guess how conscious they may have been of the fact. For example, people demonstrate how unequal society has been in the past, and use that to argue about the present-day education system. While it is not exactly wrong to make that argument, strictly speaking the case for fiddling with the school system is rather weak if one proposes to correct inequality among those for whom it has been demonstrated, since they have already left school. It would surely make better sense to take measures directly impacting on the individual, such as income redistribution, etc. However, one rarely hears that argument made: instead we just hear ever more passionate debate about the school system.

This does not apply just to schools. It is impossible to make any empirical argument about opportunity inequality except regarding the period from the past to the present; yet somehow the conversation tends to drift into the zone from the present to the future. That is of course partly due to the fact that there is nothing we can do to change things that have already happened; and yet, if there were not some tacit agreement that some kind of compensation could be arranged between the present and the future, I do not suppose we would see that narrative shift into the future tense.

In a discourse much heard in postwar Japan, a person will say how the poverty of his parents when he was a child, or the large number of siblings in his family, obliged him to give up hopes of advancing to higher levels of education and obliged him to take a job that did not really appeal to him. In the future, however, opportunities will probably open up for him to make better use of his abilities, and as for his children, they will probably enjoy even greater opportunities. When one thinks in this way, it is just like believing that one is going to be compensated for inequalities suffered by oneself. It is almost like believing that one will have another chance to play the game – only this time the rules will be fairer and one will play the game through one's 'sub-self' – one's children.

Gender: Representing a blank

Looking a little closer at the matter, we find that gender differences are also involved. Male or female adults may have male or female children to be their 'sub-selves,' but the way in which children represent their parents is strongly gendered.

For fathers, the 'sub-self' has usually been a son; or, where that has not been possible, a father has sometimes asked a daughter to play that role. Mothers, by contrast, have tended to expect their sons and daughters to serve as sub-selves in rather different ways. In the postwar nuclear family, women have suffered from opportunity inequality related to gender, as well as to parental occupation, educational background, etc. Consequently they expect their sons to achieve on their behalf the social status that they believe they should really have been able to attain themselves. To that extent they are the same as fathers, but mothers also look to their daughters to confirm the rightness of their own present situation.

In short, the meaning of a child representing its parents as a sub-self falls into two patterns divided by gender. For both fathers and mothers, boys have been the proxies of their parents in a future status attainment game that they have expected to offer greater equality of opportunity. As for girls, they have been a substitute for boys for fathers who have no sons or have not been able to place enough hope in their sons. For mothers, girls have not only been proxies in a future game, but also a presence that offers affirmation of the mother's present role by being there to succeed to it. To a mother, in her doubly excluded role, a daughter is an ambiguous thing: the mother wants her to break out of the role, but she also wants her to choose to stay in it and thereby affirm the mother's own value (Satō 2003).

On that point, it seems plausible to argue that ways of gauging intergenerational mobility from father to son have actually been applied to generational shifts with the entire family as their unit of analysis. If so, it follows that the status of 'housewife' has naturally tended to become an external item, impossible to gauge. It is well known that the status affiliation consciousness of a married woman is influenced by the income, educational credentials, etc. of her husband (see for instance Shirahase 2005, chapter 2), but I would argue that the position of a housewife bringing up her children is not only impossible to measure in terms of income or occupation, but has been a 'blank' in a much more fundamental sense. It has been taken for granted that her status is inscribed by proxy: initially her husband's status and later that acquired by her offspring – mainly her male offspring.

The concept of housewife status as a 'blank' is not the only thing that the logic of the sub-self brings to status theory. Consider for instance the starting point for inter-generational mobility. Parental occupational status is often used to define that starting point. This is the base line from which the next generation's status achievements are measured. As has already been pointed out several times, this 'intergenerational mobility' is not strictly speaking between generations. It is a form of mobility within the individual's own generation, and should be thought of as measuring the shift in status from before getting a job to after.[3] It is just that before the individual gets a job, his status is calculated using his father's occupational status as a proxy.[4]

The logic of parent-child continuity crops up not just in policy-making, but also within sociology – in status research, social mobility research, etc. Since sociology is one of modern society's ways of conducting internal observation, that is hardly surprising.

The postwar-type equal society

I hope I have now shown how social inequality is closely related to the family and to the birth and upbringing of children.

Looking at the matter historically, it is generally held that the concept of 'middle class' and 'working class' only emerged in Japan from the 1920s. Before that, there were quite a few families, mostly in the urban underclass, that could not afford to have children (see Figure 1.1). In other words, the emergence of continuity from parent to child as an issue was itself an outcome of 'basic equalitization' (Hara and Seiyama 1999), and the 1920s were a turning point for the Japanese family.

The population statistics tell the tale. Starting with the 1925–34 marriage cohort (couples married in that period), we see a drastic decline in the number of children born. The 1915–24 cohort averaged 5.2 children, but the 1925–34 cohort averaged only 4.6 children, and for the 1935–44 group, it was just 3.2 (Saitō 1996). 'Have fewer children and bring them up properly.' This was the prevailing ethos that brought the advent of the education-centered

Figure 1.1: Total number of children born to married women, 1890–1952

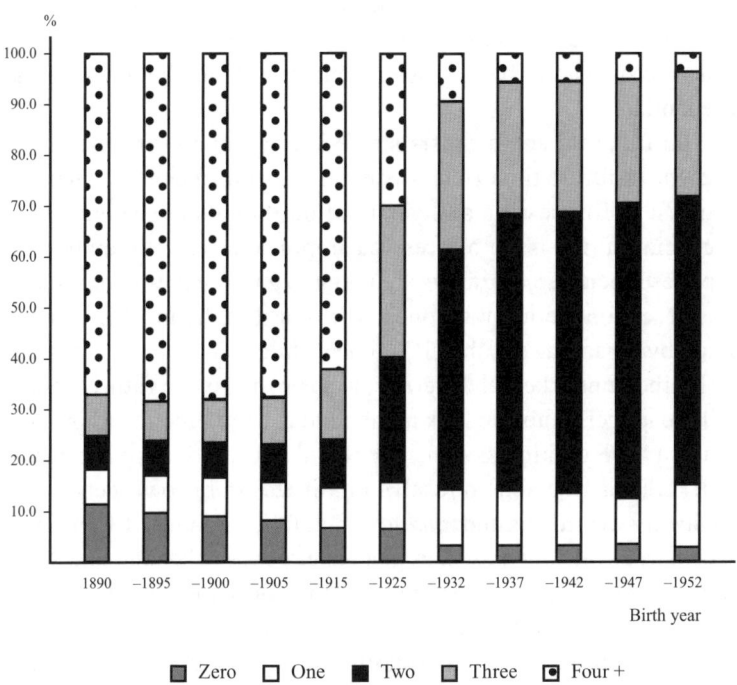

family. It was an ethos that spread widely across Japan in the postwar period. Parents worked hard to send their children to 'good schools' and then into jobs at 'good companies.' This combination of hard-working parents and hard-studying children became the de facto standard for the Japanese family.

This was all made possible by the steady narrowing of differentials that continued through the postwar period. 'Opportunity' – that name we give to the game of acquiring and distributing resources – became gradually more equal. It consequently became possible to believe that there would be a further increase in equality in the future. It was possible to believe that one's children would be playing in a fairer game than one had played in oneself, and would be accurately judged by society according to their own abilities.

The influence was felt not just among general members of society, but also within the academy. Sociologists developed a powerful interest in trends – that is, in how things would develop in future. As I mentioned earlier, if one is seriously interested in correcting unfairness in the person of the individual him/herself, then talk about the period from present to future becomes of strictly secondary importance – since it is virtually impossible to send a grown adult back to school and rewrite his/her educational credentials.

The fact that sociologists started showing an interest in the present-to-future time zone was not due just to sociology's natural interest in forecasting and verification, but also because this is a crucial policy issue of pressing importance to all members of Japanese society. How things are going to go from now on may have no direct connection with one's self, but it is the most important issue by far to one's 'sub-self' – one's child.

By the same token, if differentials do not narrow in future, people will no longer be able to look to their children to function as proxies. Not only will unfairness arise in the child's generation, but the parent will no longer be able to resolve unfairness in his own generation by seeing it compensated in the one that follows. When differentials stop narrowing, not only does that generate the 'illusion of decline': it also creates serious concrete problems for both generations.

But that is not all. At an even more fundamental level, the very nature of the family is undergoing change. It is already evident that parents can no longer take it for granted that their children will compensate for their unfulfilled aspirations through proxy attainment as 'sub-selves.' In this respect, too, the principle of equality of opportunity is running into some serious difficulties.

The end of the postwar-type family

There is quite a bit of data to back up my assertion that the mindset that sees children as proxies for their parents is crumbling – or, to be more precise, is becoming harder to apply.

Of the various indices, the easiest to understand is of course the dwindling birthrate. If a child is to serve as proxy to a parent, then the most natural approach to procreation is for everyone to get married and have two children, preferably one boy and one girl. Producing boys and girls to order still poses some challenges to reproductive technology, but it is now fairly easy to plan one's family at least in terms of number of offspring.

An Explosion of Inequality Consciousness

Japan has always had a high marriage rate, but if we look at the age cohort born before 1900, nearly 10% of married women had no children. For the 1926–32 birth cohort, i.e. the generation that started families shortly after the war, the zero-child percentage dips below 4%, while nearly half of all married women gave birth to two children. There are various factors influencing the number of children people have, but we may observe that the style of family composition emerging in this period was relatively well matched to the project of proxy attainment I have been discussing.

Recently there has been no great change in the number of children of each married couple, but the marriage rate has been falling and we have seen more people in their 30s and 40s without children.

Some more telling data comes from a regular survey on 'Japanese Value Orientations' conducted by the NHK Broadcasting Culture Research Institute, which includes the following item asking for a response to a statement approving of working mothers: 'Even if a child is born, it is better for the mother to carry on working.' In the 1973 survey, only 20% agreed with this statement, but in 2003 that figure had risen to 49%. This NHK survey also found that the percentage of people thinking girls should be educated to university level had more than doubled, from 22% in 1973 to 48% in 2003. Meanwhile, the percentage thinking that boys should be educated to university level climbed from 64% in 1973 to 72% in 1988 but fell back to 68% in 2003, thus remaining fairly even over the 30-year span, and there was only a tiny increase in those calling for boys to go to graduate school. It would appear that the rise in educational expectations for girls was not just part of a general increase, but did in fact represent a substantial narrowing of the gender gap in status attainment expectations – while doubtless leaving intact discrimination at the concrete level.

Also significant is the changing pattern of responses to a question added from the 1993 edition of the NHK survey: 'Is it only natural to have children?' In the 10 years from 1993 to 2003, the percentage of people answering 'Even if one gets married, one does not necessarily have to have children' rose from 40% to 50%, while those answering 'It is only natural for married couples to have children' fell from 54% to 44%. The majority view has changed sides on this issue.

Figure 1.2: Future/present focus of life objectives, 1973–2003

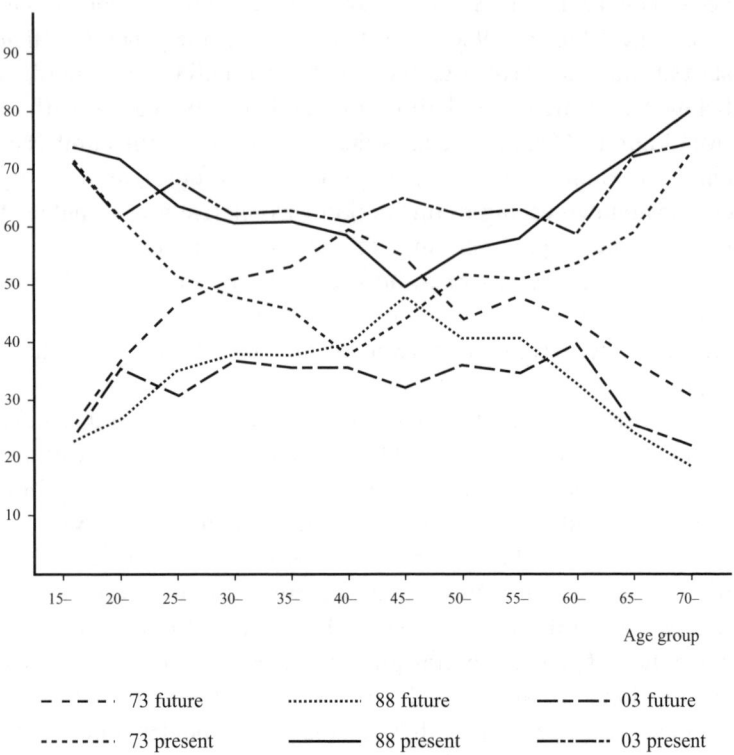

Source: NHK Broadcasting Culture Research Institute.

The vanishing future orientation

Another striking feature of the NHK surveys has been the decline of the future orientation in people's life objectives. This item is calculated from a question asking survey respondents to choose which one of the following four statements best describes their objective in life: (1) 'Live each day freely and enjoyably'; (2) 'Pass tranquil days with people close to me'; (3) 'Put together a good solid plan and construct an affluent future'; (4) 'Join forces with everyone to make the world a better place.' Scores for the first and second choices are pooled and labeled 'present orientation,' and scores for the third and fourth are pooled and labeled 'future orientation.' As we can see from Figure 1.2, present orientation has been steadily supplanting future orientation in recent years.

Looking at it in terms of age groups, the 1973 survey found a majority espousing the future orientation in the 30–50 age range. One would hardly expect the 10–20 group to be overly concerned with future social justice or affluence, since they still have so much life to look forward to, but the future orientation strengthens as people enter the childrearing years. In sharp contrast to that picture, the 2003 survey finds the present orientation outweighing the future orientation in every single age group. Moreover, from the age of 20 to the age of 65, there is virtually no change in the values for the two orientations: for decade after decade, present orientation is in the 60–70% range while future orientation is in the 30–40% range. It seems that one's position in the life cycle no longer has much bearing on orientation to present or future.

The logic of proxy achievement, by children serving as sub-selves, seeks to offset past inequality via a more equal game to be played in the future. It therefore goes hand in hand with future orientation. Indeed, while the strengthening of the future orientation in the childrearing years observable in the 1973 data does not conclusively prove the strength of 'proxy achievement logic,' the weakening of the connection between age-group and future/present orientation in the 2003 data does strongly suggest that this way of thinking is not working any more.

Looking at other past surveys, we find that 1988 is the first one in which present orientation outweighs future orientation for all age groups. However, at this point in time there is still a discernible spike in future orientation for those in their 40s, and a corresponding dip in present orientation. By the time we get to the 1998 survey, the graph line is virtually flat from 20 to 65 (NHK Hōsō Bunka Kenkyūjo 2000: 194), so we can probably locate the significant change in mindset in the 1990s.

What the 'sense of inequality' has to tell us

As I pointed out at the start of this chapter, equality of opportunity is a concept that is by its very nature impossible to measure accurately; yet correcting it requires intervention into the vital personal interests of each individual human being. It follows that eliminating inequality of opportunity is a tricky matter at the best of times, but intergenerational inequality involving families is particularly awkward to deal with. It is understood that we cannot attribute the various elements involved in inequality simply to each individual. However, since the family system acknowledges, tacitly perhaps, the continuity of personhood between family members, we cannot prevent parents from exerting influence on their children.

That is basically because, going beyond the issue of opportunity inequality, we have not been able to define the position of the family in modern society; that is to say, we have not been able to logically derive the role of the family from the fundamental principles of modern society. In modern society there is no positive logic to justify the family; consequently, when the family comes into direct confrontation with the principle of self-responsibility, we are also unable to put together a logic to mediate between the two.

Here I think the concept of correcting inequalities through the person of the child as 'sub-self' is quite a useful solution, or should I say 'dissolution' of the problem. It looks at parent-child continuity the other way round, and corrects the confirmed inequalities of the past in future time. It takes the two great problems afflicting inequality theory – the challenge of measuring what is indeterminate by nature, and the continuity between parent and child – and uses them to cancel each other out as if by magic.

Of course in postwar Japan, the people themselves were not entirely aware of how effectively this mechanism was working. There is no data we might use to establish directly how much effect it actually had on erasing consciousness of inequality. When all is said and done, this is just a hypothesis. However, we can at least say that with its long-term narrowing of status differentials, and its prevalence of nuclear families engaged in education, postwar Japan provided a good environment for that erasure of inequality consciousness to take place.

By the same token, however, now that this erasure effect is itself being erased, it is becoming very difficult to solve the problem of opportunity inequality; or, to put it better, we can see no prospect of solving it; we cannot even see any *possibility* of solving it. You could say that we are now in a situation very similar to that faced by those 17th century New England Puritans I discussed earlier. Changes in the mechanisms of postwar society are deeply implicated in the explosion of inequality consciousness we have seen since the second half of the 1990s.

Thinking along these lines, we may say that it is quite natural for people to feel that widening inequality is a really massive sea-change, something going far beyond any measurable reality. This is not just about equality and inequality as patterns of resource acquisition: another grand system, the postwar family, is implicated in the erasure and subsequent explosion of inequality consciousness. It is because people sense the enormity of a change that is engulfing the whole of society that they feel a powerful reality in the word *fubyōdōka*, or 'unequalization.'

I refuse to dismiss out of hand the fears of people obsessed with widening inequality, and I do not believe they can be written off simply as instances of victim consciousness or media-incited hysteria. Neither, however, do I simply affirm those feelings as a true reflection of actual inequality. Those are two very different things. Feelings are themselves important social facts: they come from the acute intuitions of real people who feel social change through their skin. For that very reason it is essential, when drafting policy responses or conducting sociological research, to analyze, as clearly and accurately as possible, where those intuitions come from and what sort of changes are involved in what sort of ways with those feelings. On the basis of that kind of careful analysis, we then have to reconstruct those feelings. Because it is likely that a lot of elements will be involved in a very complex system, we have to avoid over-simplification and map out that system in all its glorious complexity.

In that sense, I view it as erroneous either to affirm or deny the rationality of the explosion in inequality consciousness. Neither sociologists nor policymakers are in any position to look down upon this phenomenon and pass judgment on it as a good or bad thing. Rather we should view this topic as a challenge that we have to take on.

The mechanism of policy failures

If I were to attempt a rough mapping of the unequalization problem, I think it would look something like what I have described above.

In present-day Japan, it is gradually becoming impossible to establish a 'sub-self' in the form of one's offspring. We can no longer define parents with children who maintain continuity of the parents' personhood as a de facto standard. On the other hand, each individual *does* without question have parents. That is to say, the living individual is always somebody's child, and will inevitably be influenced by that fact. People continue to receive unequal inheritances from their parents, but many of them can no longer hope to restore a measure of equality through their children.

It follows that we are now faced with the challenge of correcting inequality of opportunity during the lifetime of each individual. People have become far more sensitive than they used to be to this problem, and the degree to which it can be solved will be bound up with trust in society at the level of its fundamental principles.

When thinking about this point, one is once again reminded of the importance of item (3) in my list of factors influencing the explosion of inequality consciousness: policy failures. At this juncture, when the old systems erasing inequality consciousness have largely ceased to work, one might expect the government to take some kind of countermeasures to ease public dissatisfaction. Instead, whether by accident or design, policies have repeatedly been adopted that have had precisely the opposite effect. Just at the time when opportunity inequality started to become very visible, the government responded with facile attempts to portray equality as a bad thing in the first place (*akubyōdō*, literally 'bad equality'), or to stress the self-responsibility (*jiko sekinin*) of the individual. Apparently believing its own propaganda, the government developed policies that denied the very existence of the problem. The timing of these moves can only be described as terrible.

There was a perfectly good reason for that terrible timing. The government started denying there was any inequality problem, not *in spite of* the failure of the old self-correcting system, but *because of* that failure. Once the traditional solution stopped working, the government went into a state of denial, turning its back upon the problem in the hope that it would go away. The anesthetic wore off and the doctor resorted to hypnotism, looking the patient in the eye and solemnly intoning 'there is no pain.'

Ironically enough, the very same mechanism of denial that we can observe behind all the talk about bad equality and self-responsibility had also been at work in the series of blunders that plunged the Japanese economy into recession a few years earlier. Take the case of bed debt, for example. Until the bubble economy went 'pop,' the banks had been able to get away with making rash loans by waiting for asset prices to rise still higher so that the borrower had the leeway to reconstruct their finances and pay back the loan. After the bubble burst, although the old remedy had ceased to work – no, *because* it had ceased to work – the banks started pretending there was no bad debt problem, juggling the accounts by shifting bad debts onto the books of subsidiaries, etc. in order to maintain the pretence. This is exactly the kind of self-delusion that we now see concerning the problem of inequality.

Perhaps this kind of behavior is only human. Certainly I do not demand god-like perfection of judgment from fallible humans with limited knowledge. However, once we are aware of the problem there can be no going back to the old ways. Today we live in a society that is growing increasingly conscious of inequality. We have no option but to honestly face that fact and look for new solutions to the problem of opportunity inequality.

Five strategies toward a new solution

So – what kind of new solution might there be? I cannot claim to have a concrete vision for the future, but I do think the lines along which we need to think can be fairly clearly laid out. Broadly speaking, I see five strategic issues on which we need to focus.

Securing the survival and participatory ability of the individual

If we are to correct inequality at the level of the individual, as opposed to his/her children, we first have to secure for each individual the possibility of living a long life, so that they survive long enough to participate fully in the game of status attainment. To put it simply, we need to concentrate on guaranteeing 'the future of the individual' rather than 'the future of the individual's children.' It follows that social security systems, particularly those concerned with maintaining health, will be of great importance.

Ishida Hiroshi's analysis in Chapter 5 of the present volume suggests that happily, there does not seem to be a very noticeable level of inequality on this point in Japan today – life expectancy and standard of health do not show big variations related to income, social status, etc., unlike in the US, UK, etc. where very concrete instances of inequality have been demonstrated. Japan's medical and health insurance systems have often been described as 'socialistic' by admirers and critics alike; if they are going to have to be reformed, there is every possibility that we may see a shift toward the Anglo-Saxon model here as in so many other aspects of society.

Guaranteeing the individual the chance of a long life and continued participation in society is an essential precondition to the other four strategies I will outline here. In general, inequality of opportunity is something that we can only grasp after the event (Satō 2000a), meaning that by the time we discover inequality it is often too late to do anything about it, and this applies in spades to inequality in lifespan and physical health. It follows that this issue requires sensitive and continuous monitoring.

Further, if we are to make it consistently possible for the individual to have a second chance at acquiring higher status, abolition of age discrimination in employment is absolutely essential.

Switching to a balance-sheet strictly based on the individual

In a system where children substitute for their parents in the pursuit of status, it is inevitable that the parents will be quite old by the time the children have reached a measurable status. Quite often the parents will already have died by then. It follows that the key issue is not so much whether or not the children really can attain status as proxies of their parents as whether or not the parents can reasonably *expect* them to do that. Indeed, this issue of reasonable expectation has been accorded much weight in Japan.

For instance, the endless meandering series of reforms of selection systems, especially university entrance examinations, may be seen as a sacrifice to this necessity to maintain future expectations of inequality redress. Constant tinkering with the entrance exam system sends out the message that 'there are inappropriate elements in the system we have had up to now, and in future these should be put right.'[5] Thus, irrespective of any changes that actually happen to selection outcomes in future, the expectation of greater equality of opportunity has been constantly renewed. Borrowing a coinage of Takeuchi Yo, it has been possible to 're-heat' (*sai-kanetsu*) the status-attainment game across the generations (Takeuchi 1995).

The demise of ways of thinking based on the 'sub-self' makes it much harder to erase consciousness of present inequality through vague hopes for the future. What is called for, then, is a thoroughgoing correction of inequality through a social security system in which the hypothetical unit of account is the individual rather than the family.

I am not saying that we have to maintain strict balance between payments and receipts for each individual. What I am saying, though, is that the profit and loss has to be made clear for each individual and we have to promote adjustment between and within generations on the basis of some clear agreement.

Aiming for redistribution that takes account of uncertainty

I will have more to say about this below, but it is of course impossible to eliminate every single element of opportunity inequality. Nor would I argue that we should attempt such a thing in the first place. In the real world, correcting inequality carries quite a heavy social cost. A series of policy compromises will be needed, but in order to judge where to make compromises we first need to establish a clear understanding of the character of the inequality-correction enterprise.

As I have repeatedly stated, correcting inequality in the person of the individual entails taking corrective measures without being able to establish for certain how much inequality there is, nor what sort of factors have caused that inequality. However, once we get tangled up in the struggle to strictly identify every element in the web of cause and effect, we can all too easily end up chasing our tails. And while that futile debate continues, a situation that clearly *is* unequal just gets more firmly entrenched.[6]

That leaves us with no option but to press forward with corrective measures even while admitting a degree of uncertainty regarding the problem we are trying to correct. Conversely, when seeking to correct inequality, it is good to seek methods in which a degree of uncertainty does not constitute a fatal flaw. Or to put it a little more precisely, in an ideal world one would accurately recalculate each individual's level of contribution to society to take account of inequality in starting position. Boldly claiming that one has succeeded in this intrinsically impossible task runs the risk of increasing a different kind of inequality by unfairly applying 'corrective' measures that do not reflect reality. It would be far better to think of redistributive measures that would apply uniformly to everyone.

Tateiwa Shinya puts the matter well when he says that even if one starts from a position of demanding only equality of *opportunity*, measures designed to correct inequalities of *outcome* are both more effective and more just, in the sense that they are less likely to generate further injustices (Tateiwa 2004). One who advocates equality of opportunity cannot reject out of hand particular policies, such as concrete methods to redistribute resources, just because they are predicated on equality of outcome. We must *fully take into account the barriers to precise measurement of inequality* before deciding to adopt or reject any given policy.

Reducing the burden on parent-child continuity

It is often pointed out that correcting equality brings a heavy burden, both economically and ethically. Indeed, any state that attempted to totally eradicate inequality of opportunity would have to gather a colossal amount of data about its citizens, about their environmental conditions and activities as well as the assets at their disposal. That would entail the creation of a gargantuan control society (Satō 2000b, 2001).

All is not lost, however, for we can choose the degree of precision with which we propose to correct inequality. Just because absolutely precise correction is impossible in reality, or is not desirable because achieving it would violate other fundamental principles such as the freedom of the individual, this does not mean we should abandon the whole project of correcting inequality. What we have to do is constantly weigh the injustices that arise from correcting inequality against those that arise from leaving inequality unchecked. Since absolute equality is impossible, we cannot use arguments based on what might happen if it actually were to be achieved, either to support or oppose corrective measures. In debating inequality, it is fine to discuss the theoretical limiting cases or conduct intellectual experiments in order to clarify the logic of the debate – but in such cases we have to start by asking whether these instances really merit serious discussion in the first place.

The problem of parent-child continuity is very much a case in point. Since the family system exists, we cannot prevent parents from influencing their children. However, we can take a selective approach, asking ourselves which forms of influence are acceptable and which are not. For instance, it would be difficult to forbid parents from becoming actively involved in their children's education, but it would be perfectly possible to establish a system of subsidies to enable children of low-income parents to attend schools with high fees. It is also possible to put limits on the ability of parents to carry on financially supporting their children after they have died – by levying high rates of inheritance tax on wealthy estates, for instance, thereby at least obliging wealthy individuals to give money to their children while they themselves are still alive. These and other measures can be taken to alleviate inequality.

We cannot denounce all the various ways in which parents influence their children and thereby create inequality of opportunity – but that does not mean we have to approve of all of them.

Clear demarcation between what is subject to individual choice and what is not

One basic issue involved in all four of the above issues is the distinction between areas of life that can be left to individual choice and those that cannot.

When one is arguing about principles, this distinction is an axiomatic premise, but when it comes to measuring what goes on in real life, it is far from easy even to define an accurate distinction. For example, it is possible to measure the average degree of influence that parents' educational level or occupation has on their children, but it is not possible, or at least not a realistic proposition, to figure out exactly which factors have had what degree of influence on the life of each individual person. There are always people who attain high levels of achievement despite being born and brought up in a poor environment, but that is not evidence that environment has no influence. Beyond a certain point, the degree of influence is always indeterminable. As I said above, we also have to assume indeterminacy when seeking to correct inequality; and, again as noted above, any attempt to argue from extreme limiting cases must start by establishing that using such instances is really appropriate.

That being so, drawing a line to distinguish that which is subject to individual choice from that which is not will inevitably be a 'social' project to some degree, rather than something that can be derived from first principles. In sociology jargon, that dividing line is 'socially constructed,' but at a more fundamental level it has to be treated as a *contract* between individuals.

The most important thing about a contract is that once it has been agreed to it should be honored. Put simply, if we are to permit the inheritance of wealth from one generation to the next, we cannot hold individuals wholly responsible for their wealth or poverty. If we accept that education can take place in the household, we cannot ascribe educational achievement entirely to the efforts of the individual. Naturally these are issues of degree, not yes/no issues, and we need to include an awareness of that fact in striving to take a consistent stance on the limits of individual choice.

Inconsistency on this point can cause an explosion of inequality that goes beyond the size of real-life differentials. Even if we cannot provide objective grounds to justify the place where we draw the line, and even if we are unable in real life to correct all the inequalities of opportunity that we identify, it is at least possible, and necessary, to show consistency in our application of the standards we use to draw the line.

Goals for equalization strategies

The five strategies I have just outlined are *not* designed to reduce inequality to zero.

Attempts to improve society by reducing inequality will always run up against the two imponderables that I mentioned above – the impossibility of accurately determining levels of inequality, and the more fundamental systemic problem of the family. We can no longer hope for some mechanism like the postwar family system to play these two problems off against each other and cancel them out.[7] Barring some drastic change in modern society as presently constituted, these barriers to equality cannot be totally eradicated. We cannot totally eradicate them, but neither can we leave them untouched. Inequality of opportunity will always be that kind of problem.

What is called for, then, is not a policy aiming at a 'final solution.' Even though total eradication of inequality is neither possible nor desirable, we still need a realistic approach that moves the game of resource acquisition and distribution in as fair a direction as possible, without wreaking irreparable damage on the lives of each individual member of society. That is the sort of solution that is called for.

This may sound self-contradictory, but the reason why the required solution is so pragmatic is precisely because equality of opportunity is a magnificent *principle*. The principles of resource distribution, and indeed social principles in general, are not just ideals that go beyond reality, but the very foundations of the trust that people invest in their society. Preserving trust does not require 100% success. It is not necessary to make everyone do well, but if certain people are abandoned or ignored right from the start, *that* is a fatal flaw in society.

Social principles are not destroyed by failure to achieve them – they are destroyed by people losing faith in them. That is a far greater loss to society. It follows that the really important thing for policies that touch upon social principles is not to totally eliminate problems and overcome challenges, but to show the highest possible degree of sensitivity to those problems and challenges. It is important to avoid policies that lead to problems and challenges being overlooked – including those that have not yet become apparent. The German sociologist Niklas Luhmann called this approach 'system rationality' (1973). Borrowing Luhmann's style of expression, we may say that the five strategies I have just outlined are solutions 'functionally equivalent' to maintaining the principle of equality of opportunity.

'Equality of opportunity' remains a very distant objective. When something is so far away, it is easier to grieve over it than to strive for it; easier to pretend we cannot see it than to learn the pain of striving for something we cannot reach. I rather fancy that this is the psychology underlying the debate on inequality of opportunity – a debate that always tends to become overly theoretical, and to become the plaything of those who enjoy theoretical argument about abstract principles.

Inequality is the kind of topic where one naturally wants to argue in terms of extremes, and where it is indeed easier to argue in terms of extremes. But I happen to believe that it is terribly boring to only walk the easy road.

2 Unequal Japan: Implications for Households and Gender[1]

Sawako Shirahase

Trends in inequality

Japan used to be celebrated as a mass middle-class society, in which the great majority of the population had a middle-class consciousness and there was no rigid class system (Murakami 1977, 1984). In every house there was a television, a washing machine and a vacuum cleaner. Wherever you went in Japan, people would be humming the same pop songs and wearing the same clothes that they had seen in the same fashion magazines. Popular writings on Japanese society emphasized the remarkable degree of homogeneity: whoever you looked at, and wherever they lived, they would be sharing the same lifestyle. Such writings, known as *Nihonjinron*, powerfully reinforced that image. This cultural uniformity, among a people who placed great emphasis on harmony, was widely identified as a key factor in the super-high economic growth of the 1960s – the so-called 'Japanese Miracle.'

The high-growth 60s hit a wall in 1973, when the first oil shock plunged Japan into a period of low growth. That year became known as *fukushi gannen*, literally the first year of the welfare era, but it only lasted for one year, and the government had to restructure the social security system while keeping a close eye on the severely stretched resources available to finance it. A new challenge emerged in 1990, with the revelation that the total fertility rate had plunged to just 1.57 in 1989 – the so-called '1.57 shock.' Why weren't women having more babies? An alarmed government started casting around for policies to support childbirth and childrearing.

From the mid-1980s, Japan developed a supercharged economy, defying a global economic turndown that brought widening trade deficits and rising unemployment to Europe and the US. Ultimately, the bubble economy brought pathologies of its own: economic logic started to warp, so that higher prices would sometimes bring better sales. The feeling spread through society that anyone could enjoy a luxurious lifestyle. But a close look at what was really going on reveals that while the rich were undoubtedly getting richer, the poor were also getting poorer.

The 1990s brought the bursting of the bubble economy: the dream of limitless wealth was over. This time low economic growth was here to stay: unemployment climbed, and even middle-aged and elderly people who had long thought themselves immune from unemployment suddenly found they were facing dismissal. It began to occur to a lot of people that Japan was a much less equal society than they had imagined. Their nascent suspicions were fuelled by books like Toshiaki Tachibanaki's *Nihon no Keizai Kakusa* (Economic differentials in Japan) (1998) and Toshiki Satō's *Fubyōdō Shakai Nippon* (The unequal society, Japan) (2000a), both of which became bestsellers.

Were income differentials really widening during this period? Based on the Comprehensive Survey of the People's Living Conditions (*Kokumin Seikatsu Kiso Chōsa*), we can obtain the following Gini coefficients[2] for Japan: .293 in 1986, .317 in 1995, and .335 in 2001. Clearly, then, inequality was indeed on the rise in this period.[3] However, the people's attitude toward inequality outstripped the differentials shown in these Gini figures (Ohtake 2005).

The terms 'differentials' and 'inequality' tend to be used interchangeably, but they are not quite the same thing. Perhaps a note would be in order about the relationship between the two. Satō (2005b) draws a distinction between economic differentials and social ones, arguing that the former term emphasizes the measurement of the degree of economic gaps whereas the latter takes into account the relative standards with which the gap is evaluated. Social differentials thus include concepts of unfairness and inequality that go beyond quantitative gaps or differences. In that sense, differentials are relative rather than absolute. On top of that, the significance of economic differentials goes beyond differences in income, albeit they are the most common representative measure: these differentials generate more all-inclusive economic advantage and disadvantage to individuals and households. When I say 'all-inclusive' I mean not just the degree to which one possesses various kinds of financial capability at any given moment, but also the degree to which one possesses the latent ability to respond to the various social risks that may befall one in the future. The difference between high income and low income includes concealed differences going well beyond any gap in annual income expressed in simple cash terms – and those differences are relative, not absolute. To elucidate those relative differences is the objective of inequality research.

In this chapter we will use the Gini coefficient as our index of income inequality. This coefficient indicates the degree to which a given population deviates from the hypothetical situation where the distribution of income is perfectly equal. However, there is room for debate as to what is the ideal level for the Gini coefficient: few would favor an ultimate policy goal of reducing it to zero. Konishi (2002) is surely right to point out the problems of description and norm that arise in using inequality indices. Any attempt to argue about inequality or unfairness must start by clarifying social norms regarding what constitutes inequality and what degree of equality should be the ultimate goal of society. The Gini coefficients used in this chapter are no more than a tool for describing degrees of income inequality, and one could not hope to argue convincingly about social norms regarding inequality using these coefficients alone.

The concept of inequality (*fubyōdō*) always interferes in debate on 'differentials' (*kakusa*), including the notion of gaps (*sa*) that cannot be accepted as just. Ignoring such morally indefensible gaps may be viewed as 'relative deprivation' (Satō 2005b). Differentials include certain given conditions that cannot largely be explained by individual ability: they are formidable obstacles standing in the way of progress. For example, one's class origin, age and gender are given conditions that cannot be controlled at one's own discretion. Lowering these barriers against equality under social justice – that, surely, is the challenge that must be overcome to achieve a better society.

Two perspectives on economic inequalities: Households and gender

It is far from easy to specify the causes of economic inequality. The aging population is certainly one major factor. One of the first scholars to apply empirical data to demonstrating the connection between the aging population and widening economic inequality was Ohtake (1994). Older age groups in Japan tend to exhibit a greater degree of income inequality than younger age groups (Genda

1994; Ohtake and Saitō 1999; Shirahase 2002; Seike and Yamada 2004; Ohtake 2005); and, as the proportion of older age groups has grown in relation to other age groups, the overall extent of income inequality has consequently widened.

However, the aging population is not a sole sufficient explanation for the widening of income inequality seen in recent years. The fact is that much attention has recently been paid to widening differentials among younger age groups, and Genda (2002) has observed that the income of younger generations has fallen relative to that of the retired generation. The phenomenon of widening differentials among younger age groups is of course closely related to the spread of irregular labor and unemployment (Higuchi 2004; Ohta 2005). The popularity of foreign-sounding words like *freeter* ('free arbeiter') and NEET (Not in Employment, Education or Training) to describe younger generation lifestyles gives us a sense of the spirit of the times. Young people today, we are told, have no interest in slaving away like worker bees for the sake of the company, wearing a white shirt and tight necktie in the heat of summer. One popular image is of young people unencumbered by the dead weight of outmoded values, gliding elegantly through the era, happy to be part-time workers if they can defend their personal freedom. In sharp contrast to that image, the number of dispirited unemployed youths who cannot get regular employment even if they do want it, has continued to rise. There are young people in Japan today struggling in desperation because they cannot get a steady job. Genda (2001; English version 2005) has aptly described their 'vague feeling of anxiety' about their working careers.

Arguments over the greater differentials in older age groups, or the expansion of differentials among the young, have a common stance that seeks to identify in as much detail as possible where the big differentials are and where differentials have been widening. In this chapter the attempt to get a clear picture of what differentials really mean will focus on households and on gender. The formation of inequality in the real world does not happen at the level of neutral individual people. Regional and national societies are formed out of households and families – the basic units of consumption. This chapter will focus on the interplay between individuals, households/family, regions and society as the multi-dimensional site where the structures of inequality are formed.

There has been some lively discussion about the household from the standpoint of social security system and social class theory (Acker 1973, 1980; Goldthorpe 1983, 1984; Hara and Seiyama 1999; Ōsawa Mari 2002; Kokuritsu Shakai Hoshō/Jinkō Mondai Kenkyūjo 2002b; Shirahase 2004). In particular, studies on the changing lifestyles of women have called into question the appropriateness of defining the household as a homogeneous unit where all family members share the identical social status represented by the head of the household (the householder; usually a man) and treating it as the fundamental unit of socioeconomic systems and status groups. In cases where the household relies on the single income of the householder, or runs its own family business, there has not been too much difficulty in defining the household's socioeconomic standing in terms of that of its head. More importantly, there has been an unstated assumption that the other members of the household share the same socioeconomic standing as the householder. However, where the wife is also working outside the home, cases can arise where wife and husband have different employment conditions. In such cases one naturally has to ask whether it is still appropriate to assume that the household is a homogeneous community. At the same time we must also remember that not all households have multiple members; that there are many households composed of a single person living alone. Indeed, a rise in the number of single-person households has been one of the striking changes in household type in recent years.

When I speak of household type, I have in mind a typology of households based on the relationships between family members, such as households composed of a childless couple,[4] or of a nuclear family, etc. The household is the site where an individual's real life takes shape. Taking the household in this way, as the infrastructure of real people's livelihoods, how can we relate it to changes in population, and to the theme of economic differentials? That is the central theme of this chapter.

Of course, household type is not a static thing – it changes with time. The same individual may graduate from college and live alone while going to work, then get married and live for a few years in a two-person household with his/her spouse, and then live in a nuclear family household if and when children are born. The household changes form as people go through different life and family stages. Cross-sectional studies that look at circumstances at a single point in time cannot hope to investigate these changes related to life stage. That said, if we pay due attention to the householder's age and household type at the point in time surveyed, we can make a pretty good guess as to the life stage of each household member. In this chapter the household will be treated as the basic unit for investigating economic differentials, and I will use the age of the householder as a proxy variable for looking at life stage issues.

My second perspective will look at the household in terms of gender. A lot of work has already been done on economic differentials and gender, mainly by labor economists (Shinotsuka 1982; Yashiro 1983; Higuchi 1991; Ōsawa Machiko 1993; Nagase 1997). However, these works have tended to focus on the position of individual women vis-à-vis men, and there has not been much work done that incorporates a gender perspective into studies specifically of the household in debating economic differentials. Broadly speaking there are two ways of looking at the household from a gender perspective: one that focuses on gender in the context of intra-household dynamism, or differences between household members; and another that looks at the head of the household, from the viewpoint of gender. Thus a study of the contribution to family earnings from the wife's employment would be an example of the former approach. Here, however, I want to take the latter approach and look at how household structure varies according to whether the householder is female or male.

Specifically, I propose to look at two kinds of household: single-person households and single-parent households. The economic status of a person living alone varies considerably according to gender. I have already discussed empirical analyses on the unfavorable economic circumstances of elderly women living alone (Shirahase 2002, 2005b). As for single-parent families, they are still a relatively small proportion of the population, accounting for less than 10% of Japan's households, but that percentage is steadily on the increase. Research on single-mother households in Japan remains far from sufficient, but the issue has been discussed to some extent, mainly in the context of poverty studies. Iwata (2004) uses a panel survey to detail the 'experience of poverty'[5] of single-mother households, identifying divorce, widowhood and separation as factors increasing the risk of falling into poverty, along with large numbers of children, low educational attainment and continued non-marriage.

The high level of employment among single mothers in Japan has already been established by a large volume of research (Shinotsuka 1992; Shimoebisu 1993; Fujiwara 2003; Nagase 2003; Shirahase 2005a). Ezawa and Fujiwara (2005) see one factor in that high level of single-parent employment to be the system of child support allowances, which includes strong employment incentives. Many single mother families are in the low-income stratum, and that of course is closely connected to the low wages that single mothers tend to earn. Abe and Ōishi (2005) observe that nearly all Japanese single mothers are in employment, and argue that cash payments to these women from public welfare authorities should be read as a policy functioning to supplement their low incomes, thereby lessening the risk of falling into the low-income bracket.

The data used in this chapter comes from the income section of the Comprehensive Survey of the People's Living Conditions, editions of 1986, 1995 and 2001.[6] This is a very valuable resource, containing as it does some of the most precise data available on incomes across Japan, derived moreover from fairly large samples. My analysis will focus on incomes, a particular strength of the Comprehensive Survey, to cast fresh light upon changes in economic differentials and the present situation. I will be looking at data for the mid-1980s, mid-1990s and the start of the 21st century, and naturally some interpretative caution is called for since the three surveys are not at uniform chronological intervals. Since the household is the unit used by the Comprehensive Survey, I will focus my analysis mainly on householders (i.e. heads of households). The kinds of household type to be covered here are (1) single-person households, (2) couple-only households, (3) nuclear families (married couples with one or more unmarried children), (4) single-parent families (one parent with one or more unmarried children), (5) three-generation households, and (6) others not covered by the first five categories. In some cases I merge single-parent families with nuclear or three-generation families to produce five categories of household type.

Changes in household type

Figure 2.1 presents the proportion of Japan's population over the age of 65 since 1960 as indices to illustrate trends in the distribution

Figure 2.1: Trends in the household structure and ageing population

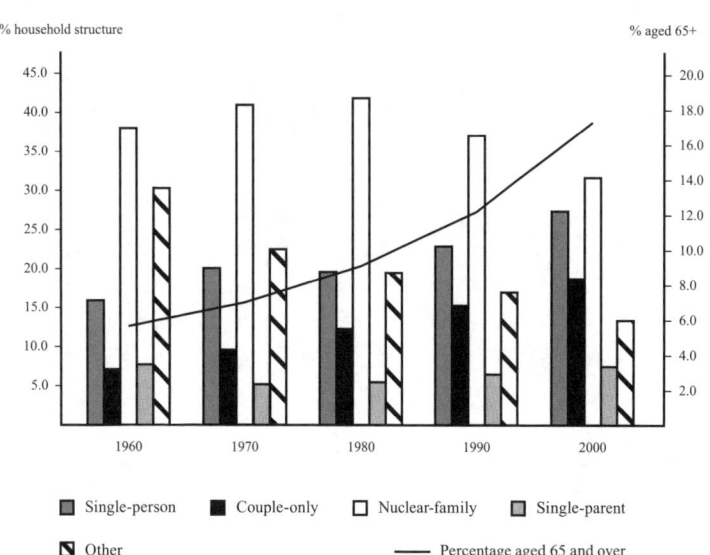

Source: Population Census of Japan (each year).

of household type along with the aging population and declining birthrate. The aging of the population and decline of the birthrate (not shown in the figure) both sharply accelerated from the second half of the 1980s. In particular the proportion of the population over the age of 65 greatly increased from the start of the 1990s. These twin trends were accompanied by changes in household type. From the 1980s onwards, single-person and couple-only households increased, while nuclear and three-generation families (included here in the 'other' category) clearly decreased. However, the economic circumstances and social significance of single-person households will naturally vary with age: life will likely be very different for a single person in his 20s to that of one in his 70s. So in Figure 2.1, I have divided data on household type from the three editions of the Comprehensive Survey into age groups.

Let us look first at households headed by people in their 20s. Changes in household type for this age group saw different pat-

Table 2.1: Trends in household structure by age of household head (%)

	20s			30s			40s		
	1986	1995	2001	1986	1995	2001	1986	1995	2001
Single-person	47.0	61.5	54.5	7.2	13.7	14.4	4.8	6.8	8.3
Couple-only	16.4	13.1	13.0	7.9	13.2	13.2	4.5	5.7	5.6
Nuclear-family	29.0	20.4	25.9	69.1	61.3	59.7	66.6	61.3	60.0
Single-parent	0.8	1.1	1.1	2.6	2.9	5.1	4.8	5.9	5.6
Three-generation	1.9	0.6	0.6	11.5	6.6	5.1	17.5	16.6	16.5
Other	5.0	3.3	4.9	1.6	2.3	2.4	1.8	3.7	4.0
Total	100.0	100.0	100.0	100.0	100.0	100.0	100.0	100.0	100.0

	50s			60s			70s and over		
	1986	1995	2001	1986	1995	2001	1986	1995	2001
Single-person	5.9	8.2	9.8	14.0	13.9	16.9	27.8	28.7	29.0
Couple-only	15.7	16.2	15.9	29.7	34.9	32.9	34.4	36.1	38.0
Nuclear-family	47.7	48.3	43.3	22.0	23.9	25.2	11.0	9.7	9.8
Single-parent	5.9	6.4	6.6	4.4	5.6	5.4	5.3	5.6	6.4
Three-generation	17.4	13.6	16.0	20.1	12.0	9.9	16.3	13.6	10.4
Other	7.4	7.4	8.4	9.7	9.7	9.6	5.2	6.2	6.5
Total	100.0	100.0	100.0	100.0	100.0	100.0	100.0	100.0	100.0

Source: Comprehensive Survey of People's Living Conditions (each year).

terns for the two periods 1986–1995 and 1995–2001. In the first period, single-person households rose very substantially – from 47% to 61.5% of the total – while nuclear families fell from 29% to 20.4%. By 2001, however, single-person households had fallen back to 54.5%, while nuclear families had rebounded to 25.9% – an increase due largely to the relative decline in singe-person households. Nuclear families where the householder is in his/her 20s are mostly young families with small children. The recent trend towards postponing marriage is bringing a decline in the absolute numbers of people married with children in their 20s, but here we are concerned with the distribution of household types *within* that group. Looking at the age distribution of the total population of householders we find that the percentage of people in their 20s declined from 6.1% in 1986 to 5.2% in 2001 – a low figure, getting lower still. The reader should bear in mind that these changes I am describing are proportional changes by the age group (householders in their 20s) which is itself a small and declining minority. In the late 1980s to early 1990s, concern over the declining birthrate cast the spotlight on the growing numbers of unmarried adults who did not become new householders but continued to live with their parents and rely upon parental economic support – the so-called 'parasite singles.' But among those people in their 20s who did become householders, there was an increase in those who lived alone. Background factors here included the rise in youth unemployment from the mid-1990s,[7] and the growing proportion of young people staying on to higher levels of education.

No consideration of this age group can afford to overlook the special situation of students. In 1986 and in 1995, some 35% of solitary householders in their 20s were students. By 2001, however, that proportion had declined to 26%. Put those figures alongside the *increasing* proportion of high school graduates going on to university, from 32.1% in 1995 to 39.9% in 2001 (Monbukagakushō Shōgai Gakushū Seisaku-kyoku 2004), and it is evident that there has been a sharp decline in the proportion of students living on their own. These figures tell us that more and more university students are commuting to campus from the parental home.

For the older generations of householders, from those in their 30s upward, we can see a fairly consistent pattern in household structural change over this period. First of all, all generations show an increase in the number of single-person households. Elderly people living alone are generally forced into an unfavorable economic position, so differences in household type are especially significant for the older age groups (Shirahase 2002). However, single-person households are also increasing for those in their 30s, 40s and 50s. The trend is especially noticeable for the 30s age-group, where the proportion of single-person households precisely doubled during this period, from 7.2% in 1986 to 14.4% in 2001. At the same time, the proportion of couple-only households in this age group rose from 7.9% to 13.2% over the same period, while that of nuclear families fell from 69.1% to 59.7%. Single-parent families also nearly doubled their proportion of the total, from 2.6% to 5.1%. While they are still a fairly small proportion of the total, the steady increase in single-parent families should not be overlooked. Overall, the changes in this age group speak to a nascent diversification in lifestyles which has seen the emergence of population groups choosing to marry later in life or to refrain from having children.

Increasing single-person households may also be observed in the 40s and 50s age groups, and there too the proportion of nuclear families has been steadily falling. Even householders in their 50s, who will have to bear the brunt of the 2007 Problem,[8] have shown a decline in the proportion living in nuclear families, from 47.7% to 43.3%. Thus from the 30s right through the 50s, we see a striking decline in the number of households with children (nuclear families, three-generation households), with the exception of single-parent families, which are increasing from a low base.

The story for householders in their 60s and 70s is that most forms of household type have been rising, at the expense of three-generation households, which have shown a sharp decline. In the past, living with the younger generations provided old people in Japan not only with the kind of care and attention they need in everyday life, but also with a degree of economic protection (Shirahase 2002). However, as the graying of society has proceeded, the number of old people living alone or with just their spouse for company has been increasing and it has become difficult for them to obtain the livelihood security they require purely within the household. The human resources within the household have declined, to the point where it is difficult for old people to receive the same level of livelihood security as in previous generations – that is the tale told by these figures on household type. Changes like this in the living places of old people have had quite a considerable influence on economic differentials.

The degree of income inequality seen from the life stage perspective

In this analysis I use the age of the householder to represent life stage. Ohtake and Saitō (1999) ascribed the widening of economic differentials in the 1980s and '90s mainly to the increase in the proportion of old people in the total population, noting that this segment of the population has particularly wide economic differentials. Iwamoto (2000) also pointed to the aging population in accounting for the further increase in income inequality observed from 1989 to 1995, and the Comprehensive Surveys have confirmed that effects seen within age groups have been a major factor. I therefore propose now to look at economic differentials within age groups, and look at diachronic changes for each householder age group. Figure 2.2 shows the distribution of householder ages and Gini coefficients within each age group. The first thing that becomes apparent is that differentials have been widening among younger groups, notably householders in their 20s and 30s, while they have actually been narrowing among those aged 65 and over.

Figure 2.2: Age distribution of household head and trends in gini coefficient by age of household head

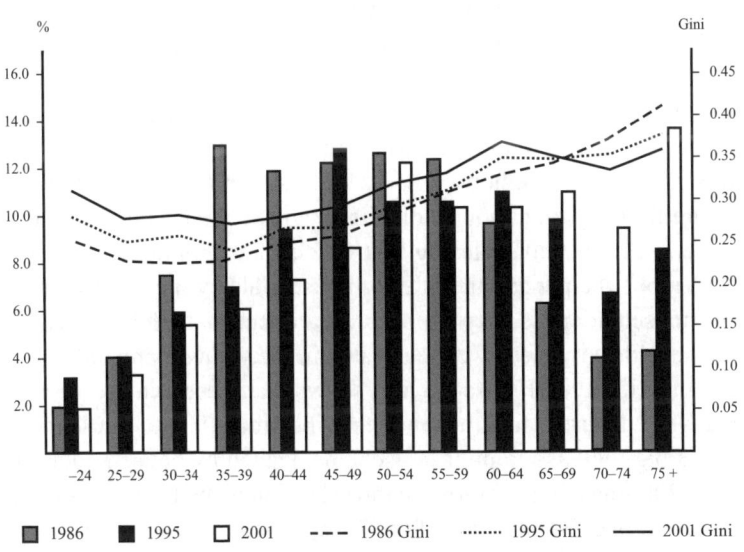

Source: Comprehensive Survey of People's Living Conditions (each year).

A look at Figure 2.2 gives us a rough idea of the connection between the changing sizes of age groups and the degree of inequality within each. The first thing we notice is that economic differentials have been widening especially sharply in the younger householder age-groups, which have been declining in size during the same period. Since the declining birthrate has decreased the size of the younger age groups, the widening differentials in these groups do not affect the overall picture as much as the aging population factor does. Hence, from the perspective of the younger generation it is not surprising if the widening differentials in Japanese society feel larger than usually described. On the other hand, the degree of income inequality has actually been declining among the expanding older age groups. Thus the relationship between size of age group and size of economic differentials varies according to which stage in the lifecycle one looks at, and this naturally confuses people's consciousness of inequality. It has been observed that the younger age groups feel inequality especially acutely, and also tend to expect society to become more unequal in future (Ohtake 2005; Shirahase 2005b). Figure 2.2 shows us that such perceptions accurately reflect what is actually going on for this generation: a particularly large increase in economic differentials. Nevertheless, even in 2001 it remains the case that Gini coefficients gradually increase with householder age, at least until the 60–64 age group.

How should we read the narrowing of differentials for the elderly age groups? It does not necessarily mean that older people overall have improved their economic status. Wider economic differentials cannot simply be equated with high levels of economic risk. In this chapter I define households with less than 50% of the median figure for equivalent household disposable income as being in the poverty group, and suffering high levels of economic risk. Figure 2.3 graphs the percentage of poor households by the age group of the householder. Its shape appears as a U-curve, with low-income households very clearly concentrated in the younger and older age-groups. However, Figure 2.3 also shows that these two age groups had very different fortunes in the period from 1986 to 2001: there was a big increase in poor households headed by householders in their 20s, and a big *decrease* in those headed by householders aged 65 and above. By the start of the 2000s, the U-shape curve shows a definite tilt towards the young end of the scale, with the percentage of poor households among those headed by householders aged

Figure 2.3: Trend in poverty rates by age of household head

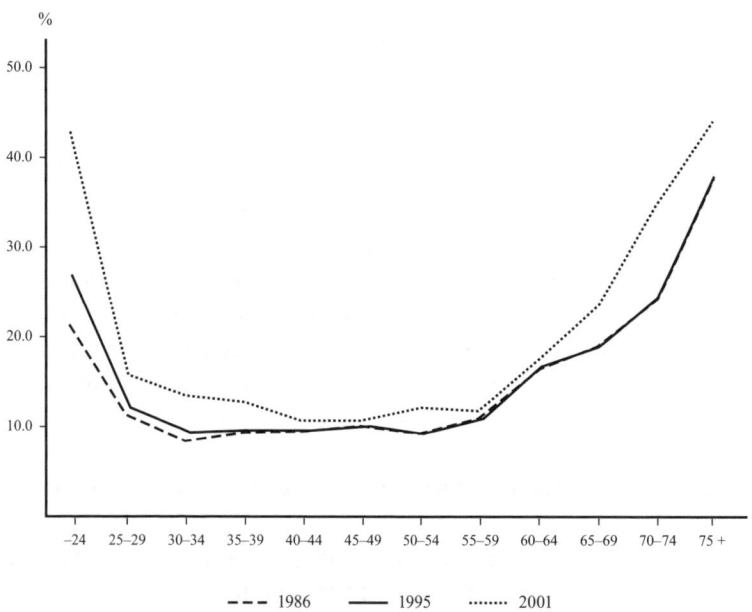

Source: Comprehensive Survey of People's Living Conditions (each year).

under 24 doubling over this 15-year period, from 21% to 42%. Meanwhile the poverty rate for householders aged 75 and above (the group with the highest poverty rate in 1986) came down from 44% to 29% in the same period. It seems reasonable to ascribe this favorable trend to improvements in public pensions and other welfare systems. As for the dramatic rise in poor households for the young generation, factors such as mounting unemployment and the spread of irregular working conditions for those who do manage to get jobs have already been widely observed (Genda 2002; Kosugi 2003; Higuchi 2004).

Finally, one more word about the position of students among householders in their 20s. The data displayed in Figure 2.3 includes students, but if we look at income sources for students we find that many are financially dependent on their parents, so that their economic circumstances, at least in terms of self-generated income, are worse than those of self-supporting householders. If we recalculate the data for the 20s age group excluding students, then the pattern of change over the 15-year period becomes less uniform, with a particularly sharp increase in inequality in the period from 1995 to 2001. Removing the student householders, many of whom fall into the poor category while depending on parental support, the bottom end of the income hierarchy rises a little higher and the picture of economic differentials for householders in their 20s looks somewhat better. However, focusing more tightly on the 1995–2001 period, we find a major increase in inequality among young householders, especially those in their *early* 20s. This reflects the growing proportion of young people who are neither students nor in regular employment. The economic facts of life are very different between students, whose lives are focused on education, and people who have already completed their education. Accordingly, I will exclude students from the analysis that follows.

Degree of income inequality seen in terms of household type

In an earlier work (Shirahase 2005c), I attempted to analyze changes in the degree of inequality among those aged 65 and over by separating factors *within* the household-type group from those *between* different household-type groups. I found that in the period from 1986 to 1989, the proportion of inter-group factors rose from 20.5% to 23.3%, but then settled down at around 20% going into the 1990s, showing that degree of income inequality *within* household type groups was of considerably greater significance. I have also found (Shirahase 2002) that in households with old people, the degree of income inequality decreased from the mid-1980s to the late 1990s, and that differences in the degree of income inequality by different household type showed an overall decline, resulting in a converging trend. Clearly, then, it is very important to take into account household type when examining income inequality.

Table 2.2 shows changes in the level of inequality classified by household type, for younger and middle-aged age groups as well as the elderly, paying due attention to differences in life-stage. For householders in their 20s, income differentials widened for every type of household except the three-generation. The wide income differentials opening up among single-person households are particularly striking.[9] The common pattern for middle-aged groups, with householders in their 30s to 50s, is of widening differentials within the nuclear family category, indicating growing income

Table 2.2: Trend in gini coefficients by household structure and age of household head

	20s			30s			40s		
	1986	1995	2001	1986	1995	2001	1986	1995	2001
Single-person	0.215	0.241	0.305	0.276	0.260	0.270	0.346	0.329	0.351
Couple-only	0.211	0.260	0.264	0.232	0.230	0.254	0.274	0.307	0.310
Nuclear-family	0.219	0.216	0.253	0.219	0.235	0.265	0.239	0.265	0.278
Three-generation	0.210	0.247	0.191	0.231	0.238	0.251	0.287	0.256	0.282
Other	0.244	0.304	0.374	0.316	0.294	0.303	0.304	0.309	0.344

	50s			60s			70s and over		
	1986	1995	2001	1986	1995	2001	1986	1995	2001
Single-person	0.414	0.398	0.405	0.421	0.412	0.431	0.392	0.383	0.366
Couple-only	0.336	0.324	0.360	0.385	0.378	0.371	0.430	0.355	0.320
Nuclear-family	0.288	0.294	0.321	0.332	0.346	0.362	0.371	0.383	0.327
Three-generation	0.282	0.288	0.291	0.288	0.295	0.316	0.294	0.293	0.305
Other	0.301	0.331	0.351	0.328	0.346	0.349	0.419	0.349	0.371

Source: Comprehensive Survey of People's Living Conditions (each year).

inequality among households with unmarried children. For the 30s age group we may further observe a similar widening of income differentials for households composed of childless couples, and even three-generation households have shown widening economic differentials in recent years. As for the 40s group, the degree of income inequality shows an overall increase across the three time-points, and here too a widening of income differentials among nuclear families is a notable feature.

Turning now to households headed by people in their 60s and over, widening differentials may be observed within the categories of nuclear families and three-generation households. Nuclear families with household heads in their 60s (and over) often include unmarried adults still cohabiting with their parents. In that sense we may say that economic differentials have been widening among households that include unmarried adult children. A similar widening of differentials may be observed in three-generation families, where the older generation typically relies upon the cohabiting younger generations for livelihood support. The three-generation household, long the representative living arrangement for older people in Japan, is rapidly declining in numbers compared with other forms of household constitution; within this dwindling category, economic differentials are steadily widening. For householders in their 60s, retirement from regular work may be followed by re-employment or by an immediate transition to life on a pension. The presence or absence of employment income leads to a greater variety of economic circumstances in this age group. It is when people are in their 60s that differences in working and living styles become most apparent, and hence this is where economic differentials are at their widest.

For householders in their 70s and over, economic differentials narrowed for almost all types of household during the period surveyed. For single-person households, the Gini coefficient fell from .392 in 1986 to .366 in 2001, while for households composed of married couples the decline was much bigger – all the way from .430 to .320. For nuclear families, Gini declined from .371 to .327. For the over-70s, hitherto the group with the biggest economic differentials, there was a narrowing of differentials, clearly distinguishing the 'old old' from the 'young old' in their 60s, for whom differentials widened.

Economic differentials are one index for gauging the degree to which wealthy and poor people are mixed together in a given population, but they do not constitute sufficient data to calculate the degree of economic risk actually afflicting people. For example, a population may be composed mainly of poor people, showing only small economic differentials within the group but still with a high proportion of people with low incomes. With that in mind, let us now look at the degree of economic risk for each type of household, taking the poverty rates as an indicator of economic risk.

Differences in economic risk according to household type

Table 2.3 shows changes across the survey period in the poverty rates for each type of household. It is immediately striking how the poverty rates rose for every household type in the 20s age group. The rise was especially noticeable for single person households (15.2% to 24.6%), and for those with children (15.7% to 22.3% for nuclear families; 6.4% to 12.5% for three-generation families). For the 30s age group too the low-income proportion rose for every kind of household except single-person households, albeit not as sharply as for the 20s group.

From the 40s upwards, all the age groups showed a decline in the poverty rate for single-person households, from 24.3% to 14.2% in the 40s, 39.6% to 31.0% in the 50s, 56.1% to 39.4% in the 60s, and 69.7% to 44.9% in the 70s. We can therefore identify a lower level of economic risk in these categories, especially marked in the two oldest age groups. Despite this improvement, however, old people are still exposed to a higher level of economic risk than young and middle-aged people: we cannot overlook the fact that nearly 40% of Japanese people living alone in their 60s, and almost half of those in their 70s and above, are in the poor group.[10] The over-60s still have the highest poverty rate, although economic differentials are narrowing for this age group.

We can also observe a marked increase in poor households where the householder is in his/her 30s, especially those with small children. We have already seen in Table 2.2 above that income differentials are widening for this age group, and the data in Table 2.3 suggests that the increasing income inequality among nuclear family households in this age group is largely caused by sinking economic fortunes at the bottom end of the economic pecking order, reflected in the increasing poverty rates. The widening income differentials

Table 2.3: Trends in poverty rates by household structure and age of household head (%)

	20s			30s			40s		
	1986	1995	2001	1986	1995	2001	1986	1995	2001
Single-person	15.2	16.0	24.6	12.8	14.0	11.1	24.3	15.8	14.2
Couple-only	4.2	7.1	7.9	3.5	3.3	4.8	8.5	7.3	9.1
Nuclear-family	15.7	21.1	22.3	8.8	9.4	13.9	8.0	9.2	9.8
Three-generation	6.5	15.4	12.5	9.0	9.2	11.1	10.6	7.3	6.4
Other	14.3	23.6	42.9	13.1	14.1	20.3	8.9	9.1	8.9
Total	13.0	16.2	22.2	8.7	9.3	12.3	9.3	9.2	9.8

	50s			60s			70s and over		
	1986	1995	2001	1986	1995	2001	1986	1995	2001
Single-person	39.6	32.0	31.0	56.1	40.6	39.4	69.7	56.5	44.9
Couple-only	10.4	7.3	8.9	16.5	14.6	15.4	37.2	22.6	16.7
Nuclear-family	8.4	8.0	10.2	12.4	13.1	14.6	25.5	25.0	19.5
Three-generation	8.9	6.6	6.7	7.0	9.1	10.8	8.0	9.5	10.2
Other	14.4	10.1	9.2	17.1	15.5	14.9	36.6	27.3	22.4
Total	11.1	9.8	11.3	19.1	17.2	18.7	39.6	31.2	25.0

Source: Comprehensive Survey of People's Living Conditions (each year).

among families with small children are a major background factor in the argument for higher levels of social security to be extended to this group, as well as to the elderly (Tsumura 2002; Kokuritsu Shakai Hoshō/Jinkō Mondai Kenkyūjo 2005b).

So far we have been looking at income differentials and poverty rates for all forms of household type. One important point that emerges is that single-person households show a high degree of income inequality and high poverty rates for all age groups. Let us therefore take a closer look at people who live on their own, and add a gender perspective to the discussion. I will use the term 'singleton' to describe householders living alone, whether through non-marriage, divorce/separation or widowhood.

Economic conditions of single-person households

What sorts of people live alone in Japan? Let us look at the singleton population in terms of gender and age. As of 2001, 35.6% of them were male and 64.4% were female. This is a very strong female majority, although it has been coming down somewhat in recent years. Figure 2.4 shows that the female proportion of the singleton population only increased in the 30s age group during the 15-year survey period, and there only marginally. In other age groups the female proportion stayed about the same or declined. The decline was particularly marked in the 40s and 50s age groups – or to put it another way, the proportion of men rose quite sharply for these groups. This reflects the growing numbers of men remaining permanently unmarried – up from 9.0% in 1995 to 12.6% in 2000[11] (Kokuritsu Shakai Hoshō/Jinkō Mondai Kenkyūjo 2005). The permanent non-marriage rate for women has also been rising steadily, though not as fast as the male rate. It stood at 5.8% in 2000 (Kokuritsu Shakai Hoshō/Jinkō Mondai Kenkyūjo 2005).[12]

There are various ways people come to live alone, and Table 2.4 shows the marital status for different age groups of male and female singletons. Not surprisingly, the vast majority of those in their 20s are never-married, and there has been no great change over time in the gender ratio for this group. However, the picture is rather different for female singletons in their 30s, where the never-married proportion rose from 84% in 1986 to 92.8% in 2001. The fact that this age group alone shows an increase in the female never-married rate doubtless reflects the trend for women to postpone marriage

Figure 2.4: Trends in the percentage of women in single-person households by age of household head

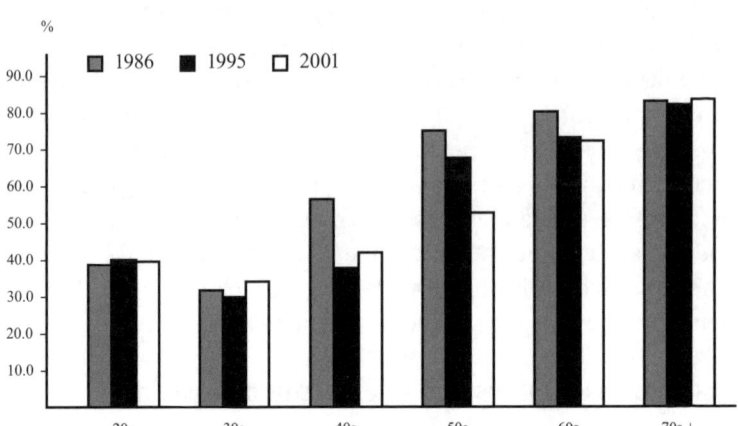

Source: Comprehensive Survey of People's Living Conditions (each year).

(*bankonka*) or refrain from marrying altogether (*mikonka*). In 1986, some 15% of female singletons were divorced or separated; by 2001 (Js: 2000) that figure had halved and over 90% of these women were never-married.

As for the men, we see no great change in marital status for the younger age groups, but for men living alone in their 50s and 60s there is an interesting rise in the number of bachelors. In 2001 over half of men in the 50s group were bachelors, while the proportion divorced or separated had fallen from 41.1% in 1986 to 35.5%. The proportion of bachelors also rose in the 60s group, but here there was also a big increase in divorced and separated men, reaching 40% in 2001. In the mid-1980s a strong majority of men living alone in their 60s were widowers, but there has been a massive change there, the proportion falling from 57.4% in 1986 to 36.6% in 2001. Going back to female singletons, we find that for them, age groups from the 40s upwards have all seen a big increase in the divorced/separated proportion. In the 50s age group particularly, that group grew from 23.4% in 1986 to 46.7% in 2001.

In Japan the postwar baby boom generation is called the *dankai* generation.[13] In 2001 these baby boomers were in their 50s, and some interesting differences were emerging between male and female

Table 2.4: Marital status of single-person households by gender and age (%)

	Male			Female		
	1986	1995	2001	1986	1995	2001
20s						
Never-married	99.0	99.4	98.7	99.8	99.1	99.5
Widowed	0.0	0.2	0.0	2.1	0.3	0.0
Divorced	1.0	0.4	1.3	1.1	0.6	0.5
30s						
Never-married	93.9	95.7	92.5	84.0	87.2	92.8
Widowed	1.5	0.3	0.5	1.6	1.4	0.0
Divorced	4.2	4.0	7.1	14.4	11.5	7.2
40s						
Never-married	75.6	77.2	76.9	67.4	52.2	58.4
Widowed	2.3	2.3	1.6	8.7	9.9	8.0
Divorced	22.1	20.5	21.5	23.8	37.9	33.6
50s						
Never-married	43.2	57.4	57.4	31.2	25.8	31.1
Widowed	15.8	11.6	7.0	45.4	38.2	22.1
Divorced	41.1	31.0	35.5	23.4	36.1	46.7
60s						
Never-married	15.7	22.3	23.0	15.4	15.3	14.3
Widowed	57.4	50.2	36.6	69.0	68.6	65.1
Divorced	27.0	27.5	40.4	15.6	16.0	20.5
70s+						
Never-married	5.1	7.1	7.8	4.0	6.8	8.6
Widowed	82.8	84.0	78.9	91.7	86.3	84.4
Divorced	12.1	9.0	13.3	4.3	6.9	7.0

Source: Comprehensive Survey of People's Living Conditions (each year).

members of the cohort. Though much discussed because of its sheer size, this group displays an internal variety of individual lifestyles hardly conveyed by the word *dankai*, originally meaning a lump or nodule of some geological substance. Traditionally in Japan, a man in his 50s was supposed to be the pillar of the household, the breadwinner of his family, and a reliable member of the middle management in the workplace, at or near the top of the remuneration pyramid. Such a man would be able to carry on supporting his children even if they remained economically dependent on him after reaching adulthood. However, in years to come a dwindling

Table 2.5: Poverty rates of single-person households by gender and age (%)

	Poverty rates		
	1986	1995	2001
20s			
Male single	13.1	13.7	22.0
Female single	19.0	19.4	28.6
30s			
Male single	8.0	10.1	9.4
female single	23.2	21.6	15.2
40s			
Male single	16.8	8.8	14.0
Female single	29.7	28.0	25.6
50s			
Male single	29.5	25.2	25.0
Female single	43.1	36.1	36.7
60s			
Male single	47.0	30.8	29.8
Female single	58.4	45.0	44.0
70s+			
Male single	52.5	40.6	28.5
Female single	73.1	61.0	48.7
Total			
Male single	21.6	18.8	21.6
Female single	50.3	44.5	42.0

Source: Comprehensive Survey of People's Living Conditions (each year).

number of men in their 50s will match that profile. More and more men reach their 50s still unmarried; more are divorced or separated; and quite a few are struggling economically.

Table 2.5 shows the proportion of single-person households in the poor group for men and women. One noticeable finding is the rise in the poverty rates among men and women living alone in their 20s – a rise that was especially sharp in the six-year period from 1995 to 2001. It is equally evident that among people who live alone, women are far more likely than men to fall into the poor group. For the entire population, no less than 42% of women were in the poverty group, almost double the figure for men. This massive gap cannot be accounted for simply in terms of gender differences in

Figure 2.5: The percentage of single-person households by decile by age of household head in 2001

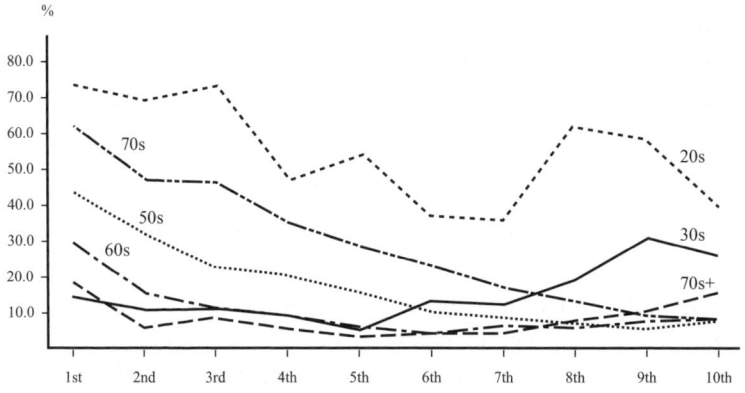

Source: Comprehensive Survey of People's Living Conditions (each year).

rates of employment. In the overall population of people living alone, the proportion holding jobs is generally high, and for women in their 50s the percentage holding down a job climbed from 70% in 1986 to 86% in 2001. Even if they have low incomes, most people who live alone do have a job. This indicates that high levels of economic risk among single-person households have more to do with low wages than unemployment.

So then, is it generally true that people living alone are suffering from a poor economic situation? Far from it. Figure 2.5 divides Japan's households into income deciles, showing the percentage of single-person households in each decile as of 2001. The most interesting feature that emerges is that for singletons in their 30s and 40s, the proportion of single-person households is U-shaped, with relatively high incidence at the bottom and top ends of the income spectrum. Certainly there are plenty of poor people living alone, but we can also observe a 'bachelor aristocracy' of wealthy singletons in the 9th and 10th deciles.[14] However, once we move into the 50s and above, we find ever higher proportions of singletons in the bottom two or three deciles while the wealthy type becomes much rarer. As people grow older, the connection between single life and economic risk becomes ever closer. One naturally wonders what becomes of those wealthy singletons once they age beyond their 40s. How many of them carry on living in solitary luxury into their old age? How many of them belatedly decide to get married or in some other way put an end to their solitude? I have no answer to these interesting questions at present.

As for people living alone in their 20s, the profile is not so much a 'U' as a ragged 'M,' with peaks observable at the third and eighth deciles. Compared with the older age groups, these young singletons show a more complex and varied relationship between lifestyle and economic wellbeing.

Economic differentials seen in terms of gender

We have seen that the economic implications of living alone vary considerably between men and women. What does this variation signify? I have set out two analytic perspectives for this chapter: one based on the household, the other on gender. People who live alone, especially those who stay that way into middle and old age, deviate more than any other group from the stereotypical Japanese life course: spending one's childhood living with parents and perhaps grandparents, getting a job and living perhaps in the company dormitory, getting married and setting up a nuclear household with spouse and children. But the significance of the solitary life course differs between the sexes. As we saw in Table 2.5, women living alone overall have somewhat improved their position, with the percentage in the poverty rate falling from 50.3% in 1986 to 42.0% in 2001. Nevertheless, high economic risk is still a fact of life for a great many women living alone, especially those in their 60s and 70s. Here, then, I would like to consider what it actually means to be a female head of household.

Table 2.6 presents data on householder gender for different kinds of household type. In 2001, 60% of households headed by a woman consisted of that woman alone, and another 24% were single-parent families. Couple-only households and nuclear families added up to just 6% of the total. This profile of female-headed households speaks to the traditionally subordinate role of a woman in Japanese society: living with her parents until marriage, then in a household headed by her husband where she bears and raises children, later to live out her old age in one of her children's households if widowed. She is never head of the household, and is always living in someone else's household – that of her parents, her husband (or husband's parents in some cases), or her children. However, as Japanese women have

Table 2.6: Trends in household structure by gender (%)

	1986		1995		2001	
	Male	Female	Male	Female	Male	Female
Single-person	4.4	54.8	7.3	57.6	7.8	60.6
Couple-only	17.4	0.5	24.4	0.5	27.6	0.6
Two-parent	55.0	5.7	47.3	5.8	42.9	5.4
Single-parent	1.2	27.6	1.2	26.0	1.4	24.2
Three-generation	17.3	4.8	13.9	3.9	13.5	3.1
Other	4.7	6.5	5.9	6.2	6.8	6.0

Source: Comprehensive Survey of People's Living Conditions (each year).

Table 2.7: Income disparity between two-parent and single-parent families (in ten thousand yen)

Median of disposable income	1986	1995	2001
1. Two-parent families	200.4	262.1	244.8
2. Single-father families	189.3	257.5	190.6
3. Single-mother families	99.1	135.4	117.0
Ratio of 2 to 1 (1 = 100)	94.4	98.3	77.9
Ratio of 3 to 1 (1 = 100)	49.5	51.7	47.8
Ratio of 3 to 2 (2 = 100)	52.4	52.6	61.4

Source: Comprehensive Survey of People's Living Conditions (each year).

taken to marrying later and later in life, if at all, and as their life expectancy has steadily risen, the proportion of women living alone has grown. We also observe a richer variety of lifestyles, seen for instance in the climbing divorce rate. However, despite this growing variety, it remains the case that women are virtually excluded from householder status unless they live alone or are single mothers.

Finally, let us take a look at the economic wellbeing of parents bringing up children alone, in terms of differentials between men and women. Table 2.7 compares median incomes for two-parent families and single-parent families led by the father and mother respectively. In the data for 2001 we see that income for male single-parent families averaged 77.9% of that for two-parent families, showing a considerable deterioration from 1995 when the corresponding figure was 98.3%. One possible reason for this appears to be the relative decline in income for male single-parent families in recent years, shown by the decline in median incomes for this type of household from 2,580,000 yen in 1995 to 1,910,000 yen in 2001. This kind of household has seen a sharp decline in economic fortunes since the mid-1990s, having enjoyed incomes close to those of two-parent families up until then.[15]

Female single-parent families also suffered a widening negative disparity relative to two-parent families during the survey period, although it was a fairly marginal deterioration, from 49.5% of two-parent family income in 1986 to 47.8% in 2001. More to the point is the fact that women bringing up children on their own struggled to make half the income of two-parent families throughout the period. The economic handicap that comes with being a single parent is far more significant for women than for men. In 2001 the average income for female single-parent families was just 61.4% of that for male single-parent families, though this figure did show an improvement from the 52.6% registered in 1995. This change was largely due to declining incomes for male single-parent families, suggesting that there may be a latent need for some kind of economic support for this sector, a group that has tended to be neglected by researchers and policymakers.[16]

Table 2.8 shows the poverty rates (defined, as before, as having less than 50% of median income for all households), categorized into two-parent families, male single-parent families and female single-parent families. That final category consistently had more than 50% of its members in poverty throughout the 15-year survey period. Single-parent families headed by mothers evidently suffer higher levels of economic risk than those headed by fathers. However, we should not overlook the sharp rise in low-income households among the latter: by 2001, nearly a quarter of male single-parent families were in the low-income bracket.

Iwata proposes indices for 'standard lifestyles' and suggests that people with experience of poverty are more likely to deviate from the standard lifestyle (2004: 224). If we take the two-parent family as a standard, then single-parent families may be described as having deviated from the standard lifestyle. If we take the life course experienced by the majority of the population as 'typical,' then single-person and single-parent households are both examples of deviation from that typical life course. Deviation from the typical entails higher levels of economic risk, and that risk is higher still for women. Clearly, the very concept of deviation from the typical is a highly gendered one. Indeed, the distribution of household types is totally different for men and women, and it is still fairly rare for

Table 2.8: Poverty rates of two-parent and single-parent families (%)

	1986	1995	2001
Two-parent families	7.5	8.1	10.1
Single-father families	12.9	17.9	24.4
Single-mother families	55.1	50.2	52.8

Source: Comprehensive Survey of People's Living Conditions (each year).

households to be headed by women. That said, the problems associated with deviation from the typical are not restricted to women. For men, too, permanent bachelorhood and divorce/separation bring higher levels of economic risk.[17] The question of how these atypical minorities should be socially supported forms one of the key issues facing anyone trying to think about policies to guarantee social security in an aging society with a falling birthrate.

Economic risk and households/gender

If we look at the degree of income inequality at each stage in the life course, we find that for old people in Japanese society, income differentials have actually narrowed and a smaller proportion are suffering from low incomes. True, households headed by elderly people are still more likely to suffer from low incomes than those headed by young or middle-aged people. However, it will be difficult to carry on with a welfare policy that provides high levels of care to elderly people just because they are old. The time is coming when older people will no longer be able to assume complacently that they will be looked after by the state. Meanwhile younger people, especially those living alone, are experiencing ever higher levels of economic risk. The fact is that the time has come to reassess Japan's social security system, which has been heavily biased in favor of elderly people. The reassessment I have in mind would not be a simple matter of indiscriminately cutting support to older people in general. Rather, I would emphasize the need to construct a welfare system based on a thoroughgoing social design that takes account of problems at every stage in the life course, including youth and middle age.

Hitherto Japan's social security system has been developed with the elderly as the center of attention. From now on, however, the younger generation is also going to need support, for households with young children, etc. From a demographic perspective, what we need is a shift in approach toward a distribution of welfare services that provides a decent level of support to minority groups throughout society. The number of older people is going to rise. From a majoritarian point of view, there is nothing particularly strange about designing social security to prioritize the needs of this particularly large group. But as the working population supporting the welfare system gradually contracts relative to the growing number of elderly people benefiting from the system, the whole concept of expecting the young and middle aged to support them is becoming unrealistic. In the coming years the question of how to support Japan's various social minorities within the overall population will become very important, necessitating great efforts to win a national consensus as to how to proceed.

In thinking about the low birthrate/aging society, we need to pay careful attention to the fact that the 'standard model' of household is becoming less and less applicable to social reality. Specifically, we are seeing a major decline in nuclear families and three-generation families, and an increase in single-person households, single-parent families and childless couple households. We have seen that families where the two parents do not live together (single-parent families), and people that do not live with their families (single-person households) are both associated with unfavorable economic circumstances. The gender issue further complicates matters, with women – especially old women living alone and single mothers – having to battle with elevated levels of economic risk.

Nowadays there is a huge amount of talk about how lifestyles have diversified in Japan, and yet there is still not enough support for people whose lifestyle deviates from what is considered 'standard.' The question of how society supports those who deviate from the standard model, who have made choices different to those made by the majority, is going to take on increasingly pressing importance as the implications of the low birthrate and aging society gradually sink in. Decisions made by the majority, for the majority will not produce a suitable principle for distribution of wealth in these changed social conditions. A new principle is called for – one that takes full account of the interests of minorities. The central challenge facing us in designing a workable society with a low birthrate and aging population is that of breaking up the privileges of those who conform to the 'standard model,' and distributing support more fairly among those who have most need of it. The low birthrate and aging society are here to stay; our task is to respond to that fact by thinking up social security systems that aptly reflect the greater variety of life ways now developing within the greatly changed circumstances of society today.

3 Young, Japanese, and Not in Education, Employment or Training: Japan's Experence with the NEET Phenomenon

Yūji Genda

Introduction

Joblessness among young Japanese has risen alarmingly since the 1990s – Japan's 'lost decade' of virtually no economic growth. Numerous pundits have attributed that rise – largely on the basis of anecdotal evidence – to a deteriorating work ethic. Here, I argue that rising joblessness among young Japanese has resulted mainly from structural change in the employment and household environments, and I offer empirical evidence in support of that argument.

Young people have been the principal victims of the overall upturn in Japanese unemployment that began in the 1990s. Unemployment in Japan, long lower than in other industrialized nations, reached 5.4% in 2002, the highest level ever recorded. Japanese unemployment peaked in the 15–19 age bracket at 12.8% in 2002, and in the 20–24 age bracket at 9.8% in 2003.

Paralleling the sharp increase in youthful unemployment has been a surge in the number of so-called 'freeters' (*friitaa* in Japanese): young people who find employment in a series of temporary jobs after leaving school. The word 'freeter' entered the Japanese lexicon in the late 1980s and is presumably an amalgam of the English 'freelance' and the German '*arbeiter*.' Japanese use the German word as *arubaitaa* in reference to part-time workers.

The 2004 edition of the Japanese Ministry of Health, Labor and Welfare's annual *White Paper on Labor Economics* documented the increase in the number of freeters. Citing survey findings by the Statistics Bureau of the Ministry of Internal Affairs and Communications, it reported that the number of freeters had more than doubled, from 1,010,000 in 1992 to 2,170,000 in 2005.

Another pressing concern is the increase in the number of working-age young people who are not seeking employment. Japanese statistics have traditionally excluded those young people from the labor force, along with full-time housewives, full-time students and the fully retired elderly, so that they are not counted as unemployed. This practice obscures the burgeoning number of young, unmarried Japanese who are out of school and not seeking employment. However, Japan has also imported a popular term that originated in the UK to characterize those young people: NEETs, an acronym of 'not in education, employment, or training.' The concept and term NEET appeared originally in the 1998 report, *Bridging the Gap*, by the British government's Social Exclusion Unit.

This chapter is to provide non-Japanese readers with a summary of empirical findings about Japan's NEET phenomenon. It consists mainly of content presented originally in Genda and Maganuma (2004); Genda, Kosugi, and the Japan Institute for Labor Policy and Training (2005); Genda (2005); and Genda (2007). Most of the analytical results presented here are from *A Special Report on the Working Environment for Youth*, issued in July 2005 by a cabinet-advisory council chaired by the author.

The NEET phenomenon has captured a great deal of attention in Japan in recent years, but the public discourse has centered on casual observations. Notwithstanding the research cited here, the phenomenon has received surprisingly little serious empirical study. Limiting the scope for analysis has been the small size of the samples of nonemployed individuals gleaned from household surveys. Nearly all of the published research in regard to nonemployment among young Japanese has pertained to samples smaller than 200. That has seriously limited the statistical significance of the survey findings.

In this paper, I draw on the much bigger samples afforded by the Japanese government's Employment Status Survey. That survey, conducted every five years by the Ministry of Internal Affairs and Communications' Statistics Bureau, covers some one million individuals aged 15 and older in about 400,000 households nationwide. It is second only to the census – also conducted quinquennially but covering all Japanese households – in the scope of its coverage of the employment picture nationwide.

Criteria and definitions

References to freeters in white papers issued by the Japanese government's Cabinet Office and by the Japanese Ministry of Health,

Labor and Welfare have been in the context of a broad age spectrum. The white papers have tended to accept an age range for freeters of 15 – the last year of compulsory education – to 34. The upper end of that age range seems justified in light of Japanese perceptions and practice. That is, the mid-30s are the upper end of what Japanese tend to regard as 'young,' and they are the age threshold above which employment opportunities sharply decline. I therefore abide by that age criterion in the following discussion of nonemployed young Japanese. All references in this paper to young people are to individuals in the 15–34 age bracket.

Excluded from the definition of nonemployed young in this chapter are people in the subject age bracket who are attending high school, university or vocational school or who are attending preparatory school with an eye to seeking admission to university. Included in the following discussion are individuals who have completed school and those who left school, for whatever reason, before completing their education.

Also excluded from the discussion are individuals who, married or otherwise, are cohabiting with another individual as a couple. I am well aware of the formal and informal barriers faced by Japanese married women who wish to participate in the workforce, and I recognize the social, economic and moral importance of eliminating those barriers. The focus of this chapter, however, is on single individuals who lack the safety-net of a caring partner.

In defining employed and nonemployed, I abide by the definitions used by the Ministry of Internal Affairs and Communications' Statistics Bureau in its Employment Status Survey, outlined as follows. Employed: individuals ordinarily engaged in income-earning work and planning to remain engaged in such work, but also including people who are temporarily not working to cope with personal illness, to care for small children or to care for ill or infirm relatives. Nonemployed: individuals not ordinarily engaged in work that yields income.

Categories of nonemployment

Japan's nonemployed young comprise, for the purposes of this paper, three categories (see Table 3.1): jobseekers; non-jobseekers who express a desire to work but who, for whatever reason, are not actively seeking work; and non-jobseekers who, for whatever

Table 3.1: Definitions of categories of nonemployed young people (aged 15–34)

Nonemployed	Individuals not ordinarily engaged in work that yields income who are not attending school and not cohabiting as a couple with another person.
Jobseekers	Nonemployed individuals who express a desire to work and are seeking employment, awaiting the results of job applications, or preparing to undertake entrepreneurial ventures.
Non-jobseekers: express desire to work	Nonemployed individuals who express a desire to work but who, for whatever reason, are not actively seeking work.
Non-jobseekers: express no desire to work	Nonemployed individuals who express no desire to work and are not actively seeking work.

reason, are not seeking work actively and who express no desire to work. NEETs, the subject of this chapter, are a combination of non-jobseekers who have never stopped desiring work and those who have never desired employment. Parsing their behavior requires careful analysis of their expressed attitudes toward work, as well as of their activity or lack of activity in seeking work.

Jobseekers include individuals who express a desire to work and who are seeking employment, awaiting the results of job applications or preparing to undertake entrepreneurial ventures. Here, seeking employment means any concrete activity toward securing work, such as obtaining introductions from public- or private-sector employment agencies and responding to help-wanted notices. Nonemployed jobseekers appear among the 'unemployed' in the findings of the monthly labor force survey by the Ministry of Internal Affairs and Communications' Statistics Bureau. The bureau predicates that classification in its monthly surveys and in its Employment Status Survey on the ability to begin work immediately should the opportunity arise.

Non-jobseekers who want to work but who have stopped seeking work actively appear neither among the 'employed' nor among the 'unemployed' in the government's survey findings. The government classifies them – along with students, full-time housewives and retirees – as 'non-labor.'

An implicit assumption in the Employment Status Survey and in this chapter is that individuals who express no interest in working are not seeking jobs or making preparations for entrepreneurial ventures. The survey dispenses with questions about job-seeking activities for respondents who indicate that they have no desire to work. Those respondents also appear in the survey findings as non-labor.

Note that what the Employment Status Survey detects is, strictly speaking, not those who might actually be interested in working but, rather, those who express a desire to work. Interviews I have conducted reveal large numbers of Japanese NEETs who, on questioning, evince a latent interest in working but who ordinarily shy away from expressing that interest (Genda 2005). A lot of those individuals, for various reasons, display a severe lack of confidence in their ability to hold a job. Faced with the difficulty of fundamentally changing their circumstances, they identify strongly with those circumstances and regard any such change as a threat to their very being. Betraying their vulnerability are comments by which they try to rationalize their situation: 'Working is not worth that much trouble.' 'I can do without the stress of a job.' 'I'm happy enough with things the way they are.'

Trends

Japan's nonemployed young (aged 15–34) numbered 2,132,000 in 2002, the year of the government's most recent Employment Status Survey. That was up from 1,710,000 in 1997 and 1,307,000 in 1992 (Figure 3.1), and this means that the nonemployed ranks of young Japanese increased by an average of about 80,000 people a year during that period. As a percentage of the young population, the nonemployed had increased to 6.3% in 2002, from 4.9% in 1997 and 3.7% in 1992.

The most prominent movement among the nonemployed in Figure 3.1 is the increase in jobseekers. They more than doubled in number, from 639,000 in 1992 to 1,285,000 in 2002. Those jobseekers appear in Japan's unemployment statistics, and their increase matches the rise in the unemployment rate among young Japanese.

Of equal concern is the growth in nonemployed young people not counted among the unemployed. Non-jobseekers who wanted to work and those who expressed no desire to work together counted for some 40% of Japan's young nonemployed population in 2002.

Although slower than the growth in jobseekers, the growth in non-jobseekers who wanted to work is also striking in Figure

Figure 3.1: Non-employed Japanese aged 15–34 by stance (thousands)

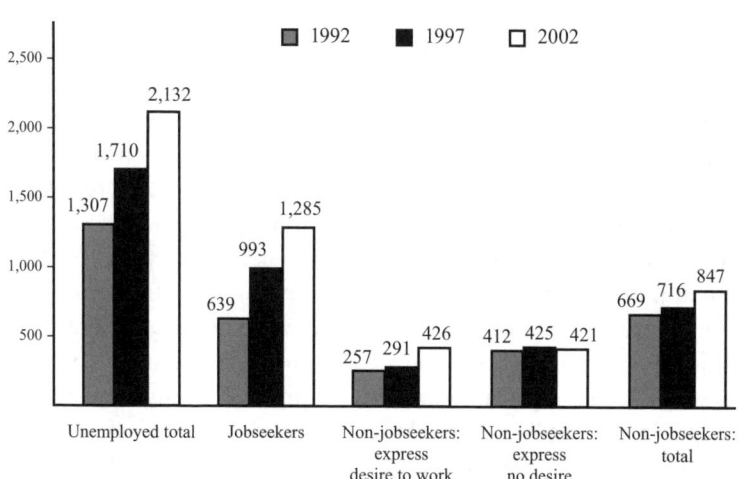

3.1. Their number increased to 426,000 in 2002, from 291,000 in 1997 and 257,000 in 1992. Prolonged unemployment became a worsening problem as the economic environment deteriorated after 1998. Growing numbers of Japanese gave up looking for work as jobs became harder to find. Physical and mental fatigue amid increasingly grueling working conditions also appears to have contributed to the increase in non-jobseekers, as I demonstrate statistically below.

In contrast with the growing number of NEETs who would if possible prefer to work has been the stagnant population of individuals who display no active desire to work. The number of non-jobseekers who expressed no desire to work hovered just above 400,000 during the 11 years covered in Figure 3.1. Nonemployed young people who do not desire to work have become a *cause célèbre* in Japan since around 2004, but we see here that they have been with us in like number for more than a decade at least.

Why NEETs can't hold down jobs

The Employment Status Survey asks non-jobseekers who express a desire to work why they can't find and retain work. The respondents choose the response that best characterizes their chief reason from among multiple choices. Readily apparent in their responses (Figure 3.2) is the adverse effect of economic sluggishness on the job market. Notable increases occurred between 1992 and 2002 in the ranks of non-jobseekers who had sought work but could not find anything, or who saw no chance of finding the kind of work they wanted.

Japan's NEETs frequently mention a sense of insecurity about their capabilities. Some report having quit jobs under the pressure of rigorous performance-evaluation systems, which are increasingly prevalent in Japanese workplaces, and having subsequently not sought work anew. The experience and feelings of those NEETs are apparent in Figure 3.2 in the rising number of respondents who express a lack of confidence in their knowledge and ability. Employers in Japan became increasingly insistent in the late 1990s that job applicants possess distinctive strengths, such as specialized skills, language ability and good communication skills. The emphasis on communication skills was especially vexing for individuals who struggled with interpersonal relationships, a common problem with NEETs.

A separate and alarming trend depicted in Figure 3.2 pertains to health. Among all the respondents who specified a reason for not seeking work, those who cited illness or injury increased the most sharply. Their number reached 104,000 in 2002, an increase of 40,000 in 10 years. Illness or injury prevented one in four of the non-jobseekers expressing a desire to work from seeking employment.

The Employment Status Survey does not gather information about the kinds of illnesses and injuries that the respondents have suffered. Informal evidence suggests, however, that psychological and mental disorders, along with physical and mental exhaustion, have increased in frequency among young workers since the end of the 1990s. Of the 104,000 survey respondents who cited illness or injury as their reason for not seeking work, fully 70,000 had work experience. We can fairly surmise that mental stress figured in the withdrawal of many of those individuals from the workforce.

Workloads became more onerous for large segments of the Japanese workforce as the economy stagnated. Performance quotas rose. Ever-longer working hours became a fact of life. A lengthening workweek is immediately apparent in the yearly editions of the 'Annual Report on the Labor Force Survey,' published by the Ministry of Internal Affairs and Communications' Statistics Bureau. The reports detail an especially sharp increase since the 1990s in

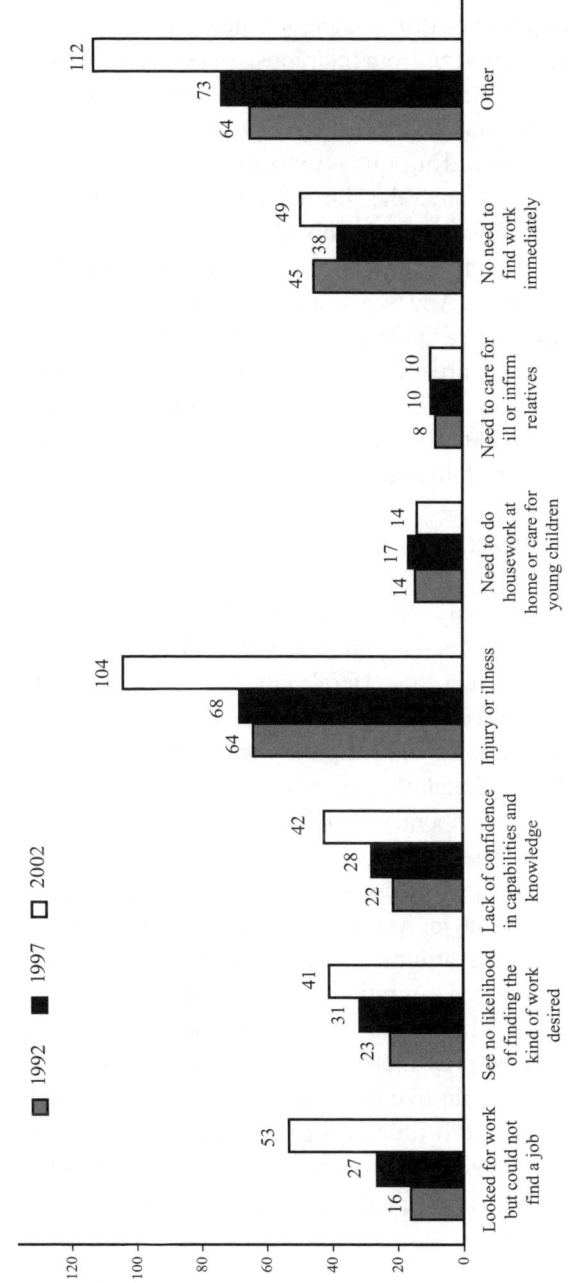

Figure 3.2: Chief reasons for not seeking work (thousands of responses)

weekly working hours for males in their 30s. About one-fourth of those workers were logging more than 60 hours of work per week.

Incidence of depression, schizophrenia and other mental disorders multiplied and drove young Japanese who would have preferred to continue working from their jobs. So pervasive was the problem in the late 1990s that most large employers adopted measures to cope with mental health issues.

Also commanding our attention in Figure 3.2 is the reason cited more than any other for the inability to work: 'Other.' Some of the respondents presumably chose that response because their reasons for being unable to work were complex and defied easy characterization. And we can assume that some respondents simply didn't have a clear notion of why they couldn't hold down jobs. Young Japanese are ordinarily conscious of their reason or reasons for quitting a job or for giving up looking for employment. But after joining the ranks of the NEETs, many gradually lose sight of why exactly they feel unable to work.

Work aspirations

A reason commonly offered for the NEET phenomenon – and for the increase in freeters – is young people's allegedly declining interest in full-time career jobs. Here's how the reasoning typically goes: Increasingly diverse values have blurred the conventional focus on full-time vocations, and temporary employment and even not working at all have become acceptable lifestyle options. The growing amenability to temporary work frees young people to seek work when and as they please, and thus eliminates the tense fixation with Japan's traditional spring hiring season. That breakdown of well-established job-seeking behavior has encouraged freeters and spawned NEETs.

The preceding argument, though seemingly plausible, is at odds with the expressed aspirations of young Japanese. That is evident in young people's responses to the government's Employment Status Survey. The survey includes questions about what kind of work respondents would like to do, and most have indicated a desire to find permanent, full-time work (Figure 3.3). More than three-fourths of the male jobseekers and more than three-fifths of the female jobseekers expressed a preference for such work in each of the past three surveys.

Figure 3.3: Percentage who desire full-time, permanent employment

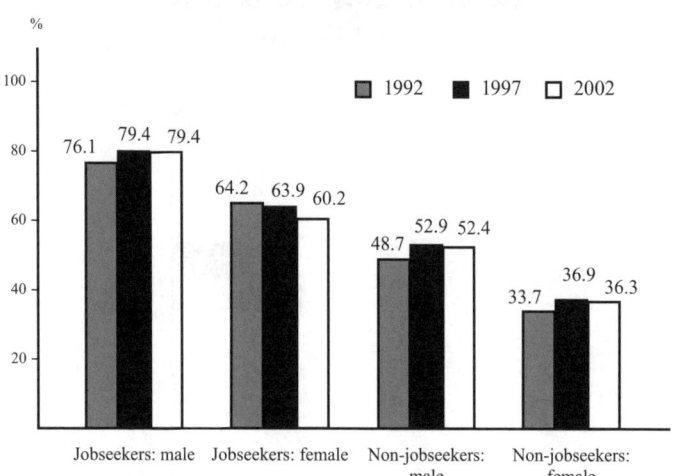

To be sure, the preference for permanent, full-time work is lower among non-jobseekers who express a desire to work: around 50% for males and lower than 40% for females. No long-term downward trend is evident, however, that would corroborate a declining interest in permanent, full-time work or a growing preference for the freedom and flexibility of temporary employment. If anything, the preference for stable employment among non-jobseekers shows a slight increase from 1992 to 2002.

An oft-heard criticism of Japan's NEETs is that they harbor unrealistic expectations. Their aspirations exceed their qualifications by far, according to the critics, and when they encounter the impossibility of finding employment consistent with those aspirations, they lose interest and stop looking for work. Belying that complaint are the responses by NEETs in the 2002 Employment Status Survey (Figure 3.4).

In the 2002 survey, jobseekers who cited a vocational preference favored technical and other specialized work. Next in order of preference for the jobseekers were office work and service-sector jobs. The top three vocational preferences were the same for non-jobseekers who cited vocational aims, though service-sector jobs displaced office work as the number two choice.

Figure 3.4: Work preference

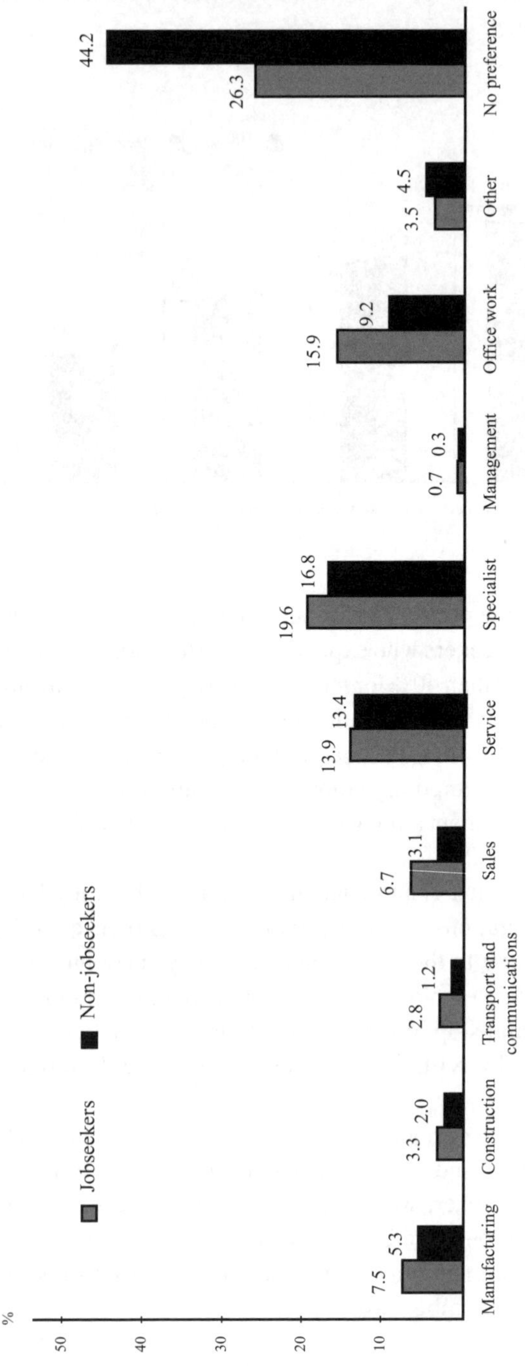

What is most striking about the findings, however, is that 'No preference' outnumbered all other responses by jobseekers and non-jobseekers. That was the response by 26.3% of the jobseekers and 44.2% of the non-jobseekers. Inordinately choosy behavior thus does not appear to be a definitive factor in nonemployment among Japan's NEETs. If anything, a lack of focus in vocational preferences might be impeding their assimilation into the workforce.

Education

Japan's nonemployed young display a strong correlation between approach to work and educational attainment (Figure 3.5). The percentage of young people who have not graduated from a four-year university, a two-year college or a postsecondary vocational school ('non-college graduates') is notably higher for the nonemployed than for the 15–34 population overall. And among the nonemployed young, the percentage of college graduates is higher for jobseekers than for non-jobseekers. In short, educational attainment is lower among the nonemployed than the employed, lower among non-jobseekers than jobseekers and lower among non-jobseekers who express no interest in working than among those who express a desire to work. Figure 3.5 presents findings of the Employment Status Survey for 2002, but similar trends are evident in the findings for 1997 and for 1992.

The percentage of job-seekers who have graduated from a four-year university course (including those who have completed postgraduate studies), is 18.2%, but the figure for non-jobseekers who express a desire to work is 5.1 points lower, at 13.1%, while that for non-jobseekers who express no interest in working is 10.6 points lower, at 7.6%. Among non-jobseekers who express no desire to work, the percentage whose education ended with high school graduation is 5.4 points higher than among jobseekers, at 52.1%, and that of junior high school graduates who have not completed high school is 12.6 points higher, at 28.6%.

Nonemployed graduates and holders of postgraduate degrees have powerful motivations to seek jobs. Remaining jobless entails the opportunity cost of failing to secure the income that their education has qualified them to earn. It prevents them from earning a sound return on the money that they – or someone – invested in their education. In that sense, nonemployed young who have only completed high

Figure 3.5: Highest educational attainment (percentage, 2002)

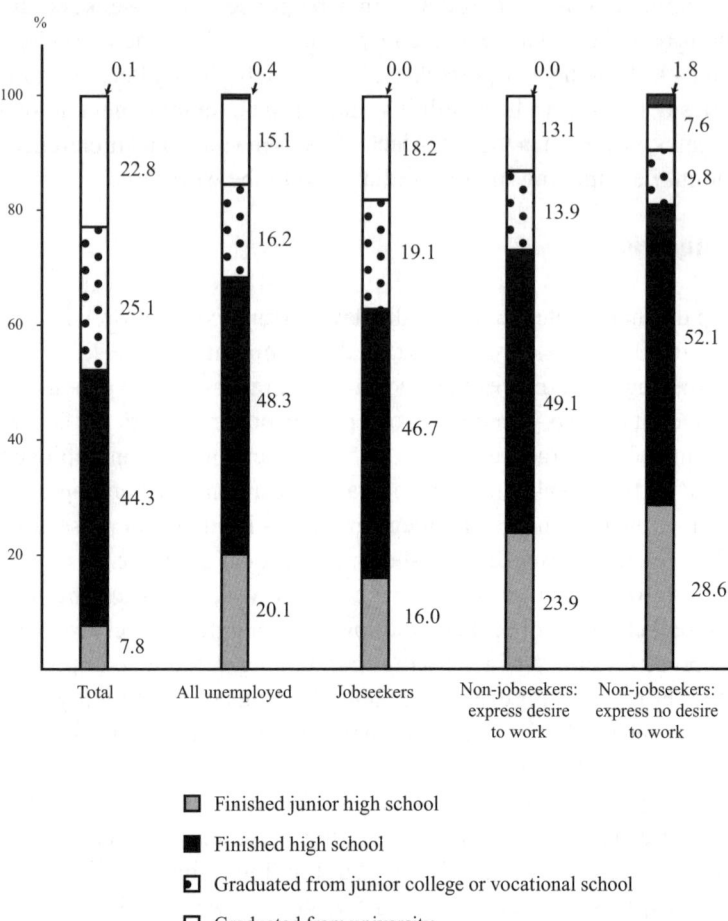

school or junior high school have less to lose from not working: they have invested little in their education, and the compensation on offer for their services in the labor market is small.

The demotivating factors are especially compelling for non-employed young who never attended high school or who dropped out. These individuals have little hope of securing work that is even the least bit fulfilling, and the compensation and workplace conditions at any jobs they are likely to find are generally unappealing. Remaining out of work is an all too easy choice for these young people. Even maintaining the desire to work can become an unsustainable chore.

Inexorable demographic trends are depleting the ranks of 18-year-old Japanese, and the day is fast approaching when anyone who wants to attend university will be able to get a place somewhere. Numerous households, of course, will lack the economic wherewithal to send children to college. Japanese will witness a growing gulf between families financially able to provide their children with comprehensive educational support and those unable to provide that support. Many of the young people unable to further their education will choose not to seek work rather than accept employment on demeaning terms. An appalling number of young Japanese are losing the opportunity to even want to work.

Japanese concern with educational attainment and employment prospects has centered on differentials in compensation for employees. Those differentials are small, however, compared with what prevails in the US and in other industrialized nations, and they have not become much of a social issue. What will command mounting attention in Japan, more than the question of employee compensation, is the difficulty of even eyeing employment for people of low educational attainment. Japanese have long prided themselves on possessing a largely classless society, but a new set of castes, based on educational attainment, is about to emerge.

Work experience

Any assistance for Japan's NEETs will need to address the characteristics of the intended beneficiaries. Some of the NEETs, for instance, express a desire to work, whereas others deny any interest in working. That distinction alone warrants different approaches in counseling, training and other modes of assistance, and other distinctions, such as differences in work experience, also require attention.

Table 3.2 presents a breakdown of work experience among nonemployed young Japanese by category: jobseekers; non-jobseekers expressing a desire to work; and non-jobseekers expressing no desire to work. Two-thirds of the nonemployed young covered in the 2002 Employment Status Survey possessed work experience. However, fewer than one in three non-jobseekers who expressed no interest in working had held a job. The lack of work experience was, as to be expected, higher toward the lower end of the age spectrum. But even at the upper end – late 20s to early 30s – former job holders accounted for less than 40% of the total. Over-30 NEETs who have never worked are a particularly daunting challenge in efforts to help people gain the desire to seek and hold jobs.

Work experience was more common, at more than 60%, among the non-jobseekers who expressed a desire to work than among their counterparts who expressed no desire to work, who registered at about 30%. But that percentage was substantially lower than the work-experienced percentage – nearly 80% – of jobseekers. Individuals who express a desire to work and those who do not constitute roughly equal portions of Japan's NEET population. So people who possessed no work experience accounted for nearly half of that population.

Table 3.2 displays a steep increase in the percentage of nonemployed in 2002 who possessed work experience, compared with 1997 and 1992. Among the nonemployed overall, that percentage had risen from 53.8% in 1992 to 65.5% in 2002. Rising unemployment among the young had become a conspicuous problem for Japan, and the percentage of jobseekers who possessed work experience rose from 70.6% in 1997 to 78.3% in 2002. The work-experienced percentage also rose among young non-jobseekers. It had surpassed 60% by 2002 among non-jobseekers who expressed a desire to work. The work-experienced percentage of non-jobseekers who expressed no desire to work remained low in 2002, at about 30%, but that was up from only 24.3% in 1997 and just 22.0% in 1992.

Something was persuading or forcing large numbers of young people to stop working. For many, health problems associated with increasingly onerous working conditions were, as noted, the reason for leaving the workforce. The growth in Japan's NEET population is thus a combination of working young people who lose the motivation to work and those who never gain that motivation sufficiently to obtain work. Remedial efforts will need to include measures for helping young working people cope with adversity encountered in the workplace, as well as measures for helping first-time jobseekers find viable positions in the workforce.

Table 3.2: Percentage with work experience

	2002			
	Nonemployed total	Jobseekers	Non-jobseekers: express desire to work	Non-jobseekers: express no desire to work
Aged 15–34	65.5	78.3	62.0	29.9
15–19	36.2	49.6	34.4	9.4
20–24	59.6	70.1	52.3	26.8
25–29	74.1	86.8	68.8	37.2
30–34	76.5	93.2	76.5	36.8

	1997			
	Nonemployed total	Jobseekers	Non-jobseekers: express desire to work	Non-jobseekers: express no desire to work
Aged 15–34	56.6	70.6	55.8	24.3
15–19	21.3	34.8	21.3	4.2
20–24	54.7	66.6	48.9	20.5
25–29	71.0	83.6	70.2	39.0
30–34	70.5	88.3	71.8	36.1

	1992			
	Nonemployed total	Jobseekers	Non-jobseekers: express desire to work	Non-jobseekers: express no desire to work
Aged 15–34	53.8	73.1	56.6	22.0
15–19	19.1	37.3	23.4	3.0
20–24	58.1	74.8	55.5	23.5
25–29	71.6	86.7	70.6	42.6
30–34	63.5	86.8	66.4	31.0

Household income

External factors weigh heavily in the discouragement of NEETs who express no desire to work. The circumstances of a NEET's household, especially, influence the individual's notions of possible vocational and career paths. Singularly important is household income. Along with social status and parental vocation, overall household income has figured decisively in the NEET phenomenon. And NEETs are more likely to be the product of economic disadvantage than of affluence, intuitive speculation to the contrary.

Figure 3.6: *Japanese aged 15–34 with an annual household income of more than ¥10 million*

Blaming the NEET phenomenon on unprecedented affluence and spoiled children was a natural response for Japanese reared in the postwar years of hardship. The data, however, tells a different story, as we see in Figure 3.6. Affluence is rarer among NEETs' households than among the households of young Japanese in general.

Annual pretax income of ¥10 million is a common benchmark for upper middle class attainment in Japan. That figure, as used here, does not include income from such one-time sources as drawing on savings, selling fixed assets, coming into an inheritance or receiving employment insurance. In 1992, annual household income exceeded ¥10 million at 21.3% of Japanese households that included members aged 15–34. The percentage edged up to 22.9% in 1997 despite Japan's economic stagnation of the 1990s, but it slipped to 19.0% in 2002, reflecting the stubbornness of the economic malaise. The affluent – more than ¥10 million – percentage was consistently lower among nonemployed young people's households: nearly five points lower in 2002, at 14.1%.

Among nonemployed young people, the affluent percentage was highest among households that included NEETs who expressed no interest in working. That percentage among those households exceeded 20% in 1992 and 1997, and it was comparable in those years to the percentage among all households that included members aged 15 to 34. The affluent percentage was conspicuously lower among

Figure 3.7: Japanese aged 15–34 with an annual household income of less than ¥3 million

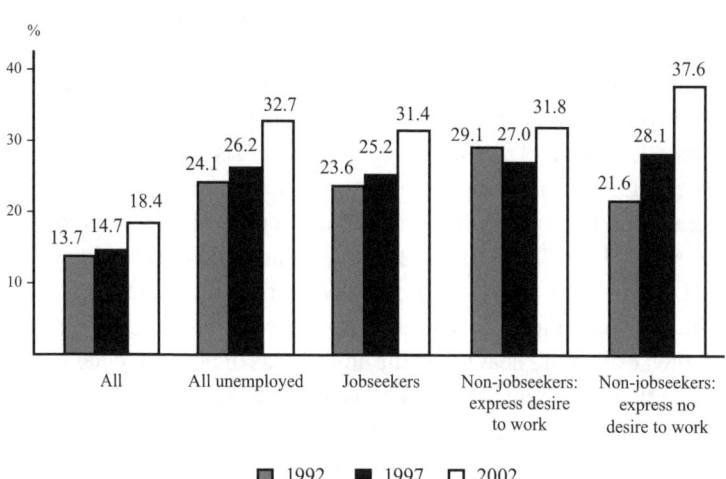

nonemployed young people's households whose nonemployed young were jobseekers or non-jobseekers who wanted to work.

Affluence might have figured in the decision by numerous NEETs not to seek work in the 1990s, but that was clearly not the case after the turn of the century. The percentage of affluent households that included NEETs who expressed no interest in working plunged from 22.9% in 1997 to 14.4% in 2002. That plunge was 4.6 points larger than the decline in the same indicator for young people's households overall. The percentage of affluent households was lower in 2002 for NEETs – both those who wanted to work and those who expressed no interest in working – than for young jobseekers, and it was substantially lower than the percentage for young people overall.

Separately, I have used 80% random resampling data from the government's Employment Status Survey and multiple statistical methodologies to identify determinants of nonemployment among young jobseekers, non-jobseekers who want to work and non-jobseekers who express no interest in working (Genda 2007). The findings indicate that the tendency to refrain from seeking work and even to deny an interest in working is strongest at the high end of the age bracket (15–34), among the individuals who have the lowest educational attainment, among females and among the individuals who have been out of employment for the longest durations. Also evident in the findings is a statistical linkage between a lack of interest in working and affluent households, but that linkage weakens over time, consistent with the trend described above.

NEETs and other nonemployed Japanese aged 15–34, meanwhile, represent a disproportionately large share of economically disadvantaged households (Figure 3.7). The percentage of low-income households – less than ¥3 million a year – was consistently more than 10 points higher for nonemployed young people than for young people overall, and the differential broadened over the 11 years covered in Figure 3.7. From 1992 to 2002, the low-income household percentage increased 4.7 points for young people overall, but increased 8.6 points for nonemployed young people. Economic stagnation thus weighed even more heavily on the households of nonemployed young people than on young people's households in general.

Bearing the brunt of economic adversity in the 1990s were the households of young non-jobseekers who were nonetheless interested in working. The low-income percentage for those households in 1992, at 29.1%, was more than twice as high as for young people's households overall, and it was nearly twice as high, at 27.0%, in 1997.

By 2002, the households of young non-jobseekers who expressed no interest in working displayed the highest low-income percentage. At 37.6%, that percentage was conspicuously higher than the low-income percentages for the households of young jobseekers, at 31.4%, and young non-jobseekers who wanted to work, at 31.8%.

The views from the affluent and the low-income ends of the economic spectrum reinforce the same message: if the NEET phenomenon was ever rooted in affluence, that relationship had played out by century's end. Young non-jobseekers who expressed no interest in working tended to be from economically comfortable households in the 1990s, but by 2002 they were over-represented among economically less-comfortable households.

Whereas the number of NEETs who wanted to work increased notably, the number of NEETs who expressed no interest in working hovered around 420,000. The lack of substantial change in the number of more-discouraged NEETs masked a sweeping change in economic circumstances. NEET was no longer – if it ever had been – a choice made amid affluence. It was becoming the face of the vicious circle of disadvantage breeding disadvantage.

Prospects

Japan's NEET population appears to be shrinking. Arithmetic based on the preliminary findings of Japan's latest census, conducted in October 2005, indicates a NEET population of 670,000. That figure is the result of simply subtracting the numbers of working people, unemployed jobseekers and students from the total number of unmarried people in the 15–34 age bracket. Performing the same calculation with the 2000 census numbers produces the much-larger figure of 940,000 for the NEET population. The census data, admittedly, is an imprecise indicator of the NEET population. That is because the data provided by people on the census forms about their job-seeking activities is frequently incomplete. But the evidence of a general trend is convincing.

NEETs multiplied amid the labor market deterioration wrought by economic stagnation and deflation. Now, economic rejuvenation, along with demographic trends that place a premium on increasingly scarce young workers, promises to help reabsorb them into the labor force. However, we must not allow the brightening economic outlook to divert our attention from the deep-rooted problems manifest in the NEET phenomenon. That phenomenon was only partly economic in its origins. Physical and mental problems have underlain the inability of numerous NEETs to find and hold jobs, and similar problems continue to prevent numerous young Japanese from seeking work or even summoning the desire to seek work. Meanwhile, onerous working conditions across a large range of the jobs on offer have also diminished the propensity to work, and it remains to be seen as to whether economic recovery will ameliorate those conditions, and if so, to what degree.

All things considered, we should expect a persistent population of Japanese NEETs in the hundreds of thousands for some time to come. And we should recognize the NEET-like trend among Japanese older than the age-35 ceiling we have adopted in our considerations here. Figure 3.8 shows nonemployment among unmarried people aged 35–49 by the same criteria we used for younger Japanese and on the basis of the same Employment Status Survey data. Whereas jobseekers outnumbered non-jobseekers among nonemployed Japanese in the 15–34 age bracket, non-jobseekers were in the majority among nonemployed Japanese aged 35–49.

Figure 3.8: Non-employed Japanese aged 35–49 by stance (thousands)

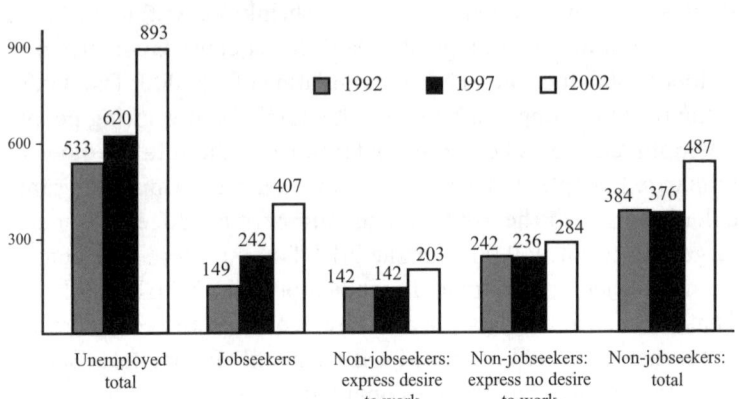

Jobseekers – the stuff of Japan's unemployment statistics – numbered 407,000 in the 35–49 age bracket in 2002. That was up nearly threefold over the 149,000 of 1992. Non-jobseekers who wanted to work numbered 203,000 in 2002. That was up from 142,000 in 1997, when their number was unchanged from 1992. Non-jobseekers who expressed no desire to work – a category that showed little 10-year change in the 15–34 age bracket – increased notably between 1997 and 2002. Their number rose to 284,000 in 2002, after edging down to 236,000 in 1997 from 242,000 in 1992.

Japan's census data underlines the presence of a large and persistent population of middle-aged NEETs. Calculating the number of Japan's 35–49-year-old NEETs on the basis of the 2000 census data yields a figure of 410,000. Arithmetic based on the preliminary data from the 2005 census yields an identical number.

Careful analysis of the Employment Status Survey data reveals that the middle-aged NEETs reflect a disproportionately large weighting of low-income households and low educational attainment. They include a startlingly large number of individuals who have never held regular jobs (Genda 2006).

Japanese can ill afford to turn a blind eye to NEETs of any age. Young NEETs tend to be dependents of their parents, but a lot of them will end up as dependents of society unless they attain some degree of self-sufficiency. As for the middle-aged NEETs, their parents are elderly, and the need to secure continuing means of support is a pressing issue for most. Employment opportunities are scarcer for middle-aged NEETs, meanwhile, than for their younger counterparts, which heightens the urgency of devising assistance.

Renewed economic vitality and a reinvigorated job market are bound to dampen concern about the issue of NEETs. That only heightens the importance of recognizing the stark message of objective labor-economic data and of adopting policies to promote wide-ranging social participation by all citizens. Social-assistance programs should include every possible precaution, of course, to encourage self-reliance and to avoid fostering a culture of dependence. But the assistance needs to be substantial, as well as motivational. More than employment is at issue here. For a large portion of Japan's NEETs, survival is at stake. Japanese authorities and civil society need to go to work forthrightly on measures for helping NEETs take their lives into their own hands.

4 Hidden Educational Inequalities in Postwar Japan: Misconceptions and Reconceptions

Takehiko Kariya

Introduction

After World War II, much influenced by the policies of the US-led occupation administration, Japan developed an education system that was extremely liberal by the global standards of the day. This was the so-called 6-3-3 system, with nine years of compulsory education divided into six years at elementary school and three at junior high school, followed by three more years at non-compulsory senior high school. In pre-war Japan, the education system had learned from European models, entailing just six years of compulsory education, after which only a small male elite would be offered the chance of middle and high school education. Compared with that, and indeed compared with mid-century education systems in Britain, France, Germany and other advanced European countries, the postwar Japanese system could fairly be described as being based on extremely progressive ideals designed specifically to realize the social ideal of equal opportunity.

Moreover, the new system was informed by a powerful spirit of egalitarianism, in some ways even outstripping the realities of the US model on which it was based. As we shall see in greater detail later on, US practices such as ability grouping and tracking, which created distinctions between students and sorted them on the basis of ability or achievement, did not gain wide acceptance in Japan's new junior high schools. At the same time, regional differences in educational environment stemming from financial differences between different school districts were kept to an absolute minimum. The net result was to make possible a degree of egalitarianism that exceeded anything seen in the US at the time.

By the time we entered the 1980s and 1990s, Japanese education was being praised by US sociologists such as Cummings (1980) and

Stevenson and Stigler (1992) for its success in turning out pupils who scored very well in international comparative tests, while also exhibiting a low degree of deviation in scores, indicating considerable success in achieving equality of outcomes. At least until the early 1990s, Japanese education was widely seen as a success story for other countries to imitate, combining high standards with equality of opportunity and outcome.

That said, there was also a negative side to the reputation of Japanese education. Competition to pass entrance examinations to elite high schools and universities had intensified to the point where 'exam hell' became a cliché; education designed to help students survive that hell was overly focused on rote memorization, stuffing students with knowledge while stifling their individuality and creativity; a highly centralized system allowed the Ministry of Education to impose a conformist approach to pedagogy that prevented teachers from acting freely and made it difficult to realize diversity in education; and so on. Eventually these criticisms started to impact on policymakers, and the 1990s saw the start of a series of educational reforms.

Let us now consider how postwar Japanese education handled the problem of educational inequality. Could it be that behind the general image of Japan as a society that succeeded in creating an egalitarian education system, inequality has in fact been spreading gradually through the system? I will also discuss the apparent paradox of a system that has aimed for equality while at the same time generating intense competition. What is the relationship between those two phenomena? And what about the recent educational reforms, designed to solve the problems of a society obsessed with educational credentials: how have they impacted on educational equality? In this chapter, while focusing on education, I will seek to clarify the complex relations between equality and inequality in postwar Japan.

First, I will review the developing relationship between education and society in postwar Japan, showing how the discourse of educationalists loudly advocating egalitarianism served to conceal elements of inequality in education. Second, I will show how the reality of an education system driven by an egalitarian ideology actually contributed to exacerbating the 'diploma disease' (Dore 1976) in Japanese society and the intensification of educational competition in a credential-governed society. Third, I will draw attention to another paradox: the fact that educational reforms rooted in a critique of the educational-credential society have actually served to further widen inequality within the education system.

Establishment of the mass education society[1]

Distaste for academic ranking of students: It's origins

Many Japanese people of the postwar generations have a strong dislike for anything that smacks of treating children differently according to their ability or school grades. Separating students on that sort of basis is seen by many as a sure way to generate dropouts and delinquents. This view is quite prevalent among both educators and lay Japanese people. Ranking students in order of ability, or treating students differently according to their grades, has been viewed as a form of discrimination, and generally thought of as a 'Bad Thing.' This way of thinking about education is deeply embedded in both Japanese people and educators' consciousness of the education profession, and is generally taken for granted.

A pioneering example of this view of education may be found in a report compiled in 1974 by the Committee to Re-examine the Education System (*Kyō'iku Seido Kentō I'inkai*), comprised of top-flight educational scholars assembled by the teachers' union, Nikkyōso. I quote:

> We categorize children according to their "grades," we rank them higher or lower in terms of their "ability," we separate those that will go on to higher levels of education from those that will not, we classify high schools into general and vocational schools, we discriminate between boys and girls, we rank schools from first rate down to n^{th} rate; we select. This gives rise to an intense but cold ideology of competition among the children. In this way, our nation's tendency towards credentialism is strengthened, and our schools become bloody battlefields of competition for educational credentials. This situation is what so-called "meritocracy" (*nōryokushugi*) has wrought. (1974: 54)

> Meritocracy is the great evil devastating education today, and should be called the root of all educational evils. (1974: 82)

From the 1960s to the late 1990s, Japanese educators were in the grip of a way of thinking that viewed the ranking of children in terms of ability and achievement as a very serious educational problem. Underlying this way of thinking was a particular understanding of the 'educational credential society.' Because Japan was a society obsessed with educational credentials, ranking inevitably happened, reflecting performance in tests and *hensachi* scores, designed to locate every child in the country along a bell curve based on standard deviation principles. That ranking led to bullying, delinquency, etc. We saw a chain reaction, as one educational problem led to another.

It therefore seems appropriate to ask ourselves how this perception, equating meritocracy with discriminatory/selective education, came into being.

The meaning of 'discrimination' as in 'discriminatory/selective education'

Japanese teachers tend to think of any attempt to treat students differently according to their ability or achievement, as 'meritocratic discrimination' (*nōryokushugiteki sabetsu*) or 'discriminatory/selective education' (*sabetsu-senbatsu kyō'iku*). However, from an international comparative perspective, this is not necessarily a universally shared perception. Even to translate the Japanese word *sabetsu* into the English word 'discrimination' creates semantic and cognitive problems.

Looking up the English words 'discriminate' and 'discrimination' in *Webster's Third New International Dictionary* (published in 1966), we find that alongside a number of neutral definitions, meaning simply to distinguish between different things and treat them accordingly, there is also the following definition that corresponds closely to what Japanese educators mean when they speak of 'discriminatory treatment' (*sabetsuteki taigū*):

> *Discriminate* "to make a difference in treatment or favor on a class or categorical basis in disregard of individual merit."
>
> *Discrimination* "the act, practice, or instance of discriminating categorically rather than individually."

Clearly the English concept of 'discrimination' does not include differential treatment caused by differences in individual ability or achievement. Rather, it pertains to *unjustly* differentiated treatment based not on qualities of the individual but on social categories such as class, race/ethnicity, gender, place of birth, etc.

This is not just a matter of dictionary definitions. A lot of research has been done by educationalists from the US and UK on the issue of equality of opportunity in education, but virtually none of it equates differential treatment based on individual ability with 'discrimination' (Kariya 1995). When Euro-American research talks about 'discrimination,' it is strictly referring to the kind of definition cited above – differential treatment based on class, race/ethnicity, gender, etc. – and not to distinctions reflecting individual ability or achievement.

That being the case, it would appear reasonable to describe the shared concern with *nōryokushugiteki sabetsu* (discrimination based on merit) and *sabetsu/senbetsu kyō'iku* (selective-discriminative education) as particular to Japanese society.

With that in mind, I will now take a look at the social and historical background to the emergence of this tendency in postwar Japan to link the concept of pedagogy differentiated according to ability/achievement with that of 'discrimination.'

The National Education Study Group and concern over the sense of discrimination among pupils

The mainstream teaching union in postwar Japan has been the Japan Teachers Union (Nihon Kyōshoku'in Kumiai), generally known by its abbreviated Japanese name, Nikkyōso. From a certain point in its development, Nikkyōso proffered a critique of the Ministry of Education that condemned its education policy as 'meritocracy' (*nōryokushugi*). Nikkyōso held its first national conference in 1952, and part of that conference was a National Educational Research Meeting (*Zenkoku Kyō'iku Kenkyū Shūkai*). Since then, Nikkyōso has continued to hold these annual research meetings right up to the present day. The proceedings are published annually by Nikkyōso under the title 'Education in Japan' (*Nihon no Kyō'iku*). A careful look through the back issues of this publication gives us a chance to trace how the debate on selective-discriminatory education developed over the years within the Japanese teaching profession.

One of the reports presented at the very first research meeting in 1952 discussed the distinction between general (*futsūka*) and vocational education (*shokugyōka*) in senior high schools. Here is a passage from that report:

> I also feel that there is a problem with occupational guidance in junior high schools. For instance, even if students go straight into employment from the general education track at senior high school, there is still a strongly lingering discriminatory consciousness regarding the general course and the vocational course, both among ourselves and in society... In the end the whole point of the 6-3 system is to keep all the students together. Or are we going to abandon that point, and start using the two types of school in all the school districts in the prefecture, in which case... the discriminatory consciousness will get bigger and bigger, and will linger on in the form of discriminatory treatment in society at large. (*Education in Japan* (EJ) 1952 1: 65)

In this report, the expression 'discriminatory consciousness' (*sabetsu-kan*) is used to refer to the pupils' preference for general education, and the teachers' tendency to prioritize the general education course, in the choice between general and vocational education. In the early 1950s, then, Japanese schoolteachers were sensitive about the distinction between these two forms of education and saw it as embodying a discriminatory consciousness.

Another distinction that caused concern was that between day schools and night schools, or in Japanese terminology those using the 'all-day system' (*zennichi-sei*) versus those using the 'fixed time system' (*teiji-sei*). Yet a third was that between those students who went on to senior high school and those who did not. There was much discussion at the research meetings about the feelings of inferiority and rejection that could result from being on the wrong side of these educational divides. Consider for example this statement, from a teacher talking about extra lessons that were provided in some education districts for pupils planning to continue their education beyond the compulsory years:

> There is a general consensus among the reports that this intensifying trend towards extra lessons brings many harmful effects, to teachers as well as pupils... particularly in the case of students who are not going on to higher levels of education, we hear it said that "schools are

obsessed with getting students into the next level, and so tend to forget about the students who are not planning to do that," and that "because of that, those students tend to get the feeling that they are a forgotten half, and start to feel inferior and wronged." (EJ 1955: 593)

Here, extra classes for students with higher academic ambitions are described as 'fundamentally warping senior high-school and junior high-school education' (EJ 1955: 593). At the same time, one of the reasons given for the problematic nature of these classes was that they did not include pupils planning to go straight into the job market from school, and hence caused them to feel 'inferior and wronged.'

This view, problematizing discriminatory consciousness, gave rise to the first use of the term 'discriminatory education' (*sabetsu kyō'iku*) during a debate at the 1958 meeting on the evils of extra classes:

> Even without being divided into separate classes, these students feel inferior and wronged. Creating separate classes will merely incite a stronger discriminatory consciousness among the pupils. (Report from Kumamoto prefecture)

> (1) Creates distortions in inter-pupil relations, such as divisions, antagonism and feelings of superiority and inferiority; (2) results in creating education emphasizing academic advancement, leading to the emergence of an advancement-oriented school within the junior high school; (3) it is impossible to make decisions on academic advancement in the second year of junior high school; (4) opposition from families to *discriminatory education*. (Report from Shizuoka prefecture, listing reasons for opposition to extra classes to prepare for entrance examinations; EJ 1958: 333. Italics added by author)

Thus, as the 1950s progressed, the tendency developed within the teaching profession to voice concern about the consciousness of discrimination among students labeled as being near the bottom of the academic pecking order, to call for moves to eliminate that phenomenon, and to describe education that created a consciousness of discrimination as 'discriminatory education.' The perception that problematized organizational structures and practices giving rise to that consciousness of discrimination was the prototype for later thinking on discriminatory education.

The poor as a minority

However, the teaching profession's perception of 'discrimination' during this period was not entirely divorced from social categories. On the contrary, the 1950s view of discrimination as an educational problem was founded on concern over a very apparent social category: that of poverty.

The inaugural meeting of 1952 included reports like the following about junior high school pupils who did not go on to senior high school:

> As for pupils who do not continue their studies, the main reason is lack of money and time...regarding these pupils' psychological state and their living conditions...they have a sense of inferiority, and generally are not blessed by favorable economic circumstances, which means that they are liable to lose their psychological equanimity even over quite small matters. Thirdly, and this is a very difficult problem, there are many students who quite casually engage in outrageous behavior. (EJ 1952: 114)

At the same sub-group where the above statement was made, numerous reports included empirical survey data to show that economic factors were the main element preventing pupils from advancing to senior high school. The following passage comes from one of those reports, linking the economically determined division of pupils into those who could and could not continue education past junior high school with feelings of inferiority and discrimination.

> Among laboring youths we find all sorts of bad conditions, including the gap between rich and poor. I tell them that it's no good always having that sense of inferiority, that discriminatory way of thinking, and I aim to create people who will stand tall in any situation, even if they are working as laborers, as free and equal human beings... The framework created by the old prewar system, with its middle schools, girls' schools, higher elementary schools and youth schools, created various distinctions between classes of people according to their various social and economic environments, but I think we have to get rid of that kind of education. (EJ 1952: 138)

In those days, the gap between rich and poor was still a very tangible reality. That, of course, is why there were so many reports at the

Nikkyōso study meetings about pupils' socioeconomic environments, extending far enough to include material on their social status origins. In that sense, problematizing the consciousness of discrimination among pupils who did not go on to senior high school amounted to making an issue of 'unjust' treatment based on the social category of poverty – 'discrimination' in the English sense of the word

Changing views of ability and meritocratic/discriminatory education

There was, however, a weakness with this simple view of what constituted discriminatory education: it made it all too easy to develop a way of thinking that emotionally shrank from any kind of ranking that could cause feelings of discrimination. I will now look at this issue, mainly by reference to the changing debate on ability grouping.

Moving into the 1960s, Nikkyōso developed a position that condemned ability grouping ('tracking' in US parlance; 'streaming' in the UK literature), as a form of meritocratic discrimination. Interestingly, though, until the early 1950s Nikkyōso had been willing to countenance academic tracking. The union's position shifted from acceptance to rejection during a period from the late 1950s to the start of the 1960s. Behind that change of position lay a major shift in the union's perception of ability differentials.

At the 1958 Nikkyōso study meeting, the sub-group on career guidance discussed plans then thought to be afoot at the Ministry of Education to introduce 'aptitude-based career guidance principles' (*tekisei tekishoku-shugi*), under which pupils would be guided towards different careers depending on their intellectual ability. Among the contributions to the debate was this one criticizing the Ministry for intellectual essentialism/determinism:

> The idea that intelligence is constitutionally innate, so that if you carry out intelligence tests you can predict future intelligence with a considerable degree of accuracy, in which sense the tests have value as a sort of preliminary examination – I would describe that idea as pretty dubious. In that sense things like the MOE's handbook "A Ready Reckoner of IQ-based Job Aptitude" (*IQ ni yoru Tekishoku Hayami-hyō*), that assume that IQ has a constant value, are worthless

and harmful because they fix permanent labels of excellence or inferiority on students, denying the possibility of future improvement, and effectively sealing their fate. (EJ 1958: 321)

'The possibility of future improvement.' The opinion quoted here is based on a certain view of school students – a view that does not see intelligence as a fixed value and recoils from any labeling of students as excellent or inferior in terms of intelligence. Suspicion about the very use of intelligence as a standard to judge students' levels emerges here as an important debating point in the argument over ability differentials.

The other side of the coin was a view that all students had equal ability – and that by extension, differences in achievement should not be viewed as fixed by innate ability, but as things that could be changed by the effort and determination (*ganbari*) of the pupils. This view can be clearly seen, for example, in this statement by a junior high school teacher at the start of the 1960s:

All the kids, or at least nearly all of them, essentially have the ability to score 100%, and I believe the fact that they do not means that we cannot say that "education," in the true sense of the word, is going on. (*Kyō'iku* journal, May 1962: 28)

By the 1960s, this kind of view of intelligence and academic ability had become a powerful position from which to criticize meritocratic education. In 1961, a report pointing to elements in the social environment and individual make-up as factors determining career choice drew a string of hostile responses, including the following:

On the subject of intelligence and lifestyle, there is a problem with the view that sees poor people as having low intelligence. (Gunma pref.)

The report sees a vicious cycle between poverty and low intelligence, but we have to critically question the meaning of intelligence tests. (Kyoto pref.)

There's some kind of hocus-pocus going on with intelligence tests. Since intelligence is not something innate, it follows that there are elements of social class in intelligence tests. (Osaka, Kumamoto prefs.)

> Intelligence is not the decisive factor in academic ability. (Osaka pref.) (EJ 1961: 296)

Furthermore, a report on deliberations at the career guidance subgroup at the 1962 meeting has this to say:

> On the subject of forming ability-based school classes, this meeting heard both the positive view (Okayama pref.) and the negative view (report from Japan Senior High School Teachers Union [*Nikkōkyō*], Hokkaido chapter). One's impression was that the positive view for introducing such classes took a severe beating, especially from junior high school participants. (EJ 1962: 253)

As this passage indicates, negative views of ability-differentiated education were widespread in the teaching profession at this time.

Views of meritocratic/discriminatory education and the mass education society

Let us now ask ourselves how postwar Japanese education and society changed in response to the acquisition of this perception of education and society. First of all, this kind of egalitarianism inevitably led to the leveling out of education, at least in its formal structures – that is to say, it led to an increasingly conformist conception of equality. During the years of compulsory education in particular, it led to an emphasis on using the same educational materials and the same standards of evaluation for all students to avoid giving them any sense that they were being discriminated against. This was considered more conducive to equality of education than the use of a variety of educational materials and evaluation standards. Standardization of curriculum, evaluation standards and evaluation procedures were promoted, and this in turn led to strengthening the notion of a single ranking system for all pupils. Why? Because applying the same treatment to all students, without isolating any of them from the mainstream, was seen as 'equal education,' that would not make anyone feel discriminated against. Bizarrely, this meant that telling a student he was in the bottom 1% of all pupils his age in the whole of Japan was supposed to make him feel good because he was not being discriminated against by being excluded from the ranking system.

Secondly, the expansion of education based on this kind of egalitarianism became a powerful engine driving the spread of mass meritocracy. The idea, as quoted above, was that anyone could get 100% if they only tried hard enough, irrespective of what sort of circumstances they had been born into. Every kid was supposed to have unlimited academic potential. The denial that ability was innate and determined led to an egalitarian view of ability, and hence to an ideology of effort, stressing that education gave everybody the chance to succeed. And so, ironically enough, while denying any role for competition in education, the argument against meritocratic education ended up playing the role of leading the masses into intense educational competition. That in turn led to an expansion of educational opportunities – of more homogeneous educational opportunities, moreover.

Thirdly, the expansion of education based on this kind of egalitarianism effectively obscured from sight the problem of structural inequality in education, what we call 'status and education,' contributing to the establishment of a mass education society. 'Equal education' signified education that did not create feelings of discrimination. As such, the very attempt to look at differences in academic ability between status groups was spurned for fear that it could lead to feelings of discrimination among children from lower status groups. True, the simple critique of discriminatory education, which problematized the sense of discrimination among pupils whose poverty stopped them from progressing to higher levels of education, included a perspective on social status and inequality in education as a matter of course. However, that simple critique of discriminatory education had difficulties with the view of 'inequality' as a *social* problem, preferring instead to focus on the *emotional* problem of the sense of discrimination stemming from differentials in ability. The result of that was to drive the problem of educational inequality itself into a blind corner, while the view that equated the creation of feelings of discrimination in the educational process with 'inequality' came to dominate the debate on inequality problems. Thus was perfected the structure that drew the masses into the battle to acquire academic credentials, without being distracted by the structural inequalities that do in fact arise in any education system.

Development and criticism of academic credentialism

The phenomenon that I called 'mass meritocracy' in the previous section was looked upon in Japan as the flourishing of the 'credentialist society' (*gakureki shakai*). Prompted by Japanese-style egalitarianism, more and more people desired more and more academic credentials and joined in the educational rat race. In fact, differentials stemming from social status still existed, both in the level of education attained and the scholastic standards achieved. But people paid no attention to such things until the early 2000s. Instead they focused on the intensity of competition for admission to elite schools, the scale of advantages in employment and promotion accruing to the graduation diploma of each university, and various educational problems that were viewed as by-products of the credentialist society such as delinquency, bullying, school drop-outs, etc.

The social rebirth of Japanese people

In January 1970, an OECD working party arrived in Japan to study the education system. Its objective was to identify problems in Japanese education and suggest solutions to them. One member of that working party, the Norwegian sociologist Johan Galtung, issued the following 'diagnosis' of Japanese education.

> The first thing to be said about this system is that it is essentially driven by an ideology of group association, so that once you are allotted to a particular group, it is extremely difficult to change your class. In this credentialist system, one's biological birth is followed by one's social birth. Taking a peek at that fact, one notices that these two births share the characteristic that one's class affiliation is determined at birth. To put it more accurately, which class one is affiliated to is determined by the entrance examination at each level... to pass an entrance exam is to be reborn; and once a person has been reborn, his status in society will be determined in the same way that a person's status is determined by the circumstances of their biological birth in a conservative society.
>
> It is essentially an ascriptive system in the sense that once one is allocated to a group it is very difficult to change one's class. It is like being born into a class, only that in a degreeocracy social birth takes place later than biological birth. More precisely it takes place at the time of the various entrance examinations, and like all births it has

its pains. There is the pregnancy period with some element of social isolation (preparation for the exam); the labour (the exam itself); and there are miscarriages and infant mortality (the high suicide rates for that particular age group, 20–24, in that particular period of the year, April). It is traumatic and dramatic; and it should be because it is the entrance to real life. Biological birth is dramatic and the social birth of fully conscious individuals even more so.

As mentioned so often in speeches: the entrance examination is to be born again, and once it has happened one's future life is as predetermined as in any Model I society,[2] only more effectively so because the society is more rational, more technically adequate. (1971: 139)

I would say that Galtung got it just about right in his analysis of Japan's credentialist society. Biological birth is indeed followed by social birth; and although obviously the individual has far more control over the latter than the former, once the outcome of entrance exams has determined one's social birth, one's status is determined and continues in much the same way as it is determined by breeding or social class in more traditional societies. Japanese entrance exams can indeed bring changes to a person's life that are dramatic enough to merit the expression 'rebirth.' That is why so many people are concerned about educational credentials, resulting in intensifying competition over entrance exams. We can trace the birth of the myth of credentialist society from the spread of this view represented by Galtung's remarks.

The truth of the 'credentialist society': International comparison

In the world of social research, a 'credentialist society' (*gakureki shakai*) is defined as 'a society in which the influence of educational credentials plays a relatively large role in determining its members' social status' (Asō 1991: 27). It follows that it should be possible to measure, fairly objectively, the degree to which that definition applies to a society. International comparative studies indicate that Japan is not necessarily such an intensely credentialist society as to stand out from the crowd.

By and large, it is true of all the so-called 'advanced industrial societies' that one's level of education defines one's social status to a certain degree. That degree does not appear to be spectacularly higher in Japan than in other countries (Ishida 1993). In other words, if we attempt to study the matter objectively, all advanced industrial societies appear to be 'credentialist societies.'

Moreover, if we investigate one stage further, and ask ourselves to what degree traditional social status factors such as parental occupation and education influence socioeconomic success among people with the same academic credentials, we do not find that those other factors are any less influential in Japan than elsewhere. Research comparing status mobility in different countries suggests that among people with the same academic credentials, parental birth will influence subsequent acquisition of occupational status in Japan to about the same degree as in the UK and the US (Ishida 1993).

Indeed, if we put to one side the matter of people's consciousness and seek to measure social patterns objectively, we find that Japan, the UK and the US all show aspects of social credentialism. Moreover the power of education to effect 'social rebirth' does not appear to be so much stronger in Japan than in other countries as to dilute the social influence of biological birth. However, no less important than the 'objective truth' is the way people *view and interpret* the realities of education and society. At the very least we can say that in Japanese society up to the mid-1980s, the belief that Japan had a more intensely credentialist society than other advanced industrial countries was strong enough to permeate widely through society.

The debate on old-boy networks and ability

In his interesting work on 'the glories and mishaps of the Japanese academic aristocracy' (1999), Yo Takeuchi, a well-known sociologist of education, recounts the following anecdote. I reproduce it here because it suggests that, at least until the mid-1960s, postwar university graduates had the same kind of status consciousness as the pre-war academic aristocracy. The anecdote concerns a passage from the speech made by University of Tokyo president Kazuo Ōkōchi at the 1965 Tōdai graduation ceremony.

> In your working lives you will presumably be treated as elites and embark on high-level career courses. That will be so, irrespective of how much ability or aptitude for your duties you may actually have.

Apparently this last remark prompted an outburst of laughter from the audience. As Takeuchi astutely observes, 'Behind their laughter lay the shared assumption that they would obviously be elites in their working lives' (1999: 313).

This episode cruelly exposes a well-known and much-criticized problem with the credentialist society. Criticism of the credentialist society has often included condemnation of the high-level careers guaranteed to those with the right credentials. The argument that academic credentials should not be equated with ability, and that the issuance of special privileges to educational elites is tantamount to creating a new caste system, has long pervaded critiques of the credentialist society.

That view has been strengthened by another common criticism of the credentialist society, which denigrates the value to the real world of education focused on passing entrance exams. 'If a guy's graduated from Tōdai, that only means he managed to win out in the entrance exam game.' 'The kind of knowledge that you stuffed into yourself to pass entrance exams is totally useless to society.' 'Too much studying for exams creates personality problems.' These are the oft-repeated criticisms of entrance exams and, by extension, of the credentialist society in general.

The appropriateness of credentialist discrimination

Having said that, it would be a little too facile to reject out of hand this kind of criticism of the credentialist society. Matters are not quite that simple.

First of all, we need to think about the kind of era people were living in when they started voicing criticism of credentialist discrimination. It was the early 1960s when people started to draw attention to the gap between credentials and ability. If we take a look at the academic credentials of the productive population (those aged 15–64) in 1965, we find that 64% had only been educated to primary level or lower, while 30% had completed junior high school and just 6.5% had completed senior high school (Monbushō 1969: 254).

Moreover, out of these people with low-level academic credentials, a substantial proportion had been prevented from proceeding to higher levels by economic, rather than academic, problems. A 1964 survey studied the fathers of 2,512 children at public elementary and junior high schools in Tokyo, Osaka, Hiroshima and Okinawa, and found that out of 770 fathers whose education had gone no further than elementary school under the old education system or junior high under the new system, 59.5% stated 'I had the ability, but was unable to do so because of economic or family circumstances' when asked for the reason why they did not proceed to a higher level of education. When the same question was put to those who had got as far as graduation from the old middle schools or new senior high schools, 62% stated that economic or family circumstances were the barrier (Shinbori 1967: 37).

The period when this generation was heavily represented in the workplace coincided with the period when the younger generation was starting to go on to higher levels of education in growing numbers. It was the generation in the workplace that had really experienced inequality at the level before the acquisition of educational credentials, many of them having been deprived by poverty or family circumstances of the chance to study for those credentials. In short, people who had experienced inequality at the stage *before* the acquisition of education credentials were feeling a grudge about discrimination *after* their acquisition. In many cases those two problems – pre-acquisition inequality and post-acquisition discrimination – were mixed together in people's consciousnesses.

However, in the 1970s and 1980s there was a rapid expansion of economic opportunities, and the pattern of educational credentials in Japanese society also underwent great change. The number of people debarred by poverty from pursuing higher levels of education rapidly declined.

Even so, critical views of the inequality problem from the 1970s onward maintained the tendency shown in the 1960s to focus only on discrimination after the acquisition of educational credentials. From the second half of the 1970s, the perspective criticizing ability discrimination in education, centering on the unfairness of the examination system that caused competition for acquisition of credentials, was the one that tended to strengthen. As a result people's social awareness of Japan as a credentialist society made it difficult for them to see problems of inequality in education prior to the acquisition of credentials.

The ambivalence of the credentialist society: Credentialism and the mass education society

Expressed as this understanding of the relationship between society and education, the critique of credentialism became widely accepted among Japanese people. But, however widely and loudly credentialism was criticized, those criticisms did not simply lead to the demolition of the system. That was because the same people who felt a grudge against the credentialist society often harbored hopes that their children would get a better deal out of it than they did themselves. There was never more than a very thin line between the grudge and the hopes of betterment, which amounted to an admiration for credentials, and this ambivalence was a definitive aspect of many people's thinking on the credentialist society.

The social perception that was credentialism implied the notion that education was a useful tool for acquiring social and economic status. It forced that notion into every nook and cranny of Japanese society, and made effective use of it. It had a powerful ability to turn people on to education – powerful enough to make them think they could be 'reborn' if they went to a better school and acquired higher-level credentials. But the credentialist perception did more than just lead status-seekers into education. It also encouraged people who had no access at all to credentials to believe that getting better credentials, even *slightly* better credentials, would be very important for the next generation.

Getting educational qualifications would lead to a life of 'stability.' Getting credentials that were even just one rank higher came to be viewed as a very significant way to fulfill the modest ambitions of ordinary folk.

Thus, as mentioned in the previous section, the credentialist perception came to form the conceptual foundation on which the mass education society was built. What I mean by a mass education society is one that takes its motivating power from the impulse to destroy the 'academic aristocracy' (Takeuchi 1999), while at the same time mingling rebellion against that academic aristocracy with a certain fascination for it on the part of the ambivalent masses. First of all, there was a powerful movement to sweep away all aspects of the academic aristocracy, a system viewed as a feudal relic. But then there was a second powerful movement in the opposite direction, one of fascination with the academic aristocracy that made people want the chance to join the aristocracy themselves, by acquiring credentials. We may see the mass education society as the bastard offspring of these two conflicting impulses.

The result was to trigger a quantitative expansion of education. Every year more people joined in the competition over entrance exams. It was hoped that the expansion of education would expunge discrimination after the acquisition of credentials. Thus was born the mass education society, based on the social perception of the credentialist society but actually leaving in place inequality of educational opportunity.

Escaping from the credentialist society: The 'unintended consequences' of educational reforms

The 'concealed logic' driving the educational reforms of the 1990s was a perception that the credentialist society was the root of all evil. A sense that credentialism led to excessive exam competition, which in turn led to various other educational problems, was the starting line for those reforms. The great theme of the reform trend that started in the 1990s was to do battle with the credentialist society and save the nation from the scourge of what had come to be seen as a major social pathology – 'diploma disease' in Ronald Dore's famous expression (1976). Let us therefore take a look at the ideals and perceptions underlying the reforms. This will lay bare the characteristics of these reforms that were hatched in the context of a mass education society.

Why the search for 'breathing space in education'?

Significant changes were made to the manual guiding instruction in Japanese schools (*Gakushū Shidō Yōryō*) in the year 2002. The reforms thereby enacted included the final abolition of Saturday classes to leave a five-day school week, and a new objective to foster 'living power' (*ikiru chikara*). These reforms originated in the first report of the 15th session of the Central Council for Education (*Chūō Kyō'iku Shingikai*, or *Chūkyōshin* for short), released in 1996. That first report, entitled 'On the state of Japan's education, with a view to the 21st century,' included the following statement:

> First of all, the children of today live their lives in the midst of material plenty and convenience; but on the other hand, quite a lot of their time is taken up in school life and in studying at cram schools and at home, so that they may not be getting enough sleep and in general have busy lifestyles with no "breathing space." Perhaps because of that, quite a few children use their free Saturday mornings just to take it easy.

We also gather that they spend quite a bit of time hooked up to the television and other mass media, so that their virtual experience or indirect experience increases while their actual experience of life and nature is noticeably lacking, and they also spend very little time indeed on household chores.

The word translated here as 'breathing space' is *yutori*. This difficult word is sometimes translated as 'relaxation' or 'leisure,' and *yutori kyō'iku*, education designed to foster *yutori*, is translated as 'relaxed education,' 'laid-back education,' 'pressure-free education,' etc. *Yutori* signifies that feeling that you have the time and freedom to do something different and creative, and *yutori kyō'iku* was supposed to give pupils that feeling, and encourage a lively interest in the world around them that would foster the development of their own interests and study methods rather than sitting in straight lines and memorizing the same page of the textbook as everyone else in the class. Behind the calls for more breathing space in education lay the perception that entrance exam competition had reached a pathological level, as expressed in this passage from the Council's report:

> In order to secure "breathing space" for the children, and to foster "living power," it is necessary to provide an environment in which children are able to live that way. To do that… there are various challenges to be met, but we felt that a particularly serious problem was the need to ease the overheated competition over entrance examinations. There is a view that thinks excessive exam competition is gradually easing as the decline in the birthrate continues, but we believe that on the contrary, the situation is getting even worse at present: increasing attendance at cram schools and the ever younger age at which exam competition commences are symbols that many children and their parents are getting caught up in exam competition to get into universities and senior high schools, and the trend is even spreading to some elementary school pupils. Excessive exam competition is a major factor overburdening children's lives and depriving them of breathing space. As things stand, children have their nerves worn down by excessive entrance exam competition, lack sufficient opportunities to have the kind of life experiences, social experiences and natural experiences that are desirable in youth, and find it difficult to lead a spiritually fulfilling life. A situation where

even elementary school children are studying at cram schools until late at night cannot possibly be good for personality formation.

This concept, of exam-oriented education depriving children of their breathing space, was the central element dominating the thinking behind Japan's education reforms. And although it is not specifically stated as such, if we look back at the course of deliberations at the Council's 15th session, and at the 14th session that preceded it, it is clear enough that the root of the evil of excessive exam competition was seen to be the credentialist society. The prescription for the ills of such a society was sought in educational reforms designed principally to increase pupils' breathing space (*yutori*) and thereby strengthen their 'living power' (*ikiru chikara*). These associations may clearly be seen, for example, in the following passage from the Council's second report of June 1997, where it is expressed in the form of a call for a change in *gakuryoku-kan* – the way academic ability is defined:

> The exclusive emphasis on volume of knowledge memorized in selecting successful examinees tends to twist children's style of learning in the direction of stuffing themselves with knowledge to pass exams, and represents a major obstacle to imparting "breathing space" to children's lives, including their school lives. Moreover, this kind of selection system is in serious conflict with the view that "living power" is an all-encompassing force, including not only academic ability but also a rich personality, etc., and with the great shift in perception of academic ability itself, from a simple acquisition of volumes of knowledge to a concept including the ability to study for oneself and think for oneself. (Central Council for Education, "On the state of Japan's education, with a view to the 21st century," second report, June 1997)

To sum up, then, the council's call for *yutori kyō'iku* was a prescription for education to stop concentrating on simple acquisition of knowledge, and aim rather to foster the ability to study and think for oneself. This would be the way to strengthen 'living power.'

The two council reports, of 1996 and 1997, had a powerful impact on education policy. A series of initiatives was set in motion, designed to ease exam competition and enhance 'breathing space.' That said, we should note that the spirit embodied in the Council's reform had already made its appearance some years before. The trend toward abolishing Saturday-morning classes had already started – from 1992, public schools had one Saturday off per month, rising to two Saturdays off from 1995, and the content of the public school curriculum had been carefully adjusted to work with the reduced teaching hours. In 1989 the Course of Study Guidelines (*Gakushū Shidō Yōryō*) had been revised to introduce education based on a 'new view of academic ability' (*atarashii gakuryoku-kan*) that focused on the children's appetite for study. Now, the Council's reports prompted another, more ambitious set of revisions to the classroom guidelines. From April 2002, Saturday classes were abolished completely, the content of the curriculum was drastically reduced, and time for 'general studies' was added to the timetable at the expense of time for more traditional subjects.

Changes from 1989 to 2001

What sort of influence did these seemingly idealistic educational reforms have on the problem of inequality in education? Let us take a look at the results of some empirical analysis based on data taken from surveys relating to this problem.

Unfortunately, no data exists that can directly and clearly demonstrate changes in the influence on academic ability of birth status factors, such as parental academic credentials or occupation. The best we can do here in our attempt to establish the influence of the 1990s educational reforms is to analyze survey data relating to elementary school pupils, including scholastic achievement tests in arithmetic/mathematics and Japanese, which pertains indirectly to these issues.

At this point, let me give a brief outline of the survey I will be discussing. It was carried out in some urban areas of western Japan in November 2001 by a research team including myself (Kariya and Shimizu 2004). We revisited elementary schools covered in a survey on 'Academic ability and general life circumstances' carried out in 1989 by a group from Osaka University, in order to compare the situation before and after the educational reforms of the 1990s.[3]

Among the items included in both surveys were questions put to children on their basic lifestyle practices, which may be assumed to reflect strong influence from the home environment and on early childhood experiences such as whether they had had stories read to them by their parents. These items were seen as possible keys to investigating changes in the stratification of academic ability. These changes in turn would give us an insight into the influence of the educational reforms.

The survey included six questions on basic lifestyle practices: 'Do you get up by yourself in the morning?,' 'Do you eat breakfast?,' 'Do you brush your teeth in the morning?,' 'Do you greet your family on leaving the house and on returning?,' 'Do you get ready for school the day before?,' and 'Do you go to sleep at a regular time?' In the following analysis, I have used the answers to those six questions to divide the fifth-grade elementary school students surveyed into three groups: the high group, answering yes to five or six of the questions; the middle group, answering yes to four of the questions; and the low group, answering yes to three or fewer of the questions.

Using these variables, I conducted a multiple regression analysis with test scores for arithmetic and Japanese language as the dependent variables. Other explanatory variables employed were sex (a boy dummy with one for a boy and zero for a girl), district (one for a *dōwa* district,[4] zero for others), daily time spent on study at home (in minutes), attendance at cram schools (one if attending, zero if not). We used a dummy for the top one of the three basic lifestyle groups (one if in the top group, zero if not), a middle group dummy (one if in the middle group, zero if not), and another dummy for the experience of being read to when young (one if read to, zero if not).

Let us first look at the results relating to arithmetic scores. As we can see from Table 4.1, a change did occur between 1989 and 2001 in the factors influencing test scores. There was a general increase in the influence on test outcomes of the selected factors as a whole, shown in the rise in adjusted R-square, which more than doubled from .072 in 1989 to 0.183 in 2001. Looking now at specific factors, we can see that the basic lifestyle practices, the items that particularly interest us here, showed a substantial increase in correlation with test scores. Compared with the low group, the high group had a rather slender advantage of 2.9 points in 1989, but by 2001 the gap had widened to 7.3 points. The middle group also increased its advantage vis-à-vis the low group, from 1.47 in 1989 to 3.57 in 2001. In the case of the middle group, moreover, the influence on test scores was not statistically significant in 1989, but it had become so by 2001. Even if we treat the other variables

Table 4.1: Regression analysis for arithmetic test scores – by elementary school fifth-graders

	1989		2001	
	Unstandardized coefficients	Standardized coefficients	Unstandardized coefficients	Standardized coefficients
Constant	72.243	-[a]	68.907	-
Boys	0.573	0.016	−8.975	−0.245[c]
District	−2.234	−0.050	−9.379	−0.194[c]
Time spent studying at home	0.091	0.200[c]	0.058	0.127[c]
Cram school attendance	3.885	0.099[c]	4.500	0.111[c]
Basic lifestyle practices (top)	2.913	0.081[a]	7.304	0.190[b]
Basic lifestyle practices (middle)	1.466	0.039	3.566	0.093[c]
Read to when young	2.131	0.058[c]	1.113	0.028[a]
Adjusted R-square	0.072		0.183	

Note.
a = p < 0.5; b = p < 0.1; c = p < 0.01.

Table 4.2: Regression analysis for Japanese language test scores – by elementary school fifth-graders

	1989		2001	
	Unstandardized coefficients	Standardized coefficients	Unstandardized coefficients	Standardized coefficients
Constant	72.690	-[a]	64.137	-[c]
Boys	−2.686	−0.090[b]	−3.025	−0.072[a]
District	−2.940	−0.078[b]	−8.380	−0.151[c]
Time spent studying at home	0.093	0.243[c]	0.080	0.153[c]
Cram school attendance	1.244	0.039	3.813	0.083[a]
Basic lifestyle practices (top)	2.104	0.070	6.590	0.151[c]
Basic lifestyle practices (middle)	0.906	0.029	1.465	0.033
Read to when young	2.518	0.083[b]	0.885	0.020
Adjusted R-square	0.160		0.090	

Note.
a = p < 0.5; b = p < 0.1; c = p < 0.01.

as statistically controlled, the basic lifestyle factors still show an increase in influence. The one item that seems possibly to show the opposite trend is that of 'experience of being read to,' which showed a slight decline in influence from 1989 to 2001.

Looking at the other factors surveyed, the male dummy showed increased influence in 2001, and had gone from positive to negative, meaning that boys' scores had fallen below girls' scores since 1989. The *dōwa* area dummy also showed a considerable increase in influence in the 2001 survey.

Now let us take a look at the results relating to Japanese language scores. Here, too, we can confirm that basic lifestyle practices show an increase in influence. Even controlling statistically for other factors, the top group widened its advantage over the bottom group from 2.10 in 1989 to 6.59 in 2001. Results for the middle group were not statistically significant in either year. And as with the arithmetic test, the influence of being read to in early childhood declined somewhat in significance. The impact of attending cram school increased in 2001, as did that of living in a *dōwa* area.

Overall, our results confirm that if we look at academic ability in terms of paper test scores in arithmetic and Japanese language, the degree to which children have mastered basic lifestyle practices showed a marked increase in significance during the 1990s.

If we take the mastery of basic living skills as an index of cultural environment in the home, then these results indicate that the influence of that home environment on academic performance increased during the 1990s. If we take it that parental socioeconomic status differentials are a background factor influencing home cultural environment, then we can read the results of this analysis as indicative of widening status differentials in academic ability during the 1990s. The concealed inequalities in 1980s education persisted through the 1990s, getting wider but still remaining concealed.

Conclusion

In this chapter we have traced the changes in people's consciousness of education in postwar Japan, showing how dislike of 'meritocratic discrimination' gradually strengthened and became the consciousness defining the egalitarian ideology of Japanese education. We clearly saw how this view of education, which particularly dislikes competition, ironically had the effect of drawing many more people into educational competition, encouraging the spread of meritocracy to the masses. I further showed how the nature of the problem of the 'credentialist society' that was thereby established prompted moves to reform education to ease competition and increase 'breathing space' and respect for the individual. Finally, I used empirical data to show

how the educational reforms that started in the 1990s, in another ironic twist, contributed to widening inequalities in education.

What can we draw from these findings regarding the problem of inequality in Japanese education? In this concluding section I will consider what might be called the definitively Japanese features of the problem.

The first feature that we can mention is the strength of feeling in postwar Japan against 'meritocratic discrimination,' and the influence that feeling had on the conceptualization of equality in postwar Japan. In the languages of Euro-American countries it is not as clear as in Japan that treatment differentiated on the basis of merit can be viewed as 'discrimination.' Compared with those countries, the debate on educational (in)equality in Japan has tended to place weight not so much on whether or not substantial inequalities of outcome are generated as on the possible emotional effect on children's psyches of discriminatory treatment in the educational process. This kind of feeling was at work in the demand for conformist education based on a national curriculum, and in the development of a highly centralized system using a common standard to pursue uniform practices in the placement and treatment of teachers. In that sense, we can say that the educational ideology that promoted and supported equality in Japanese education – an ideology much discussed by western researchers – emerged as an instinctive avoidance of 'meritocratic discrimination.'

A second significant feature is that ironically enough, the creation of this view of education with its highly uniform standards of evaluation, while it did have some degree of success in causing more equal outcomes of educational attainment, it also made it harder to spot inequalities in educational achievement hidden behind it – those inequalities stemming from the status group into which one was born. There can be no doubt that the equality of treatment rigorously enforced by the Japanese education system did lead to a real reduction of inequality in actual academic or educational attainment. In that sense, it is fair enough to view the statistical fact that Japanese children show relatively little variation in distribution of academic ability, much praised by western researchers, as the fruit of that kind of egalitarian education. But that is not to say that inequalities in academic or educational attainment disappeared altogether. They continued to exist, but they ceased to be observed or criticized. In this way, too, Japanese-style egalitarian ideology in education contributed to concealing the problem of inequality until recently.

Thirdly, and even more ironically, the preparation of a uniform, standardized educational environment promoted the spread of academic meritocracy to the masses. As a result, the pathology known as the 'credentialist society' came to be recognized as the predominant problem with Japanese education. The rapid increase in the provision of opportunities to acquire educational credentials was paralleled by an intensification of competition for *more desirable* credentials. This in turn created fertile ground for the emergence of other educational problems, such as bullying, delinquency, non-attendance, etc. That instinctive dislike for ranking based on competition, and for differences in treatment based on such ranking, led to very intense competition and highly sophisticated grading systems. That, for me, is the paradox at the heart of Japanese education.

Fourthly, this paradox did not stop at causing an intensification of competition. The various reforms adopted to deal with problems born of the credentialist society actually ended up *widening* inequalities in education. The educational ideology that hated meritocratic discrimination, which had until then contributed to concealing inequality in education, now closed its eyes to the possible widening of educational inequality and lent a helping hand to idealistic, child-centered educational reforms.

This kind of mutual interplay between emotion and reality cannot be observed in western countries and may perhaps be described as a feature peculiar to postwar Japan. Then again, it may be a feature common to East Asian countries, since 'exam hell' is also a well-known problem in South Korea and Taiwan. That would be a very interesting theme to pursue in comparative sociology. Meanwhile, as I write, the widening inequality in Japanese education is becoming steadily more apparent, and the government of Japan has started to question the whole idea of 'breathing space' in education and to move toward a new set of reforms, informed this time by neo-liberalism. Japanese educationalists, myself included, have pointed to the risk that these reforms could further widen educational inequalities. The fact that such reforms are being pursued despite such evident risks is a sign of the times.[5] We live in an age of globalization, in which the welfare state is being reconsidered and the complexity of issues of educational equality and inequality is becoming more apparent than ever before.

5 Health and Inequality[1]

Hiroshi Ishida

Introduction

Health is the most basic issue affecting human survival. Article 25 of the Constitution of Japan guarantees that 'all people shall have the right to maintain the minimum standards of wholesome and cultured living,' but in present-day Japan, with its falling birthrate and aging society, is this guarantee really being fulfilled for all the nation's citizens? The aging of society means that the average lifespan of Japanese citizens is lengthening and people are tending to survive longer. Do all people have the same chance to live longer while maintaining a good quality of life? Are there no social disparities concealed behind the issues of longevity and health? These questions form the basis of this chapter.

Interest in health is running high in contemporary Japan. Many books and magazines are being published on health issues, and one can easily buy a wide range of health foods and dietary supplements in supermarkets and convenience stores these days. According to the 2002 National Nutrition Survey (Kenkō/Eiyō Jōhō Kenkyūkai 2004), some 60% of Japanese men and 70% of Japanese women regularly weigh themselves. When asked why, many stated simply 'I am concerned about my weight,' but many others stated 'I want to be healthy.' In the case of those aged over 60, no less than 70% gave 'I want to be healthy' as the reason for regularly checking their weight. A survey conducted in 2005 by the *Nihon Keizai Shinbun* newspaper in the three major metropolises of Tokyo, Osaka and Nagoya found that some 40% of respondents were using some kind of health food or dietary supplement. For women the figure was 51%, well ahead of the 33% figure for men. Some 60% said that they spent less than ¥5,000 a month on these products, but the reported outlay was higher for older people of both sexes, and for those aged 50–60 some 30% reported spending over ¥10,000 a month.[2]

There is also a high level of interest in preventive health measures such as medical check-ups. According to the 2004 Comprehensive

Survey of Living Conditions of People on Health and Welfare (*Kokumin Seikatsu Kiso Chōsa*) by the Ministry of Health, Labor and Welfare (MHLW 2005), about 60% of all Japanese people had undergone some kind of medical check-up in the previous one year. Men were more likely than women to give a positive response, registering 66% against 55% for women, while people in employment registered 68% against 49% for those who were not.

These relatively high figures reflect an underlying uneasiness about personal health. In another MHLW survey, the 2002 Survey on Trends in Healthcare and Welfare (*Hoken Fukushi Dōkō Chōsa*; MHLW 2004), 37% of respondents described their health as 'good' or 'fairly good,' while 44% chose 'ordinary' and 18% chose 'not very good' or 'not good.' These figures may not suggest a national health crisis, but answers to another question on the same survey gave a rather different picture. Asked if they had any anxieties about their health, more than two-thirds of respondents (68%) stated that they were 'very worried' or 'rather worried' about their health. This suggests that there are quite a lot of people who consider themselves to be in a not-too-bad state of health but who nonetheless are worried about their health. We may conclude that Japanese people tend to have a high level of awareness of health issues, and also a high level of anxiety about health.

Let us then ask ourselves whether there are any socioeconomic differences to be observed in people's state of health. Numerous studies in Europe and the US have reported that people's health conditions are associated with their socioeconomic positions. Britain perhaps has the strongest record of all. In 1977 the British government set up the Working Group on Inequalities in Health, and carried out a large-scale survey on the subject. The results may be found in the Black Report of 1980, named after the chairman of the Working Group on Inequalities in Health, Sir Douglas Black. The report had a powerful impact, not only in Britain but around the world (Working Group on Inequalities in Health 1980, Townsend and Davidson 1982). The report drew a vivid picture of huge differences between occupational groups in health indices such as mortality rate, morbidity rate, etc. For example, the infant mortality rate for children of unskilled workers in the first month after birth was double that for children of professional and managerial workers, while the mortality rate for unskilled workers aged 15–64 was 2.5 times higher than the corresponding rate for professional and managerial workers. The report also found that families of unskilled workers made far less use of the health services than those of other occupational groups.

Social differentials in health are not by any means restricted to occupation. Numerous studies in Europe and the US have found that income, educational level and assets are related to mortality rates, morbidity rates, depression, smoking and drinking behavior and subjective perceptions of health condition. Moreover, social differentials in health are found not only at the level of individuals and families, but also at the macro level between residential communities and geographical regions. These studies (usefully surveyed in Robert and House 2000 among others) suggest the need for analysis that takes full account of both micro- and macro-level factors. For instance, some recent research has indicated that regional health disparities are related not only to the average income level of the region but also to the degree of income inequality within it (Kawachi and Kennedy 2002).

In contrast to this accumulation of knowledge about social stratification and health in Europe and the US, there are very few studies looking at the relationship between socioeconomic positions and health in Japan. The lack of studies on the inequality of health may simply reflect the fact that there are no socioeconomic differentials in health in Japan. Indeed, Japan is known as a country of longevity. The average life expectancy at birth has remained highest in the world, recording 78.4 years for men and 85.3 for women in 2002. The average healthy life expectancy is also highest in the world at 72.3 years for men and 77.7 for women in Japan.[3] The infant mortality rate fell to four per thousand births in 2002, one of the lowest in the world (World Health Organization 2004).

Japan's longest average lifespan is often attributed to healthy diet and the national health system. Japan has a universal health insurance system that was initiated in 1961. The system is believed to have created an excellent health and medical service that was indicated as one of the best in the world by the World Health Organization (2002). In principle, all Japanese citizens are supposed to be enrolled in one of the health insurance programs that ensure access to medical care.[4] The universal health insurance system is designed to guarantee healthcare services to every citizen in the country, regardless of class, education and income. Because of the universal coverage of healthcare, it is not surprising to find that Japanese people assume equal access to health services and no apparent difference in health conditions according to socioeconomic factors.

The absence of studies on the social inequality of health is closely related to the lack of empirical data to address the issue of health inequality. There are a number of studies on health by medical doctors and public health specialists. These studies, however, tend to concentrate on biological and environmental factors in explaining health outcomes, paying less attention to socioeconomic factors (but see Kondo 2005, and Kawakami et al. 2006 for exceptions). Alternatively, studies on social stratification in Japan have accumulated surveys and analyses of the Japanese stratification system. However, the surveys such as Social Stratification and Mobility National Surveys (SSM) that produced collections of studies on Japanese stratification did not include questions on health until 1995 (see for example, Ishida 1993; Kōsaka (ed.) 1995; Satō 2000a; Hara and Seiyama 2005). The 2005 SSM included questions on health for the first time, and Katase (2008a, 2008b, 2008c) examined the effect of education and occupation on health items (self-reported health, stress, etc.).

National surveys conducted primarily by the Ministry of Health, Labor and Welfare contained information on both health and socioeconomic factors. Although the secondary analyses of the national surveys are restricted, Shibuya, Hashimoto and Yano (2002) is one of few exceptions which utilized these government surveys. Using the comprehensive survey of the living conditions of people on health and welfare conducted by the former Ministry of Health and Welfare, they found that people who lived in prefectures with higher medium income were more likely to report good self-reported health than people who lived in those with a lower medium income level. In addition, individual level characteristics affected self-perceived health. Women, people with lower income and older persons were more likely to report ill-health than men, people with a higher income and younger persons. Kojima (2003) used the same survey conducted by the former Ministry of Health and Welfare and examined the relationship between income and subjective health among the elderly. He concluded: 'there is no clear tendency for those in ill-health to be concentrated among the poor elderly and those in good-health to be concentrated among the wealthy elderly' (2003: 89).

Yamazaki (ed.) (1989) examined the mortality records of the administrative districts in large metropolitan areas and found that those with a high proportion of manual labor workers and self-employed tend to show high mortality rates and those with a high proportion of professional, managerial, clerical workers and farmers tend to exhibit low mortality rates. Tsutsumi and his colleagues (Tsutsumi et al. 2001; Tsutsumi 2006) report that male blue-collar workers are more likely to suffer from hypertension than white-collar workers, even after adjusting for age and job-related stress conditions. Nakata (1999, 2001) reports based on his survey of elderly in the northern city of Sapporo that occupational prestige and individual income affect subjective health and depressive feelings. Saito and his colleagues (Suthers, Saito and Crimmens 2003; Lee, Saito and Chuang 2005) find that functional difficulty is associated with income and that emotional wellbeing is associated with income and education among the Japanese elderly population.

Ishida (2004) presents the results of one of the first national surveys on health and social inequality, and the main findings are as follows. First, when he examined the onset of chronic diseases, there was very little difference by social class, income or education. People who were not employed (including those who were retired and those who were unemployed) were more likely to have chronic diseases diagnosed by medical doctors, but among those who were working there was virtually no difference according to the kinds of occupations people were engaged in. When he uses self-reported health (that is, whether the respondents feel that their health is good or bad), similar results were found. Aside from the difference between those who work and those who do not, there was very little difference by class/occupation, income or education. This result can be explained by the following interpretation. Those people who are chronically-ill are usually too sick to be engaged in paid work, so only healthy people were engaged in work regardless of their occupation. This is called 'the healthy worker effect.'

There are two problems with this set of analyses. First, Ishida used the current occupation in order to explain the current health conditions. Ideally, we would like to examine how the social positions held in the past affect later health conditions. Therefore, we need to have information on past job histories. Second, the analysis included respondents aged 20–89 years. However, younger people are generally healthier, and it is among the older population whose health conditions vary.[5] So we need to focus on the older population.

In order to address these two problems, this study employs a national survey on elderly health. It analyzes older people aged 65 and over and uses their previous social position to predict present health conditions. The study assesses the effect of class, education, and income on various aspects of heath conditions. Given previous research in other countries, we propose to evaluate the following four hypotheses about the effects of socioeconomic factors on health-related outcomes.

1. Among the socioeconomic factors, our primary attention is given to social class – the positions within the labor market. We hypothesize that non-manual workers, especially professional-managerial workers, will have better health conditions than manual workers because their working conditions are relatively more favorable than those of the manual working class. Manual work is physically more demanding than non-manual work. The exposure to unfavorable and physically demanding working conditions is likely to increase the risk of chronic medical conditions, physical pain and activity restriction, and will eventually lower general health conditions and perceptions.

2. We hypothesize that educational attainment increases the likelihood of maintaining good health. Medical knowledge and information on healthcare are likely to be increased by educational attainment, so people with higher levels of education are expected to be more health conscious and capable of coping with changes in health conditions – thereby maintaining better health – than people with lower levels of education.

3. Income level is hypothesized to affect health-related outcomes. People with higher incomes are able to buy special services and have better access to medical technology, and they should be able to maintain superior health conditions in comparison to those with lower income. These wealthy individuals are also more likely to avoid the negative consequences of ill-health such as physical pain and activity restrictions than those with limited financial resources.

4. The effects of socioeconomic factors on health-related outcomes are mediated by health-related daily activities (smoking and drinking behaviors as well as daily exercise) and access to medical information. Socioeconomic differentials in health-related outcomes are likely to be produced in part by the socio-

economic differences in smoking and drinking behaviors and daily exercise, as well as access to medical information.

Data and variables

The data set used in this paper comes from the Health and Living Survey among the elderly conducted in Japan in November and December, 1999.[6] A sample of 6700 individuals aged 65 years and over were selected from 340 sampling districts in Japan. The respondents were interviewed face-to-face. In a small number of cases where the respondents were not able to respond to the questions, the representatives (usually the relatives taking care of the respondents) were interviewed. The response rate of 74.6% yielded the usable sample of 4997 cases.[7]

The survey asked a number of questions related to the respondents' health conditions. Six health-related outcomes are used in this paper. The first variable, chronic medical conditions, was constructed based on the question about chronic illness. The respondents were asked to report any chronic diseases diagnosed by a doctor and were given a list of 16 common illnesses as well as a chance to report a disease not on the list. The list included such conditions as heart disease, high blood pressure, diabetes, asthma and cancer. The responses were dichotomized so that the variable represents the presence of any chronic medical condition. The second variable measures visits to a doctor's office. The respondents were asked to report the number of times they visited a doctor's office (including a dentist's office) in the past year. Those with at least one visit and those who never visited doctors were distinguished. The third variable measures the presence of physical discomfort. The respondents were asked whether they had any physical discomfort in the past month. Those who reported the responses of 'applicable,' and 'sometimes applicable,' are grouped together. The fourth variable relates to the respondents' physical ability. A number of questions were asked as to whether the respondents had to restrict household and daily activities due to their physical conditions and illness in the past month. Respondents who reported that they had difficulty in going shopping for daily items were given a score of one, and zero otherwise.

The fifth variable is a measure of depression. A series of questions related to CES-D (Center for Epidemiologic Studies Depression

Scale) developed by the US National Institute of Mental Health were introduced in the questionnaire. The respondents who scored higher than 18 were designated as having symptoms of depression.[8] Finally, the sixth variable, self-reported health, is constructed as follows. There are two variables, one related to present health, and the other related to change in health. The present health variable is based on the following question: 'How do you feel about your present health? The respondents who reported that their present health was 'not good' or 'poor' were given a score of one, and a score of zero otherwise. There was another question related to self-reported health. This question deals with the change in health condition compared with a year ago. If the respondents felt that their health was 'worse,' they were given a score of one and, a score of zero was given when the respondents answered 'the same' or 'better.'

Socioeconomic variables include the following: social class, education, income and assets. Our prime independent variable, social class, is measured by the employment held by the respondent for the longest time, and it is operationalized by the Erikson-Goldthrope-Portocarero (1979) class scheme (see also Ganzeboom, Luijkx and Treiman 1989; Erikson and Goldthorpe 1992). The class categories are constructed using the questions related to employment status, managerial status and occupation. The five-category version of the EGP class schema is used. The categories are as follows: (1) the professional-managerial class (I/II); (2) the routine non-manual class (III); (3) the urban self-employed (IVab); (4) the farming class (IVc/VIIb); and (5) the skilled and unskilled manual working class (V/VI and VIIa). The first category (I/II) is used as the base reference group in the logistic regression analyses reported below.

Education is measured by years of schooling. The original responses contained four categories (years of education attached to each category are shown in parentheses): (1) elementary and higher elementary schools in the pre-war system of education and junior high schools in the postwar system (nine years); (2) old middle schools in the pre-war system of education and senior high schools in the postwar system (12 years); (3) vocational schools after senior high school and junior colleges in the postwar system (14 years); and (4) old high schools and universities in the pre-war system of education and four-year universities in the postwar system (16 years). Income is measured by the approximate yen amount. The respondents were asked to choose one of 13 categories representing their household income. The midpoints of each category were used to estimate the household income of the respondent in each category. Because about one fifth of the respondents did not report their household income, we included a dummy variable representing this group.

Three variables that represent daily activities related to health are considered in the study. These are smoking, drinking and walking. If the respondents drank or smoked at the time of the survey or in the past, they were given a score of one, and zero otherwise. The respondents who walk everyday were given a score of one, and zero otherwise. The question that purports to measure the access of medical information was introduced. The respondents who replied that they were able to obtain sufficient information about the relevant medical institution were given a score of one, and zero otherwise.

Finally, the gender and age of the respondent were included as control variables. The analyses were based on a series of binary logistic regression models that are conducted separately for six different health-related outcomes. For each dependent variable, we consider models that include different sets of independent variables. Since our prime independent variable is social class, we first enter social class, gender and age into the equation (Model 1). We then add other socioeconomic variables (education and income) into the equation (Model 2). Except for the analysis of determining chronic conditions, we introduce an additional model (Model 3) in which we add the variable measuring chronic medical conditions into the equation as an independent variable. For the analysis of the determinants of subjective perceptions of health, we consider an additional model (Model 4) that includes visits to doctors as an independent variable.

Analysis

Health-related outcomes

Table 5.1 presents the descriptive statistics for the variables used in this chapter. The first six rows present the proportion of health-related outcomes. In our sample, respondents with at least one chronic health condition account for 73.2%. Chronic diseases

Table 5.1: Descriptive statistics

Health-related variables	
Chronic health condition	0.733
Visit to doctor's office	0.736
Physical discomfort	0.238
Activity restriction (shopping)	0.103
Depression present	0.292
Self-reported health (poor, not good)	0.299
Change in self-reported health (got worse)	0.267
Independent variables	
Gender	
Male	0.513
Female	0.487
Age	
65–69	0.342
70–74	0.280
75–79	0.209
80 +	0.169
Age medium	72.000
Social class	
Professional-managerial	0.138
Routine non-manual	0.184
Self-employed	0.213
Farm	0.185
Manual	0.280
Education	
Junior high school level	0.598
Senior high school level	0.301
Junior college/technical college	0.031
University/graduate school	0.070
Average years of schooling	10.551
Household income	
Below 1 million yen	0.135
1 million to less than 1.5 million yen	0.094
1.5 million to less than 2 million yen	0.117
2 million to less than 3 million yen	0.188
3 million to less than 4 million yen	0.125
4 million to less than 5 million yen	0.069
5 million yen or more	0.089
Income missing	0.183
Medium income in million yen	2.500
Daily activities	
Smoking	0.454
Drinking	0.499
Walking	0.598
Access to medical information (% good)	0.443

include any chronic medical conditions diagnosed by doctors. The most frequent responses (multiple answers possible) include high blood pressure (31.5%), heart diseases (16.8%), digestive diseases (15.6%) and neuralgia (15.0%). About three-quarters of the respondents (73.7%) visited a doctor's office at least once during the last year. About 28% of the respondents made visits on less than 10 days, while 14 % made visits on more than 30 days. In response to the question about physical discomfort, about a quarter (23.7 %) reported that they experienced pain and discomfort. When they were asked whether their regular activities (such as shopping) were restricted due to physical conditions, about 11% responded positively. Close to 30% (29.2%) of the respondents showed depressive symptoms. Finally, respondents were asked to report their health condition: 30% reported that their health was 'poor' or 'not good.'[9] Similarly, respondents were asked to report whether their health conditions got 'better,' were 'about the same' or 'got worse' compared with a year ago. More than a quarter (27%) reported that their health 'got worse.'[10]

There are significant correlations among these health-related variables. However, these correlations are not exceptionally high. Among the highest ones are those between self-reported health and activity restriction (r=.397), between self-reported health and physical discomfort (r=.367), and between chronic condition and visits to doctors (r=.486). Other correlations are less than .300. These results suggest that these variables are related but draw on different aspects of respondent's health conditions.

The distributions of independent variables are also reported in Table 5.1 above. Our sample includes more males than females and contains a relatively large proportion of older people (two-thirds are those over the age of 70). The distributions of social class and of education are similar to those of other national surveys. The distribution of household income shows that about one fifth of our sample (18.3 %) did not report income level. Since this constitutes a relatively large segment of our sample, we included a variable representing those whose household income was missing.

Determinants of health-related outcomes

Table 5.2 reports the results of logistic regression predicting chronic medical conditions. There are two models shown in the table. Model

1 includes our prime independent variable, social class, along with control variables (gender and age). We find no significant effect of social class. Men are more likely to report chronic conditions, and the occurrence of chronic conditions increases by age. When the bivariate relationship between social class and chronic conditions was examined, there was no significant association either.

Model 2 adds education and income into the equation. Age and gender continue to exert a significant effect on chronic conditions, but education and income do not show any significant impact. We do not find any socioeconomic differentials in the chances of occurrence of chronic medical conditions. Class, education and income do not seem to influence the chances of the occurrence of chronic diseases.

Table 5.3 reports the results of the logistic regression predicting visits to a doctor's office. Models 1 and 2 contain the same independent variables as those shown in Table 5.2. As depicted in these two models, we find a strong and significant effect of age. The older the respondent, the more likely they are to make a visit to a doctor. The only significant effect among socioeconomic factors pertains to the effect of farmers. Farmers (IVc/VIIb) are less likely to go and see doctors than the professional managerial class (I+II). The effect is persistent even after controlling for gender, age, education and income. Model 3 in Table 5.3 introduces chronic diseases, in addition to all the variables in Model 2. The model assesses the effect of socioeconomic variables on doctor's visits after controlling for medical conditions. The overall picture does not change even after medical condition is held constant. Age increases the likelihood of visits. Farmers are less likely to visit doctors than the professional-managerial class. The persistent effect of farmers may be due to the fact that access to doctors is restricted in rural villages.

It is probably important to recognize that income does not show any significant effect. This suggests that access to medical facilities is not affected by the amount of income, at least visits to a doctor. We do not know the quality and nature of treatment people received, but the amount of income does not seem to deter people from going to doctors. This finding is probably due to the establishment of the national health insurance system in 1961.

Table 5.4 shows the results of logistic regression predicting the presence of physical discomfort. Models 1 through 3 contain exactly the same variables as those reported in Table 5.3. Five findings stand

Table 5.2: Logistic regression predicting chronic health conditions

Independent variables	Model 1	Model 2
Male	0.184[b]	0.197[b]
Age	0.047[a]	0.046[a]
Class (prof-managerial)		
Routine non-manual	0.161	0.111
Self-employed	0.066	−0.015
Farm	0.006	−0.087
Manual	0.017	−0.101
Education (years)	–	−0.023
Income (in 10 millon yen)	–	−0.003
Income missing	–	−0.150
Intercept	−2.455[a]	−2.031[a]
−2 Log likelihood	4,601.190	4,460.911
Sample size	3,998	3,875

Notes.
a: $p < 0.01$, b: $p < 0.05$.
The category in parentheses for the class variable is the base reference.

Table 5.3: Logistic regression predicting visits to doctor's office

Independent variables	Model 1	Model 2	Model 3
Male	−0.095	−0.079	−0.230[a]
Age	0.051[a]	0.050[a]	0.036[a]
Class (prof-managerial)			
Routine non-manual	−0.054	−0.096	−0.198
Self-employed	−0.004	−0.072	−0.082
Farm	−0.326[b]	−0.380[b]	−0.432[b]
Manual	−0.090	−0.161	−0.141
Education (years)	–	−0.014	−0.003
Income (in 10 millon yen)	–	−0.002	−0.001
Income missing	–	0.018	0.128
Chronic conditions	–	–	2.317[a]
Intercept	−2.653[a]	−2.437[a]	−1.832[a]
−2 Log likelihood	4,542.992	4,415.868	3,602.572
Sample size	3,973	3,853	3,853

Notes.
a: $p < 0.01$, b: $p < 0.05$.
The category in parentheses for the class variable is the base reference.

out from these four models. First, there is no gender difference in reporting physical discomfort. Although men are more likely to have chronic medical conditions than women, the level of physical discomfort does not seem to vary by gender.

Second, age increases the likelihood of physical pain. However, the age effect is due in part to the fact that older people are more likely to have chronic medical conditions. Once the presence or absence of chronic disease is controlled, age effect is reduced but continues to be significant. Aging comes with the deterioration of physical function and increased physical discomfort, regardless of chronic medical condition. Third, the self-employed, farmers and manual working class are at least one and a half times more likely to report physical discomfort than the professional-managerial class and the routine non-manual class. There is a clear white-collar/blue-collar divide in the presence of physical discomfort. The division may be derived from the fact that blue-collar workers are subject to more physically demanding working conditions than white-collar workers. Fourth, income exerts significant effect. The higher the income, the less likely one reports physical discomfort. People with greater financial resources may be able to avoid the risk of physical discomfort and pain, by purchasing additional service or equipment. Fifth, those with chronic medical conditions are three times ($e^{1.156} = 3.2$) more likely to report physical discomfort than those without.

Table 5.5 reports the results of running logistics regression predicting whether the respondents experienced restrictions on their daily activities due to physical conditions. Models 1 through 3 include exactly the same independent variables as those in Table 5.4. First, age has a strong positive effect on restrictions on daily activities: the older the respondents, the more restriction they face. The age effect is not explained by the fact that older people are more likely to have chronic diseases than younger people, or that chronic conditions are positively associated with activity restriction. Second, there is no significant gender difference. Even though men are more likely to have chronic medical conditions, they do not seem to experience a greater degree of activity restriction. Third, the professional-managerial class has the least likelihood of experiencing activity restriction. In contrast, the self-employed and manual working class are most subject to activity restriction. These class differences remain significant even after controlling for education and income.

Table 5.4: Logistic regression predicting physical discomfort

Independent variables	Model 1	Model 2	Model 3
Male	−0.086	−0.051	−0.079
Age	0.038[a]	0.034[a]	0.028[a]
Class (prof-managerial)			
Routine non-manual	0.234	0.182	0.172
Self-employed	0.680[a]	0.603[a]	0.617[a]
Farm	0.406[a]	0.300[c]	0.326[c]
Manual	0.468[a]	0.343[b]	0.377[b]
Education (years)	−	0.004	0.009
Income (in 10 millon yen)	−	−0.009[a]	−0.008[a]
Income missing	−	−0.039	−0.018
Chronic conditions	−	−	1.156[a]
Intercept	−4.041[a]	−0.703[a]	−3.504[a]
−2 Log likelihood	4,267.167	4,102.691	3,971.768
Sample size	3,936	3,819	3,819

Notes.
a: $p < 0.01$, b: $p < 0.05$, c: $p < 0.10$.
The category in parentheses for the class variable is the base reference.

Table 5.5: Logistic regression predicting activity restriction

Independent variables	Model 1	Model 2	Model 3
Male	−0.188	−0.114	−0.125
Age	0.124[a]	0.118[a]	0.114[a]
Class (prof-managerial)			
Routine non-manual	0.500[b]	0.438[c]	0.424[c]
Self-employed	0.698[a]	0.588[b]	0.588[b]
Farm	0.509[b]	0.300	0.299
Manual	0.703[a]	0.527[b]	0.549[b]
Education (years)	−	−0.017	−0.014
Income (in 10 millon yen)	−	−0.009[b]	−0.009[b]
Income missing	−	0.159	0.167
Chronic conditions	−	−	1.415[a]
Intercept	−11.550[a]	−10.654[a]	−10.903[a]
−2 Log likelihood	2,461.624	2,377.074	2,298.248
Sample size	3,986	3,864	3,864

Notes.
a: $p < 0.01$, b: $p < 0.05$, c: $p < 0.10$.
The category in parentheses for the class variable is the base reference.

Fourth, the level of income is negatively associated with the presence of activity restriction: the higher the income level, the less likely the activity restriction. Since this effect persists even after controlling for chronic conditions, the respondents with sufficient income are probably much more effective in using their financial resources to avoid being physically constrained than those with limited resources. Their income probably makes a difference in continuing daily activities without much restriction and facilitating geographical mobility. Fifth, the presence of chronic medical conditions affects the chances of activity restriction. The respondents who have chronic diseases are about four times ($e^{1.415} = 4.2$) more likely to experience activity restriction than those without chronic conditions.

Table 5.6 presents the results of the determinants of mental health. The results in many ways parallel those of physical discomfort and activity restriction. First, aging promotes the chances of depression, independently of chronic medical disease. Second, men are less likely to exhibit the symptoms of mental illness than women, and this gender gap persists regardless of socioeconomic characteristics and chronic medical conditions. Third, the onset of depression is related to social class. The professional-managerial class and the farming class are less likely to suffer from depression than the routine non-manual, self-employed and manual working class. These class differences are observed even after controlling for chronic medical conditions. Fourth, income is negatively associated with the occurrence of depression. Those with sufficient income may be able to resort to means that reduce the onset of mental illness. Fifth, chronic disease and depression are positively related. Those who have chronic disease are twice ($e^{0.619} = 1.9$) as likely to experience depression.

Finally, Table 5.7 presents the results of logistic regression predicting self-reported health. There are two kinds of self-reported health. The first (Table 5.7a) pertains to the perception of how good or bad the respondent feels about their current health condition. The analysis is based on predicting the response of 'poor' or 'not good' health. The second (Table 5.7b) pertains to the perception of change in health status. The analysis is based on predicting the response of health condition as deteriorated (that is, became worse).

Models 1 through 3 include exactly the same independent variables as those in Tables 5.3 through 5.6. Model 4 adds into the equation 'visit to a doctor' as an independent variable. Since major

Table 5.6: Logistic regression predicting depression

Independent variables	Model 1	Model 2	Model 3
Male	−0.216[a]	−0.171[b]	−0.189[b]
Age	0.036[a]	0.031[a]	0.027[a]
Class (prof-managerial)			
Routine non-manual	0.479[a]	0.383[b]	0.390[a]
Self-employed	0.373[a]	0.291[c]	0.307[b]
Farm	0.110	−0.065	−0.046
Manual	0.458[a]	0.308[b]	0.334[b]
Education (years)	–	−0.013	−0.009
Income (in 10 millon yen)	–	−0.007[a]	−0.007[a]
Income missing	–	−0.054	−0.039
Chronic conditions	–	–	0.619[a]
Intercept	−3.558[a]	−2.922[a]	−2.780[a]
−2 Log likelihood	4,246.880	4,130.018	4,082.549
Sample size	3,487	3,392	3,392

Notes.
a: $p < 0.01$, b: $p < 0.05$, c: $p < 0.10$.
The category in parentheses for the class variable is the base reference.

findings are very similar for both the perception of current health and that of change in health condition, I summarize them in five points. First, there is no clear gender difference in self-perception of health. Even though men are more likely to be diagnosed with chronic medical conditions than women, men are not more likely to report that their health is not in good condition than women. Second, age is positively associated with perceived ill-health and change in ill-health. The older the respondent, the poorer their self-reported health. This perception is in part explained by the fact that older people are more likely to suffer from chronic diseases, but even among those with the same medical conditions, older elderly tend to report that their health is poorer than younger elderly.

Third, regarding our prime independent variable, social class, we find that there are class differences in self-reported health. The professional-managerial class is the healthiest. Self-employed and the manual working class report the least favorable health perception. These class differentials are present even if we control for chronic conditions and visits to a doctor. In other words, even among those who have the same chronic conditions and accessibility to healthcare, respondents' social class still makes a difference in their subjective

Table 5.7a: Logistic regression predicting self-reported health

Independent variables	Model 1	Model 2	Model 3	Model 4
Male	−0.103	−0.047	−0.097	−0.077
Age	0.048[a]	0.041[a]	0.033[a]	0.029[a]
Class (prof-managerial)				
Routine non-manual	0.287[c]	0.194	0.177	0.215
Self-employed	0.401[a]	0.317[b]	0.336[b]	0.376[b]
Farm	0.280[c]	0.111	0.138	0.224
Manual	0.516[a]	0.348[b]	0.407[a]	0.455[a]
Education (years)	–	−0.004	0.003	0.010
Income (in 10 millon yen)	–	−0.013[a]	−0.013[a]	−0.013[a]
Income missing	–	−0.258[b]	−0.244[b]	−0.273[b]
Chronic conditions	–	–	1.865[a]	1.436[a]
Visit to doctor	–	–	–	1.128[a]
Intercept	−4.409[a]	−3.680[a]	−3.758[a]	−3.788[a]
−2 Log likelihood	4,809.153	4,607.261	4,263.133	4,134.999
Sample size	3,992	3,870	3,870	3,848

Notes.
a: $p < 0.01$, b: $p < 0.05$, c: $p < 0.10$.
The category in parentheses for the class variable is the base reference.

perception of health. Class differentials in perceived health may be reflecting the findings reported in earlier tables that there are class differences in physical discomfort, activity restriction and depression. Fourth, household income shows a strong and significant effect on self-reported health: the higher the income level, the better the perceived health status. The effect is very strong, especially for the perception of current health conditions, and is not influenced by the introduction of chronic health conditions and visits to a doctor's office. Those with sufficient income probably feel that their financial resources offer better protection at the time of sudden changes in their health and feel more secure about their health conditions than those with limited financial assets. Fifth, the presence of chronic disease and visits to a doctor's office negatively affect both the perception of current health and that of change in health condition.

Daily activities, access to medical information and health

The final section of the analysis will examine how daily activities and access to medical information are related to class, income and

Table 5.7b: *Logistic regression predicting change in self-reported health*

Independent variables	Model 1	Model 2	Model 3	Model 4
Male	−0.165[b]	−0.129[b]	−0.156[a]	−0.150[c]
Age	0.049[a]	0.047[a]	0.042[a]	0.040[a]
Class (prof-managerial)				
Routine non-manual	0.553[a]	0.520[a]	0.514[a]	0.531[a]
Self-employed	0.497[a]	0.467[a]	0.478[a]	0.485[a]
Farm	0.412[a]	0.379[b]	0.396[b]	0.431[a]
Manual	0.442[a]	0.410[a]	0.434[a]	0.439[a]
Education (years)	–	−0.001	0.002	0.005
Income (in 10 millon yen)	–	−0.004[b]	−0.004[c]	−0.003[c]
Income missing	–	−0.091	−0.072	−0.089
Chronic conditions	–	–	0.890[a]	0.692[a]
Visit to doctor	–	–	–	0.428[a]
Intercept	−4.642[a]	−4.449[a]	−4.358[a]	−4.296[a]
−2 Log likelihood	4,550.264	4,396.617	4,303.052	4,256.849
Sample size	3,968	3,847	3,847	3,826

Notes.
a: $p < 0.01$, b: $p < 0.05$, c: $p < 0.10$.
The category in parentheses for the class variable is the base reference.

education. Here we consider three activities, smoking, drinking and walking, in addition to accessibility to medical information. It has been reported by the medical profession that these activities and access to medical knowledge are related to the onset of chronic medical conditions, such as diabetes. Table 5.8 shows whether there are socioeconomic differentials in smoking, drinking and walking behaviors and access to medical information.

Major findings are summarized as follows. First, with regard to smoking, men are 24 times ($e^{3.2} = 24$) more likely to smoke than women; the older the respondent, the less likely they smoke; farmers are less likely to smoke than other classes; and the higher the level of education, the less likely is smoking behavior.

Second, with regard to drinking alcohol, men are nine times ($e^{2.2} = 9.0$) more likely to drink than women; the older the respondent, the less likely they drink; the professional managerial class is more likely to drink than the self-employed, farmer and manual working class; and the higher the income, the more likely one drinks. If drinking leads to bad health, it does not make sense to find that

Table 5.8: Logistic regression predicting smoking, drinking, walking and access to medical information

Independent variables	Smoking		Drinking	
	Model 1	Model 2	Model 1	Model 2
Male	3.221[a]	3.250[a]	2.241[a]	2.219[a]
Age	−0.013[c]	−0.015[b]	−0.040[a]	−0.035[a]
Class (prof–managerial)				
Routine non-manual	0.172	0.049	−0.198	−0.108
Self-employed	0.126	−0.032	−0.390[a]	−0.307[b]
Farm	−0.527[a]	−0.725[a]	−0.581[a]	−0.416[a]
Manual	0.251[c]	0.052	−0.253[b]	−0.106
Education (years)	–	−0.045[c]	–	0.022
Income (in 10 millon yen)	–	−0.002	–	0.004[b]
Income missing	–	−0.319[b]	–	−0.063
Intercept	0.513	1.077[c]	2.894[a]	2.228[a]
−2 Log likelihood	3,591.331	3,470.253	4,344.404	4,208.171
Sample size	3,985	3,863	3,972	3,853

Independent variables	Walking		Medical Information	
	Model 1	Model 2	Model 1	Model 2
Male	0.087	0.079	0.113	0.050
Age	−0.045[a]	−0.046[a]	0.002	0.007
Class (prof-managerial)				
Routine non-manual	−0.155	−0.280[b]	−0.473[a]	−0.314[b]
Self-employed	−0.239[b]	−0.386[a]	−0.441[a]	−0.292[b]
Farm	0.461[a]	0.317[b]	−0.552[a]	−0.303[b]
Manual	0.093	−0.106	−0.571[a]	−0.353[a]
Education (years)	–	−0.075[a]	–	0.036[c]
Income (in 10 millon yen)	–	0.005[a]	–	0.006[a]
Income missing	–	−0.042	–	0.002
Intercept	3.700[a]	4.450[a]	−0.354	−1.242[b]
−2 Log likelihood	5,296.848	5,110.593	4,771.540	4,635.381
Sample size	3,985	3,863	3,410	3,319

Notes.
a: $p < 0.01$, b: $p < 0.05$, c: $p < 0.10$
The category in parentheses for the class variable is the base reference.

the professional-managerial class and those with higher incomes are more likely to drink, because we already found that members of this group are less likely to suffer from physical discomfort, activity restriction and mental health issues. It turns out that there is a positive association between drinking and good health. The relationship between daily activities including drinking and health will be discussed in detail below.

Third, with regard to routine exercise (walking), the older the respondent, the less likely they exercise; the farming class exercises most frequently while the urban self-employed exercise least; the higher the education, the less likely people are to exercise; and the higher the income, the more likely people are to exercise. Fourth, with regard to access to medical information, it is clear that the professional-managerial class stands out in terms of having exceptionally good access to medical information. In addition, those with better education and income have relatively good access to information. There seems to be no age and gender difference in access to medical information.

Finally, we examine how daily activities and access to medical information are associated with various health-related outcomes. Table 5.9 summarizes the associations after controlling for gender, age, class, education and income. Significant positive associations are indicated by plus signs (one plus for the 5% level and two pluses for the 1% level of significance), and significant negative associations are indicated by minus signs (one minus sign for the 5% level and two for the 1% level of significance). Smoking is significantly associated with the likelihood of onset of chronic medical conditions and physical discomfort. The result is consistent with those of epidemiological studies. However, because smoking is not related to other health-related outcomes and chronic conditions are not affected by socioeconomic factors, smoking cannot act as a mediating factor between socioeconomic factors (class and income) and health outcomes.

Associations involving drinking, on the other hand, are more complicated than those of smoking. Drinking reduces (not increases) the chances of activity restriction and perceived poor health, while it is not related to other health outcomes. If we take the results literally, drinking contributes to good health. Epidemiological studies usually report negative association between the amount of alcohol consumption and good health: the greater the consumption of alcohol, the worse the health condition. Our study does not measure drinking by the amount of drinking but rather by the presence of drinking, either in the present (at the time of survey) or in the past. The respondents who were drinking at the time of

Table 5.9: Relationship between health-related activities and health outcomes

	Smoking	Drinking	Walking	Medical information
Chronic disease	++		– –	
Visit to doctor			– –	
Physical pain	+		– –	– –
Activity restriction		– –	– –	
Depression			– –	– –
Self-reported health (poor health)		– –	– –	– –
Self-reported health (got worse)			– –	– –

Note. The relationship is apparent after controlling for gender, age, class, education and income. When there are two signs, the effect of health-related activities is significant at .01 level. When there is one sign, the effect is significant at .05 level. When there is no sign, there is no statistically significant association.

the survey were those who did not experience activity restriction and believed that they were healthy. In other words, we should not interpret the result as indicating that drinking leads to healthy outcomes. Rather, the result implies that those who are healthy enjoy alcoholic beverages.

Similar interpretation applies to the associations involving exercise. Walking is significantly associated with all health outcomes. The results may imply that walking leads to reduced chances of having chronic disease, visiting doctors, experiencing physical discomfort, activity restriction and depression, as well as better perceived health in general. However, it is possible that those who can exercise are those who are healthy to begin with. It is impossible to establish the causal direction from our data. Daily walking may be the result of health, not the cause. In other words, it is not possible to conclude from these results that walking acts as a mediating variable between socioeconomic factors and health outcomes.

Finally, when we examine the associations involving access to medical information, we find that it is related to physical discomfort, depression, subjective perceptions of current health and perception of change in health status. Respondents who reported to have sufficient medical information were less likely to experience physical discomfort and depression and to have good subjective health perception. Since it is very unlikely to think that health outcomes are the causes of access to medical information, accessibility to information may act as an important mechanism linking socioeconomic factors (class and income) and health outcomes. We speculate that favorable health conditions of the professional-managerial class and those with high incomes are in part explained by their superior access to medical information.

Discussion

This paper examined the relationship between socioeconomic factors and health-related outcomes. We identified six different health-related outcomes and examined the effects of various socioeconomic variables separately for each outcome. The first major conclusion from the analyses pertains to the finding that the effects of socioeconomic factors depend on the different health-related outcomes. The presence of chronic medical conditions and visits to doctor's offices are largely independent of socioeconomic factors. Age is the major determinant predicting these outcomes. The other four outcomes, the presence of physical discomfort, activity restriction, depression and self-reported health, are affected by socioeconomic factors. The lack of the effects of socioeconomic factors on chronic diseases is contrary to our original hypothesis. The emergence of chronic diseases is largely driven by genetic and constitutional factors that may be independent of socioeconomic differences. The differences in working conditions by social class affect the presence of physical discomfort and fatigue and activity restriction, but probably do not directly influence chronic medical conditions, except for occupationally driven symptoms and diseases.

Studies conducted in the West consistently report class differentials in mortality and infection rates. Why did our study in Japan fail to report socioeconomic differences in the onset of chronic diseases? We need to conduct further studies to come up with definitive conclusions, but there are a few possibilities. The first possibility is diet. Traditionally, the Japanese diet relied on fish as the main source of protein, and it was believed to be related to lower rates of heart disease, colon cancer and breast cancer (Marmot and Smith 1989). This kind of diet was probably widespread regardless of class and income during the 1970s when longevity was rapidly increased. Another possibility is the Japanese health system, including the national health insurance scheme that was enacted in 1961. Along with the national health insurance system, the former Ministry of Health and Welfare established public health centers all over Japan. These centers have contributed to reducing infectious diseases, especially tuberculosis, as well as infant mortality rates. Among the 191 national members of the WHO (World Health Organization), Japan's health system is ranked at the top (World Health Organization 2002), and the system was probably successful in providing universal health coverage, regardless of class and income. However, more recently there has been a problem of non-payment of the premiums for the national health insurance system. The rate has been increasing steadily, reaching 8.7% in 2000 (Kokumin Kenkō Hoken Chūōkai 2002). Therefore, there is a possibility that socioeconomic differences will emerge in the future.

When we move our attention beyond chronic medical conditions and consider more comprehensive health-related outcomes (physical discomfort, activity restriction, depression and subjective perceptions of health), differentials by social class and income are clearly apparent. The professional-managerial class is the most advantaged in these health-related outcomes, while the urban self-employed and the manual working class are the least advantaged. The exposure to unfavorable and physically demanding working conditions experienced by the manual working class is likely to increase the risk of physical pain and fatigue and eventually lower general health conditions and perceptions. The petty bourgeoisie also tend to have lower rates of health conditions than the professional-managerial class, and this difference is probably derived from the longer working hours of the petty bourgeoisie. All these findings suggest that the positions in the labor market have a profound influence on the workers' health. Income also exerts a significant influence on all health-related outcomes, except for chronic medical conditions and visits to a doctor's office. People with greater financial assets are probably able to derive various resources that help them avoid being physically constrained at home and feel more secured even when their health condition worsens. It is important to note that these differentials in health by class and income persist even after controlling for chronic medical conditions. In other words, class and income differentials are found among both the chronically ill and those who do not suffer from chronic diseases. In summary, socioeconomic inequality of health is documented when we use a more comprehensive measure of health-related outcomes that take into account the quality of life related to health.

The second major finding of this study relates to the predictive power of different socioeconomic factors. Social class, our primary independent variable, and income are the two most important factors in predicting health-related outcomes. In contrast, education has virtually no effect on predicting people's health conditions and perception. What makes a difference in people's health is not how much schooling they had. Instead, work positions in the labor market and financial resources affect people's physical wellbeing. The lack of the effect of education is striking, so we need to think about possible explanations. First, the respondents were aged 65 or more, so it has been more than 40 years since they undertook their formal education. Moreover, many of them went to school under the old pre-war educational system. The passing of so much time would naturally be expected to reduce the direct effect of education on present health outcomes. Second, as shown in Table 5.1, 60% of respondents had a minimum level of education. We were not able to distinguish the quality of schooling among those in this category. The result is that there is not much spread in the educational distribution, and the skewed distribution may have been another factor preventing us from fully detecting the impact of educational factors.

The third major finding of this study pertains to the role of daily activities and access to medical information in explaining the linkage between socioeconomic positions and health outcomes. Smoking, drinking and daily exercise do not seem to act as a mediating factor between socioeconomic positions and health outcomes. In particular, drinking and daily walking are better understood not as a mediating factor, but as a consequence of health conditions. Respondents who have relatively good health are able to enjoy drinking and exercising, rather than a causative link between drinking and walking and good health. In contrast, access to medical information probably acts as a mediating factor. Respondents who reported to have sufficient medical information are less likely to experience physical discomfort and depression and to have good subjective health perception. We speculate that favorable health conditions of the professional-managerial class and those with a high income are in part explained by their superior access to medical information.

Finally, with regard to our two control variables, age and gender, there are two conclusions. First, any study of health must take age into account. The aging process is closely related to the health condition of the individual, and there is usually a positive linear effect of age on poor health. Our results clearly support this point. In all six of our health-related outcomes, age is a powerful determinant. It should be noted, however, that part of the effect of age goes through chronic conditions. Older elderly are nonetheless more likely to visit doctors and have ill-heath perception than younger elderly, regardless of their chronic diseases. This is because older people are more likely to suffer from health-related problems than younger people, even though they do not have any chronic diseases. Second, gender differences are found in some health-related outcomes. Although men and women do not differ in their chances of having chronic medical conditions, men are less likely to visit doctor's offices, less likely to have depression and less likely to report that their health worsened. Therefore, men seem to be healthier, at least on these aspects of health-related outcomes.

The differentials in quality of life relating to health in old age may be viewed as a 'hidden disparity' in contemporary Japan. The labor market is the source of socioeconomic differentials, and even after one has retired from it, the nature of the work one was engaged in prior to retirement continues to exert a permanent effect on one's life, even extending to the domain of health – the most fundamental condition of human life.

6 Inheritance, Pensions, Childbirth, Childrearing and the Inequalities They Bring: A Case Study of Impact on Net Financial Assets

Katsumi Matsuura

Differentials in matters where one has no choice

There are all sorts of opinions as to when a situation can be described as 'fair.' However, few would accept as such a situation where economic differentials between people widen to the point of no return due to factors over which they have absolutely no control. Once people start to feel that their social status and livelihood are threatened by the factors causing those differentials, or the scale of the disparity, their dissatisfaction will become deeper still.

Parental socioeconomic status and children

Historically speaking, one of the biggest factors influencing people's social status and economic conditions has been the social standing and economic capacity of their parents. Modern society has destroyed the old class system whereby the lives of children were constrained by the social origins of their parents. Practically no one mourns the passing of the class society, for the simple reason that since children cannot choose their parents, rigid class systems appear obviously unfair. There is less consensus, however, as to whether one can tolerate the existence of socioeconomic differentials inherited by children from their parents, and if so, to what degree they can be endured. A society in which children's economic circumstances are substantially influenced by parental assets and their transfer through gift or inheritance, to the point where economic differentials are so wide that they cannot be overcome by a lifetime of hard work – such a society cannot be considered healthy.[1] This would lead to further problems too, since 'inequality of outcome' in the parental generation leads directly to 'inequality of opportunity'[2] in that of their children (Kunieda 2002).

Cohorts and the pension system

Along with their parents, another thing that children cannot choose is the timing of their birth – the cohort into which they are born, to put it in sociological terms. The young cohort subsidizes the old through the public pension system, and this is not much of a problem so long as economic conditions permit children to believe that tomorrow will be more prosperous than today, that their generation will enjoy a more affluent lifestyle than that of their parents. If the children's generation has become wealthy, or expects to become so, its members will feel they can afford to support the relatively impecunious parental generation. But in a situation where tomorrow will *not* necessarily be more prosperous than today, the public pension system becomes a mechanism that transfers wealth from a young cohort that is relatively poor to an old one that is relatively wealthy. When that happens, and particularly when the speed of the transfer systematically accelerates, the relatively poor younger cohort will naturally start to feel that things are less than fair. In Japan, the advent of the low birthrate/ultra-aging society means that an absolute decline in the population is a certainty. The forced transfer of income from the young generation to the old through the public pension system will inevitably pose a threat to the livelihoods of succeeding generations. The problem is that Japan tried to build a pension system based on a *savings model*, in which each generation would pay for its own pensions by saving money while economically active, but has ended up with one based on a *tax-and-spend model*, in which unfair premiums effectively function as a tax on younger cohorts to help pay for the pensions of older ones.

How childbirth and childrearing widen differentials

The bearing and rearing of children are activities closely related to the intergenerational transfer of income through inheritance and public pensions. If there are no children, then there is no incentive for the parental generation to leave money to be inherited. When there are few children, a minority of them will inherit a larger amount of wealth than before. Thus there is a strong possibility that the declining birthrate will have the effect of widening differentials.

Under the present pension system with its unfair treatment of cohorts, one of the big problems that arises when the population goes into absolute decline is that income tends to be transferred from households bringing up relatively many children to those with relatively few or none at all. Giving birth to children is a voluntary choice made by parents, and bringing them up should be a source of happiness. Children will support society in the future, and a society without children cannot survive. In that sense, childbirth and childrearing are activities endowed with profound social significance. In Japan the social support for those activities is far from adequate, as I have tried to show in previous research on the lengths of time children have to wait for a place at a day-care center, and on the difficulties faced by women who want to combine childbirth and mothering with regular employment (Matsuura and Shigeno 1996, 2005). This inadequate level of care imposes a heavy economic burden on families that tends to put them at the wrong end of widening differentials. Worse still, it also tends to transmit those wider differentials to the next generation, since families with many children will have to share inherited wealth more thinly than those with few children.

Objective of this chapter

In this chapter I propose to look at the impact on economic differentials between people caused by inheritance and the pension system – two things over which people have no personal influence – and how it varies according to family childrearing circumstances, for which I will use types of family (numbers of adult and child members, etc.) as a proxy. I will examine differentials specifically in terms of net financial assets,[3] using the 1996 and 2002 editions of the Survey on Family Budgets and Savings (*Kakei to Chochiku ni kan-suru Chōsa*) carried out by the Ministry of Posts and Telecommunications (MPT) and an agency of the Post Office.[4]

Nineteen-ninety-six was a year in which the economy showed a slight recovery. Gross National Income (GNI) grew by 3.2% in real terms, the household saving rate was 9.9%, the unemployment rate[5] was 3.4% and the TOPIX stock index averaged 1470.9 for the year. In 2002 GNI showed a real-term 0.4% decline, the household saving rate was 6.4%, the unemployment rate was 5.4% and the TOPIX stock index averaged 843.3. Hence, the analysis in this chapter will be comparing a year in which Japan was doing relatively well, despite occurring in the wake of the bursting of the bubble economy and being a year in which the recession got a lot worse due to a series of financial crises. We will be able to look for connections between the severity of Japan's economic problems, on the one hand, and the causes and degree of differentials, on the other.

The argument will be structured thus. Following the introductory remarks, I examine the situation regarding inheritance with special reference to taxation, analyzing the differentials between cohorts in terms of benefits and burdens. I also break down the costs associated with marriage, childbirth and childrearing. I then outline differentials in net financial assets among groups of people defined according to whether or not they have experienced inheritance of wealth and receipt of pensions. I also discuss differentials in levels of consumption between age cohorts. In the penultimate section I present the results of GMM (Generalized Method of Moments) estimates for correlations between net financial asset accumulation and patterns of inheritance, pension receipt and family formation. I then outline my conclusions. If I may briefly state those in advance, I find the following substantial differences between 1996 and 2002, both in the factors causing differentials and in the scale of differentials.

1. The experience of inheriting wealth, or the expectation of doing so, had a major influence on household accumulation of net financial assets. The effect was in the order of ¥4–5 million in 1996, swelling to ¥8.2–10.2 million in 2002.
2. The effect on net financial assets of receipt of pensions and enrollment/non-enrollment in a pension program was not clearly discernible in 1996. But in 2002 differentials were clearly observable, both in relation to receipt/non-receipt of pensions and regarding type of pension. Net financial assets of households not enrolled in pension programs showed a deficit of ¥2–2.2 million relative to households that were enrolled in programs but not yet receiving pensions.
3. Family type, the variable used to study the effect on net financial asset accumulation of childbirth and childrearing,

showed no influence in 1996. But in 2002 the net financial assets of families with one or more children were lower than those without children. The deficit was around ¥3–4 million for nuclear families (parents + children), and ¥6.2–7.2 million for three-generation households.
4. Net financial assets declined when people were in the age range of 30–33, which nowadays is the peak period for marriage and childbirth.

Problems in contemporary Japan with inheritance tax, the pension system and childrearing

Inheritance patterns

There is very little published research on the proportion of household assets accounted for by inheritance, reflecting the severe lack of data on this topic.[6] Even the definition of assets held by the children's generation varies from one analyst to another (Ishikawa 1991).[7] Among the few studies that have been published, my own collaboration with Toshiaki Tachibanaki uses data from surveys on household budgets and savings trends from the Management and Coordination Agency (MCA; Sōmuchō) for the period 1986–89, when land and stock prices were at all-time highs (Matsuura and Tachibanaki 1993), and finds that during that period inheritance accounted for 36.6–40.0% of family assets, including financial assets, land, housing and leaseholds. Tachibanaki and Takeda (1994) used another MPT survey, on 'Household Budget Asset Selection' (MPT 1990) to estimate that inheritance accounted for 40% of net assets and 5% of financial assets.

Let us now consider what kind of government policies have been taken in connection with inheritance. Since the late 1980s, the government of Japan has pursued a policy of reducing inheritance tax. In 1987 the top rate of inheritance tax was 75%, but it was reduced to 70% in 1988 and further to 50% in 2003. The threshold at which the tax kicks in was also raised, from ¥40 million per deceased + ¥8 million per inheritor in 1990 to ¥50 million per deceased + ¥10 million per inheritor in 1995. These various measures had the combined effect of reducing the average rate of inheritance tax across the inheriting population from 22.2% in 1991 to 10.8% in 2004. In contrast, the rate of taxation levied on interest income is a standard 20%. Even the interest on the slender savings of a person living below the poverty line is taxed at 20%. That gives you some idea of just how favorably inherited wealth has been treated in recent years.

One outcome of the inheritance tax reduction policy has been to reduce the number of people who have to pay it. In the late 1980s, some 6–7% of those who died left estates large enough to be subject to inheritance tax. By 2002, that figure had fallen to 4.5%.[8] In that year the mean value of assets acquired per inheritor was about ¥2.9 million. Inheritance tax targets particularly wealthy individuals, and even among that group the population is skewed toward higher income brackets. For instance, according to the annual report from the National Tax Agency, in 2002 estates valued in excess of ¥1 billion accounted for 2.3% of cases and 16.8% of total taxable value; those in the ¥500 million to ¥1 billion range accounted for 6.0% of cases and 16.9% of value; those in the ¥100 to ¥500 million range for 73.0% of cases and 59.7% of value; and those in the sub-¥100 million range for just 18.7% of cases and 6.7% of value.

The policy of reducing inheritance tax on wealthy individuals was designed to make it easier to transfer wealth to the next generation, and for the owners of small and medium-sized enterprises (SMEs) to pass on management of those enterprises to their children. The owners of SMEs constitute the wealthiest status group in Japanese society. The objective of facilitating the transfer of assets between generations for this group constitutes a deliberate attempt to translate outcome inequality in one generation into opportunity inequality for the next. This kind of clear and deliberate widening of differentials has been a feature of government policy in Japan since the 1990s.

One important caveat is required before we go any further. The surveys that I use in this chapter on family budgets and savings include hardly any of the super-wealthy households that might be expected to have estates worth in excess of ¥1 billion. The same goes for other big Japanese government surveys such as the National Survey of Family Income and Expenditure and the Survey of Household Economy, and for similar surveys conducted in Europe and North America. The kind of super-rich people who make it into the *Forbes* magazine rankings do *not* make it into the survey data we are about to analyze. To put it another way, there is a distinct possibility that analysis based on the available survey data will underestimate the inequality of distribution in Japan and other industrialized countries alike.[9]

The following estimates will verify that the net financial assets of inheriting households (including those likely to inherit in future) are larger than those of non-inheriting households (including those not likely to inherit in future).[10] I call this hypothesis 1.

The pension system and cohorts

In Japan there are three main types of public pension: (1) mutual-aid pensions (*kyōsai nenkin*) for public employees; (2) employee pensions (*kōsei nenkin*) for workers at large and middle-sized corporations; and (3) national pensions (*kokumin nenkin*) for the self-employed and employees at small businesses. Of the three, the national pension scheme was the last to be launched, back in 1961. Its inauguration marked the start of a universal pension system, in which everyone in the country was supposed to be enrolled in one or another of the three programs.[11] This is often cited as one of the biggest systemic differences between Japan and the US, where only a relatively small part of the population is covered by public pensions.

Since the tripartite system is based on occupational distinctions, it follows that in Japan the kind of pension fund you pay into, and the kind of pension you receive, will reflect your occupational history. The first two systems entail the employer and employee each paying 50% of the premiums. In some big corporations, it is not unknown for the employer to pay a share of the premiums in excess of the 50% stipulated by law. Compared with employees of small businesses, those working for big businesses or for the state tend to enjoy greater stability of employment and higher remuneration, so it is often the case that their pension premiums are also far higher. Consequently the pensions paid out by the mutual-aid and employee programs are generally higher than national pensions.

If public pensions are based on sound actuarial principles, designed to insure against the risk of pension recipients living longer than expected, then the system will be fair and there can be no transfer of income between generations, since the amount paid by each cohort in premiums will match that received in pension payments (Tajika, Kaneko and Hayashi 1996). However, if the system works on the taxation model, transferring income from young to old cohorts, there is a possibility that the scale of the transfer will be bigger for the mutual-aid and employee pension systems than for the national pension system, since the former two cover people with higher pre-retirement incomes.

Benefits received by cohorts: Much research has already been published on the topic of just how big the gap between generations has grown regarding the burdens and benefits of pension systems.[12] The 2003 Economic White Paper carried out broad-ranging accounting of financial burdens and benefits between generations, including social security, taxation, etc. It found that the cohort born before 1941 had received a net ¥64.99 million; the 1942–51 cohort had received a net ¥1.94 million; the 1952–61 cohort had suffered a net loss of ¥9.52 million; the 1962–71 cohort a net loss of ¥17.32 million; the 1972–81 cohort a net loss of ¥18.81 million; and the cohort from 1982 onwards was looking at a net loss of ¥52.23 million (per household). Looking just at the employee pension system, the White Paper found that the total of employer and employee contributions had greatly exceeded pensions paid out for those born in 1930, but that for those born in 1970 the pattern had reversed, with pension payments likely to exceed premium contributions.[13]

The pension system and expectations of negative returns: There is a further serious problem with public pensions that impacts on social security and economic differentials. The calculations used to set premiums and pay-outs have consistently over-estimated future birthrates and interest rates (Yashiro 1999, etc.). This continued inaccuracy in forecasting has had the effect of increasing the lifetime income of old cohorts more than might otherwise have been expected, while correspondingly decreasing the lifetime income of young cohorts beyond expectations. The generation currently receiving pensions can hardly be expected to pay back the ¥400 trillion by which pension commitments are now thought to exceed reserves. That would entail a massive cut in pension payments. Nor would a massive hike in taxation for the working generation be a realistic option. This means that younger cohorts will inevitably receive less in pensions than they pay in premiums, so that the public pension programs effectively become a form of forced investment in an instrument that is bound to show negative returns. No rational householder would invest in an asset that is bound to show a negative return. If one invests, of one's own free will, in an asset that turns out to generate a loss, then that is one's own responsibility. But when one is forced to invest in an asset that can only result in the investor incurring a loss, and when that investment actually threatens one's lifetime financial planning, then one will naturally be deeply resentful. That is the situation for younger cohorts in Japan right now.

In the estimates that follow, I will verify two further hypotheses: that households receiving pensions have greater net financial assets than those that are not receiving pensions or are not enrolled in pension funds (hypothesis 2); and that differences in pension payments between the three different types of public pension create a further set of differentials among people enrolled in different programs (hypothesis 3).

The private burden of childbirth and childrearing and inadequate public support

In Japan some 70% of women quit work on the occasion of marriage or childbirth. Especially where two or more children are born, the inadequate provision of day-care centers and other support sometimes means that the mother is effectively forced to resign from her position. If a woman quits work because of marriage or childbirth, it is extremely difficult for her to return to the workforce later on in a position with favorable working conditions. The main reason for this is that age discrimination in employment is legal in Japan. It is legal, for example, to restrict a job opening to applicants under the age of 30, or 25. Indeed, there is an age limit of 29 for sitting the examination for employment doing ordinary clerical work as a public official. For career-track public officials, the age limit is 33. The average age at first marriage for a woman living in metropolitan Tokyo is 30. If she gets married, has a baby and quits work, she will almost certainly be debarred from future employment as a public official because of legalized age discrimination.[14] This means that in most cases having a baby effectively forces the mother to abandon her career. This is another striking difference between Japan and the US, where age discrimination is illegal.

In Japan, most women who seek to return to the labor market some years after giving birth end up in part-time employment, earning hourly wages that correspond to somewhere between one third and one half of the effective hourly remuneration for similar work done as a regular employee. Let us see what that means in terms of wages earned over a lifetime, using mean figures from the 1997 White Paper on the National Lifestyle (*Kokumin Seikatsu Hakusho*). A woman who graduates from a two-year junior college and gets employed in a clerical position that she holds until the age of 60 can expect to earn a total of ¥236 million in her lifetime. If she quits that job for childbirth/childrearing and manages to get a similar position as a regular employee five years later, her lifetime earnings will total ¥173 million – a loss of ¥63 million. If, however, she returns from her five-year absence and secures a part-time job, her lifetime earnings will pan out at ¥51 million – a loss of ¥185 million. Faced by this yawning chasm in earning potential, it is hardly surprising that many women choose not to give birth, or limit themselves to a single child.[15]

Big intergenerational differentials in pension payments and the problem of accumulated pension fund deficits create concerns about Ricardian equivalence and the interconnectivity between generations. Under Japanese law, it is not possible for negative assets to be inherited within a single household, since children have no legal responsibility for their parents' debts. However, if uncovered pension debts are passed on to later generations then that is a form of negative inheritance between cohorts. The inability of the pension system to function as originally planned is a problem intimately linked to the falling birthrate.[16] Under such a pension regime, it is advantageous to the household economy to have as few children as possible and rely upon other people's children to subsidize one's future pension (Matsuura and Shirahase 2002). In short, the pension system itself contains the potential to further depress the birthrate.

Even if we leave the topic of pensions for a moment, there are plenty of other connections between childbirth/childrearing and economic differentials. Just take a look at some of the reasons cited for feeling uneasy about childrearing by householders in a 2004 survey on social consciousness carried out by the Prime Minister's Office (Naikakufu 2004).[17]

No less than 39.1% of those surveyed chose the response 'Children's future education will cost money,' and 18.1% chose 'Bringing up children when they are still young will cost money.' In addition to these simple economic concerns, 21.6% chose the response 'I will lose my free time,' and 12.8% chose 'I won't be able to work the way I want to.' It is easy to surmise from these responses that the economic burden of raising children is contributing to the widening of differentials. Even so, public assistance for childbirth and childrearing remains feeble (Matsuura and Shigeno 2005). The fact that marriage and childbirth are likely to bring women a massive decline in financial asset ownership and a major new economic burden in childrearing costs suggests that there are differences in the acquisition of net financial assets according to life-cycle phase and household type.

I will therefore seek to verify two more propositions in my analysis below: that households with children have fewer net financial assets than those without children (hypothesis 4) and that even for younger people, net financial assets do not just rise in a single steady trend, but show a temporary downturn in the course of marriage and childbirth (hypothesis 5).

Differentials in assets and the like seen in data sets and groups

Data

As mentioned earlier, in this analysis I will be using the 1996 and 2002 editions of the Survey on Family Budgets and Savings (*Kakei to Chochiku ni kan-suru Chōsa*), which I will refer to simply as the 1996 survey and the 2002 survey.[18] The 1996 survey had 3,942 respondents and the 2002 survey had 5,596. Excluding respondents who gave no answer on the items necessary for my analysis, the samples number 2,281 in 1996 and 4,534 in 2002.

In this chapter I am focusing on the influence on household net financial assets of inheritance and pensions, but in this regard the survey items are slightly different between the 1996 survey and the 2002 survey. For example, on the question of pensions, the 1996 survey asks whether the householders and/or their spouses are receiving an employee pension, a mutual-aid pension, a national pension or no pension. The 2002 survey asks whether or not the householder is already receiving a public pension of some kind, and does not directly ask about the spouse. It uses the same categories of pension as in 1996, but adds one extra category – *onkyū*, an old form of employee pension paid to retired soldiers, etc.

As for annual income, the 1996 survey asks about tax and social insurance contributions, making it possible to calculate disposable income. Those items were omitted from the 2002 survey, meaning that we only have data on pre-tax income. Consequently I have had to use somewhat different explanatory and instrumental variables for the two surveys.

Differentials in net financial assets and the like according to presence/absence of income through inheritance and pensions

Table 6.1 shows the households in the sample population broken down into four groups according to (1) whether or not the household has experience of inheritance and (2) whether or not the head of household is receiving a public pension, and tabulates annual income, financial assets, debt, net financial assets and home ownership for each group. Comparing 1996 with 2002, we can see at once that there was a sharp decline in mean and median levels of financial assets and net financial assets for all four groups. Clearly, the very poor state of the Japanese economy from 1996 to 2002 had an impact across the board on household asset accumulation.

In both 1996 and 2002, net financial assets were highest for the group with inheritance and pension income, and lowest for that with neither. In 2002, the median net financial asset level for the group with both was ¥10 million, while that for the group with pensions but no inheritance was ¥5.5 million, indicating the substantial effect of inheritance.

The home-ownership ratio is clearly higher for the inheriting groups: in the 2002 survey, for example, 94.8% of respondents (householders) in the group with pension and inheritance owned their own house, whereas only 75.3% of those with a pension but no inheritance were home-owners. Likewise in the no-pension groups, 59.9% of those with inheritance were home-owners against 40.3% of those with neither pension nor inheritance. This suggests that inheritance and pension patterns are connected to net financial assets, or, through differences in housing acquisition, to more general asset differentials.

Consumption levels: One measure of welfare is consumption, defined here as monthly living expenditure divided by a scale equivalent to the square root of the number of household members. In 1996 monthly consumption averaged ¥165,800 for the group with inheritance and a pension, ¥167,000 for the group with inheritance but no pension, ¥159,800 for the group with a pension but no inheritance and ¥162,800 for that with neither pension nor inheritance. The test statistic for equality of means between categorized groups by values of pension and inheritance F was 0.78 and p=0.50, so that there was no significant difference between the four groups. In 2002, however, the corresponding figures for the four groups were ¥170,700, ¥170,900, ¥153,200 and ¥160,500. The test statistic F was 15.18 and p=0.00, so that a statistically significant difference had emerged between the four groups. The emergence of differentials in living standards as expressed in consumption levels probably was a factor making people more aware of differentials between groups.

Differentials in consumption levels between old and young cohorts

When we speak of the children's generation being more prosperous than that of the parents, we mean that the younger generation enjoys a higher level of consumption. Using equivalent scale to calculate consumption across cohorts, I propose to investigate whether this condition has been established in Japan (see Figure 6.1). The low level of consumption among younger cohorts born after 1960 is very striking. In 2002 the cohort born in 1960–64 had average monthly consumption of ¥157,700, and the 1965–69 cohort ¥152,500. The parental cohorts born in 1930–34 and 1935–39 registered ¥163,300 and ¥162,700 respectively. The younger cohorts were clearly consuming less than the older ones. Under normal circumstances, retired generations are supposed to spend less than active ones because they are spared work-related expenditure. But the results here are the other way round, giving the impression that the era when each generation could expect to do better than the one before is already over, and we are now in reverse mode. Under such conditions, it will surely not be possible to obtain broad cross-generational support for a policy under which the younger generation is forced to subsidize the older one through the public pension system. The highest level of consumption in 2002 was ¥179,400, registered by the 1947–49 cohort – the so-called *Dankai* generation. This cohort, the cherished offspring of the high-growth era, conspicuous in so many ways, also continues to stand out from the crowd in terms of consumption.

Table 6.1: Net financial assets in terms of inheritance and pensions

	1996 survey					2002 survey				
	Mean	Median	Maximum	Minimum	Standard deviation	Mean	Median	Maximum	Minimum	Standard deviation
Inheritance and pension (n = 208)						*Inheritance and pension (n = 620)*				
Annual income	690	592	5,839	46	576	675	494	9,100	36	684
Financial assets	2,616	1,415	40,000	0	4,473	1,934	1,115	20,100	0	2,514
Debt	258	0	5,000	0	765	328	0	12,000	0	1,090
Net financial assets	2,358	1,230	35,000	−3,240	4,274	1,605	1,000	18,100	−12,000	2,788
Home ownership	96.6%	1	1	0	0.181	94.8%	1	1	0	0.221
Inheritance and no pension (n = 310)						*Inheritance and no pension (n = 1,157)*				
Annual income	905	800	4,800	6	589	717	600	15,070	0	665
Financial assets	1,767	1,113	14,500	0	2,045	1,015	490	23,184	0	1,672
Debt	600	0	22,000	0	1,649	577	10	15,000	0	1,177
Net financial assets	1,167	805	14,500	−14,500	2,408	437	200	23,184	−13,400	2,055
Home ownership	88.1%	1	1	0	0.325	59.9%	1	1	0	0.490
No inheritance and a pension (n = 356)						*No inheritance and a pension (n = 1,022)*				
Annual income	552	480	4,080	8	397	429	340	3,800	30	363
Financial assets	1,679	1,047	14,950	0	1,938	1,264	645	14,650	0	1,755
Debt	168	0	4,000	0	500	139	0	7,956	0	517
Net financial assets	1,511	912	14,950	−3,644	2,003	1,124	550	14,650	−7,356	1,854
Home ownership	81.7%	1	1	0	0.387	75.3%	1	1	0	0.431

	No inheritance and no pension (n = 1,407)					No inheritance and no pension (n = 1,735)				
Annual income	713	650	5,900	10	424	536	480	3,500	0	357
Financial assets	986	570	25,700	0	1,539	578	200	19,400	0	1,119
Debt	412	0	6,000	0	840	470	0	20,000	0	1,087
Net financial assets	574	320	25,700	−4,990	1,697	107	50	19,400	−20,000	1,546
Home ownership	53.5%	1	1	0	0.499	40.3%	0	1	0	49.1%

Note.
The unit of 'mean' is 10,000 yen.

Figure 6.1: Consumption level differentials between cohorts

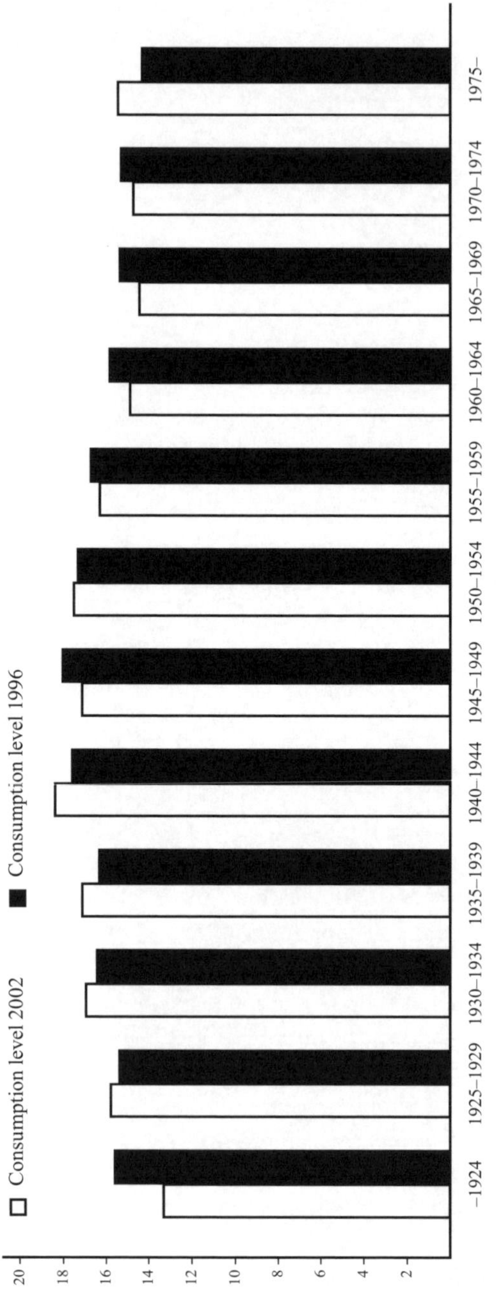

Note. Calculation made by the author.

Factors creating differentials in net financial assets

Formulation

Concrete estimation formula: In the analysis that follows, I will look at the effect on accumulation of net financial assets of (1) experience of inheriting wealth; (2) receipt of pension and type of pension; (3) family type; and (4) age. To do so I will mainly use equation 1 below:

Equation 1
Net financial asset.$_i$ = Constant + ΣA_j Age variable.$_i$ + ΣB_j Pre-tax income variable.$_i$ + C Home-ownership dummy$_i$ +D Inheritance dummy.$_i$ + ΣE_j Pension variable.$_i$ + ΣF_j Family-type variable.$_i$ + Error term.$_i$

The inheritance dummy includes the prospect of receiving inheritance as well as actual experience of inheritance. This seems appropriate because the prospect of inheriting can influence household budget activity just as the reality of inheriting can do so.

Before I commence this analysis, allow me to remind the reader that when discussing pensions, 'employee pensions' (*kōsei nenkin*), 'mutual-aid pensions' (*kyōzai nenkin*) and 'national pensions' (*kokumin nenkin*) are all sub-categories of 'public pensions' (*kōteki nenkin*).

In my analysis of the 1996 survey data, my variables related to pensions fell broadly into the following three sets:
1. 'Receiving employee pension' dummy, 'receiving mutual-aid pension' dummy, 'receiving national pension' dummy and 'not enrolled in public pension' dummy.
2. 'Receiving national pension' dummy, 'receiving public pension' dummy and 'not enrolled in public pension' dummy.
3. 'Aged 65-plus and receiving public pension' dummy, 'aged 65-plus and receiving national pension' dummy, 'aged under 65 and receiving public pension' dummy and 'aged under 65 and receiving national pension' dummy and 'not enrolled in public pension' dummy.

In all three cases the dummy for 'enrolled in public pension scheme but not receiving a pension' is a default value.

As for the 2002 data, I divided it into the following three sets:

1. 'Receiving public pension' dummy x 'householder enrolled in employee pension scheme' dummy, 'receiving public pension' dummy x 'householder enrolled in mutual-aid or *onkyū* pension scheme' dummy, 'receiving public pension' dummy x 'householder enrolled in national pension scheme' dummy and 'not enrolled in public pension' dummy.
2. 'Receiving public pension' dummy, and 'not enrolled in public pension' dummy.
3. 'Aged 65-plus and receiving public pension' dummy, 'aged under 65 and receiving public pension' dummy, 'aged under 65 and receiving national pension' dummy and 'not enrolled in public pension' dummy.

In all three cases the dummy for 'enrolled in public pension scheme but not receiving a pension' is a default value.

There were two reasons for the somewhat different choice of variable sets: one is the differences in the questions used in the two surveys, the other is that a difference was identified in the effect of national pensions between the two years. This enables us to get a grasp of the pension system's effect on pure financial asset accumulation between 1996 and 2002.

In my analysis of family types I divided the sample into single-person households, married couples without children, married couples with children, three-generation households and others. I used married couples without children as my default value. 'With children' was the sum of married couples with children and three-generation families.[19] As for age, bearing in mind the possibility that its influence could be affected by lifestyle effects and could decline during the marriage and childbirth period, I included not only age but also its square and its cube. Likewise for annual income, I included the item itself and its square. I use the home-ownership dummy as a substitute variable for property assets.

Coding conditions

It is predicted that the code for coefficient D (inheritance) will be positive. It is predicted that the code E relating to variants connected to pension receipt will be positive for all coefficients relating to pension receipt dummies where income transfer arises from the pension system. If the effect on income transfer varies according to the type of pension received, it is predicted that there will be statistically significant differences in the coefficients for each type of pension. The code for the 'not enrolled in public pension' dummy coefficient will probably not be fixed in advance. However, if the reason for non-enrollment is economic hardship revealed by inadequate accumulation of assets, then that coefficient is predicted to be significant and negative when compared with the fixed value for 'enrolled in public pension scheme but not receiving a pension.'

Turning now to coefficient F for the family-type dummy, where the economic burden of childrearing costs on the household budget is great, the code for the coefficients relating to the two dummies for childrearing budgets of married couples with children and three-generation households will probably be significant and negative.

In order to clarify the effects of the explanatory variables for the pension-receiving dummy and the family-type dummy, a Wald test was also carried out to estimate values for variables other than those found not to be statistically significant.

In this estimation, since pre-tax income and the dummy for home-ownership are endogenous variables, and the variables relating to income and assets are treated as explained and explanatory variables, error terms are expected to show a heteroskedastic distribution. Therefore an econometric method using GMM techniques was applied. In order to facilitate reading of the results, the values of net financial assets are divided by a hundred and shown in units of 1,000. Since this is a linear function, the value shown for each coefficient is its limit effect.[20] Descriptive statistics are given in Table 6.2.

Estimation results for 1996

Results were as displayed in Table 6.3. Columns 1, 3 and 5 display results where all explanatory variables are included; columns 2, 4 and 6 show results after applying a Wald test to exclude pension-receipt and household-type variables not found to be statistically significant. First of all, if we look at orthogonality conditions for over-identification, results in all six columns reach the 10% level. We may therefore conclude that there is no problem with orthogonality conditions between instrumental variables and error terms.[21] Results of the Wald tests lead me to choose the results in columns 2, 4 and 6. I will mainly address those results in my discussion below.

Table 6.2a: Descriptive statistics for 1996

	Mean	Max	Min	Standard deviation
Net financial assets/1000	0.9633	35	−14.5	2.273
Age	48.96	95	20	13.600
Age squared/100	23.97	90.25	4	13.591
Age cubed/10,000	117.36	857.38	8	109.71
Pre-tax income/1000	0.7122	5.9	0.006	0.471
Pre-tax income squared/1,000,000	0.5072	34.81	0.000	1.609
Home ownership dummy	0.6655	1	0	0.472
Inheritance/prospect of inheritance	0.2271	1	0	0.419
Receiving employee pension dummy	0.1324	1	0	0.339
Receiving mutual aid pension dummy	0.0561	1	0	0.230
Receiving national pension dummy	0.0587	1	0	0.235
Receiving public pension dummy	0.2473	1	0	0.432
Aged 65+ and receiving public pension dummy	0.1464	1	0	0.354
Aged 65+ and receiving national pension dummy	0.0447	1	0	0.207
Aged under 65 and receiving public pension dummy	0.1008	1	0	0.301
Aged under 65 and receiving national pension dummy	0.0140	1	0	0.118
'Not enrolled in public pension' dummy	0.0513	1	0	0.221
Single-person household dummy	0.0859	1	0	0.280
Married couple (no children) household dummy	0.1776	1	0	0.382
Married couple + children household dummy	0.5081	1	0	0.500
Three-generation household dummy	0.1175	1	0	0.322
Other family type dummy	0.0210	1	0	0.144

Note.
n = 2,281.

Effect of experience/prospect of inheritance: The experience or prospect of inheritance was positive and significant at the 1% or 5% level for all cases. The coefficient was 0.51 (column 2), 0.38 (col. 4) and 0.40 (col. 6). The net financial assets of households with experience or prospect of inheritance amounted to some ¥4 to 5 million more than those without. That figure exceeded the median net financial assets of the no inheritance/no pension group, which was only ¥3.2 million, and was about 50% of the median figure for the group receiving a pension but no inheritance, which stood at ¥9.12 million (Table 6.1).

A Case Study of Impact on Net Financial Assets

Table 6.2b: Descriptive statistics for 2002

	Mean	Max	Min	Standard deviation
Net financial assets/1000	0.6256	23.184	–20	2.031
Age	51.64	90	18	15.662
Age squared/100	26.67	81	3.24	15.881
Age cubed/10,000	137.71	729	5.832	130.706
Pre-tax income/1000	0.5771	15.07	0	0.517
Pre-tax income squared/1,000,000	3.3330	2,271.049	0	38.675
Home ownership dummy	0.6065	1	0	0.489
Inheritance/prospect of inheritance	0.3919	1	0	0.488
Public pension dummy x employee pension enrollment dummy	0.3622	1	0	0.481
Public pension dummy x mutual aid and '*onkyu*' pension enrollment dummy	0.2239	1	0	0.417
Public pension dummy x national pension enrollment dummy	0.0468	1	0	0.211
Receiving public pension dummy	0.0873	1	0	0.282
Aged 65+ and receiving public pension dummy	0.2464	1	0	0.431
Aged under 65 and receiving public pension dummy	0.1158	1	0	0.320
Respondent not enrolled dummy	0.0532	1	0	0.224
Single-person household dummy	0.2349	1	0	0.424
Married couple (no children) household dummy	0.2201	1	0	0.414
Married couple + children household dummy	0.4091	1	0	0.492
Three-generation household dummy	0.1030	1	0	0.304
Other family type dummy	0.0124	1	0	0.110

Note.
n = 4,534.

Effect of receiving pension: No statistical significance could be observed for the 'receiving employee pension' dummy or the 'receiving mutual-aid pension' dummy (col. 1), nor for the 'not enrolled in public pension' dummy (cols. 1, 3, 5), nor for the 'under 65 and receiving pension' dummy or the intersect 'under 65 and receiving pension' dummy x 'receiving national pension' dummy (I confirmed by Wald Test). The coefficient for the 'receiving national pension' dummy was statistically significant at the 1% level and negative, registering -0.72 (col. 2) or -1.04 (col. 4). The dummy for 'receiving public pension' was statistically significant at the 5%

Table 6.3: Estimation results for 1996

Net financial assets/1000	(1) Coefficient	(1) Standard error	(2) Coefficient	(2) Standard error	(3) Coefficient	(3) Standard error	(4) Coefficient	(4) Standard error	(5) Coefficient	(5) Standard error	(1) Coefficient	(1) Standard error
Constant	4.3786	1.214[a]	4.4981	1.035[a]	3.7917	1.069[a]	2.9869	0.893[a]	3.3159	1.155[a]	3.0257	0.906[a]
Age	−0.4241	0.097[a]	−0.4079	0.085[a]	−0.3278	0.079[a]	−0.2733	0.070[a]	−0.2915	0.084[a]	−0.2779	0.072[a]
Age squared/100	0.9131	0.200[a]	0.8913	0.177[a]	0.7216	0.167[a]	0.6184	0.149[a]	0.6454	0.183[a]	0.6293	0.152[a]
Age cubed/10,000	−0.0547	0.013[a]	−0.0534	0.012[a]	−0.0431	0.011[a]	−0.0371	0.010[a]	−0.0383	0.012[a]	−0.0378	0.010[a]
Pre-tax income/1000	4.7614	1.872[b]	3.6175	1.148[a]	2.5851	1.064[b]	2.1214	0.755[b]	2.4633	1.048[b]	2.2195	0.801[a]
Pre-tax income squared/1,000,000	−1.5390	0.806[c]	−1.4718	0.545[a]	−0.7232	0.432[c]	−0.5642	0.349	−0.6786	0.423	−0.6882	0.369[c]
Home ownership dummy	−1.1473	0.279[a]	−0.7685	0.234[a]	−0.9309	0.235[a]	−0.8283	0.209[a]	−0.8853	0.234[a]	−0.7682	0.197[a]
Inheritance/prospect of inheritance	0.3821	0.157[b]	0.5094	0.154[a]	0.3411	0.136[b]	0.3841	0.132[a]	0.3495	0.132[a]	0.4010	0.135[a]
Receiving employee pension dummy	0.3060	0.187	—	—	—	—	—	—	—	—	—	—
Receiving mutual aid pension dummy	0.5609	0.325	—	—	—	—	—	—	—	—	—	—
Receiving national pension dummy	−0.4758	0.346	−0.7159	0.277[a]	−1.1293	0.268[a]	−1.0447	0.262[a]	—	—	—	—
Receiving public pension dummy	—	—	—	—	0.3430	0.170[b]	0.3354	0.158[b]	—	—	—	—
Aged 65+ and receiving public pension dummy	—	—	—	—	—	—	—	—	0.7296	0.501	0.3712	0.215[c]
Aged 65+ and receiving national pension dummy	—	—	—	—	—	—	—	—	−2.0744	1.228	−1.2586	0.346[a]
Aged under 65 and receiving public pension dummy	—	—	—	—	—	—	—	—	−0.0066	0.416	—	—
Aged under 65 and receiving national pension dummy	—	—	—	—	—	—	—	—	1.4176	3.154	—	—
'Not enrolled in public pension' dummy.	0.2117	0.225	—	—	0.1423	0.195	—	—	0.0470	0.205	—	—

A Case Study of Impact on Net Financial Assets

Single-person household dummy	0.1263	0.254	—	—	−0.1637	0.194	—	—	−0.1296	0.198
Married couple (no children) household dummy	−0.2084	0.175	—	—	−0.1910	0.159	—	—	−0.2635	0.182
Married couple + children household dummy	−0.1406	0.167	—	—	−0.1287	0.149	—	—	−0.1381	0.154
Three-generation household dummy	0.2434	0.258	—	—	0.1931	0.231	—	—	0.2006	0.232
Other family type dummy	0.6549	0.503	—	—	0.3857	0.476	—	—	0.2288	0.490
SER	2.4985		2.5925		2.2134		2.1830		2.2274	
	χ^2	p value	χ^2	p value	χ^2	p value	χ^2	p value	χ^2	p value
Test of overidentifying restriction	18.548	0.183	20.899	0.231	28.180	0.105	30.933	0.156	27.990	0.110

(continued, final columns):

	—	—
	—	—
	—	—
	—	—
	—	—
SER	2.2348	
	χ^2	p value
	31.779	0.133

Notes.
n = 2281.
'a', 'b', 'c' denote statistical significance at the 1%, 5% and 10% levels.

level and positive, registering 0.34 (col. 4). The coefficient for the intersection '65+ and receiving pension' dummy x 'receiving national pension' dummy was significant at the 10% level and positive (0.37, col. 6), and the coefficient for the '65+ and receiving pension' dummy was statistically significant at the 1% level and negative (-1.26, col. 6). In the 1996 data the coefficient for the non-enrollment dummy was not statistically significant while the 'receiving national pension' dummy was significant and negative. At this juncture the net financial assets of those not enrolled in public pension programs were no less than those of households that were enrolled but had yet to start receiving payments; indeed, we get a picture of the low level of accumulation by households receiving national pensions. That said, the coefficients for the 'receiving employee pension' dummy and the 'receiving mutual-aid pension' dummy were not significant, so that the overall picture of how public pensions influence net financial assets remains unclear.

Family type: Where family type was factored into calculations, coefficients for the five categories (single-person household, married couple, married couple with children, three generation, other) all proved not to be statistically significant at the 10% level (see cols. 1, 3 and 5). The Wald test based on the null hypothesis that all these coefficients were zero came up with figures of 8.02 (p value 0.16), 5.59 (0.35) and 5.59 (0.35), so that the null hypothesis was not rejected. We therefore cannot observe any influence from family type on net financial assets at the 1996 stage.

Effect of age etc: If a simple life-cycle hypothesis applies, then we would expect coefficients for the primary values relating to age to be significant and positive, the square value coefficients to be significant and negative, and the cube value coefficients not to be statistically significant. However, if assets are declining at the stage of marriage, childbirth and childrearing, we would expect coefficients for the primary values relating to age to be significant and negative, the square value coefficients to be significant and positive and the cube value coefficients to be significant and negative. Looking at the results, we find that at the 1% level of statistical significance, for all cases coefficients for the primary values were significant and negative, the square value coefficients were significant and positive and the cube value coefficients were significant and negative. Looking at the age range for net financial asset accumulation, we find the nadir at ages 30 to 33 and the zenith at ages 78 to 81. This pattern, of net financial assets declining from the age of 30 to 33, and increasing thereafter before turning down again between the ages of 78 and 81, supports the supposition that the economic burden of marriage and childbirth is a major factor.

Estimation results for 2002

Results for 2002 are as shown in Table 6.4. Once again, columns 1, 3 and 5 display results where all explanatory variables are included; columns 2, 4 and 6 show results after applying a Wald test to exclude pension-receipt and household-type variables not found to be statistically significant. As with the 1996 data, the results in columns 2, 4 and 6 are suited to analysis. Orthogonality conditions for over-identification were satisfied for all cases at the 10% level.

Effect of inheritance: The coefficients for experience or prospect of inheritance were significant at the 1% or 5% level and positive. Using the data in columns 2, 4 and 6, we find that the marginal effect of inheritance experience on net financial assets was about ¥8.2 to 10.2 million. Since the corresponding figure for 1996 was ¥4 to 5 million, the influence exerted by this factor on differentials appears to have doubled. If we look at the results in Table 6.1 for the group receiving pensions (which we may assume to have relatively many older people in it), mean net financial assets for the sub-group with inherited wealth or the prospect of inheriting wealth was ¥16.05 million (median 10 million), while for the sub-group without inherited wealth, mean net financial assets were ¥11.24 million (median ¥5.5 million). This leads us to think that for those households that do not inherit, the ¥8.2–10.2 million inheritance effect constitutes a differential that will be almost impossible for them to catch up during a single lifetime.

Pension receipt effect: In 2002 the pension effect was very different from in 1996. In 2002 the coefficients for receiving employee and mutual-aid pensions were significant at the 1% level and positive, and the coefficient for non-enrollment was significant at the 5% level and negative. However, no significant result could be obtained regarding the national pension (see col. 2). Interestingly, the coefficient for mutual-aid and *onkyū* pensions was 0.93 and that for employee pensions was 0.52, with the result that the null hypothesis that these two coefficients would be the same

Table 6.4: Estimation results for 2002

	①		②		③		④		⑤		①	
Net financial assets/1000	Coefficient	Standard error	Coefficient	Standard error	Coefficient	Standard error	Coefficient	Standard error	Coefficient	Standard error	Coefficient	Standard error
Constant	6.4547	0.941[a]	6.1904	0.843[a]	7.3079	1.130[a]	6.4882	0.791[a]	7.1934	1.211[a]	6.5853	0.805[a]
Age	−0.5650	0.068[a]	−0.5490	0.072[a]	−0.6053	0.073[a]	−0.5887	0.067[a]	−0.6010	0.073[a]	−0.5966	0.068[a]
Age squared/100	1.2670	0.151[a]	1.2096	0.157[a]	1.3367	0.162[a]	1.2810	0.148[a]	1.3259	0.161[a]	1.2950	0.150[a]
Age cubed/10,000	−0.0804	0.010[a]	−0.0762	0.010[a]	−0.0842	0.010[a]	−0.0801	0.010[a]	−0.0831	0.011[a]	−0.0803	0.010[a]
Pre-tax income/1,000	3.8882	0.859[a]	3.8473	0.810[a]	4.8032	0.933[a]	4.7928	0.832[a]	4.8230	0.940[a]	4.9607	0.856[a]
Pre-tax income squared/1,000,000	−0.0993	0.036[a]	−0.0926	0.037[b]	−0.1579	0.044[a]	−0.1424	0.038[a]	−0.1568	0.044[a]	−0.1502	0.039[a]
Home ownership dummy	−2.4161	0.615[a]	−1.7895	0.511[a]	−2.2653	0.705[a]	−1.7847	0.605[a]	−2.3429	0.715[a]	−1.8924	0.622[a]
Inheritance/prospect of inheritance	1.0242	0.433[b]	0.8220	0.333[b]	1.4521	0.558[a]	1.0799	0.345[a]	1.4317	0.615[b]	1.0169	0.354[a]
Public pension dummy x Employee pension–enrollment dummy	0.5317	0.152[a]	0.5162	0.143[a]	—	—	—	—	—	—	—	—
Public pension dummy x mutual aid and 'onkyu' pension enrollment dummy	0.9822	0.211[a]	0.9317	0.206[a]	—	—	—	—	—	—	—	—
Public pension dummy x national pension enrollment dummy	0.2427	0.170	0.2141	0.161	—	—	—	—	—	—	—	—
Receiving public pension dummy	—	—	—	—	0.5826	0.165[a]	0.5523	0.148[a]	—	—	—	—

A Case Study of Impact on Net Financial Assets

	J stat value	p value	J stat value	p value	J stat value	p value	J stat value	p value	J stat value	p value	J stat value	p value
Aged 65+ and receiving public pension dummy	—	—	—	—	—	—	—	—	0.5120	0.272[c]	0.4156	0.205[b]
Aged under 65 and receiving public pension dummy	—	—	—	—	—	—	—	—	0.6243	0.163[a]	0.5969	0.155[a]
Respondent not enrolled dummy	-0.2958	0.110[a]	-0.2259	0.096[b]	-0.2429	0.116[b]	-0.1913	0.101[c]	-0.2595	0.123[b]	-0.2161	0.106[b]
Single-person household dummy	-0.2567	0.595	—	—	-0.8112	0.799	—	—	-0.7541	0.925	—	—
Married couple (no children) household dummy	-0.0062	0.564	—	—	-0.6243	0.761	—	—	-0.5557	0.901	—	—
Married couple + children household dummy	-0.3346	0.568	-0.2967	0.090[a]	-1.0339	0.777	-0.3877	0.098[a]	-0.9570	0.933	-0.3624	0.102[a]
Three-generation household dummy	-0.5426	0.575	-0.6173	0.181[a]	-1.1975	0.758	-0.7180	0.202[a]	-1.1374	0.899	-0.6751	0.209[a]
Other family type dummy	0.2378	0.648	—	—	-0.4617	0.853	—	—	-0.376813	0.996	—	—
SER	3.4321		3.2010		5.1246		4.5730		5.0876		4.8001	
Test of overidentifying restriction	1.815	0.969	7.645	0.469	9.223	0.237	15.057	0.130	9.375	0.227	13.711	0.133

Notes.

n = 4534.

'a', 'b', 'c' denote statistical significance at the 1%, 5% and 10% levels.

was rejected at the 5% level (χ^2 stat value = 6.162, p value = 0.013). These results indicate that net financial asset differentials have arisen, such that recipients of mutual-aid and *onkyū* pensions are at the top, followed by recipients of employee pensions, recipients of national pensions, those who are enrolled in public pensions but not yet receiving them and finally those who are not enrolled.

The coefficient for public pension receipt as a whole was also significant at the 1% level and positive (col. 4). The dummy for people aged over 65 and receiving a pension showed a coefficient significant at the 5% level, and that for people aged under 65 and receiving a pension was significant at the 1% level (col. 6). However, the null hypothesis that the coefficients for pension recipients under 65 and over 65 would be equivalent was not rejected in the Wald test (χ^2 stat value = 1.02, p value = 0.313).

The estimations presented above indicate that while no clear differential could be ascribed to the pension system in 1996, by 2002 the pension system *was* exerting an influence on asset differentials. Using the coefficient for the non-enrolled group, we find that these households show net financial assets some ¥2 to 2.2 million below those of households enrolled in public pensions but not yet receiving them. Considering that the effect of public pensions overall was around ¥5.5 million, it would appear that we cannot afford to ignore that differential. To put it another way, the results suggest that there is a status group that does not enroll in public pension programs due to weak accumulation of assets.

Family type: The effect of family type differed between 1996 and 2002. The coefficients for single-person households, married couples (no children) and 'other family types' did not appear statistically significant (cols. 1, 3, 5). The null hypothesis that all these coefficients would be zero also scored 5.12 (p value 0.12), 2.75 (0.43) and 3.06 (0.38) on the Wald test (cols. 1, 3, 5). In contrast, coefficients for the 'married couple with children' dummy and the 'three-generation household' dummy were significant at the 1% level and negative (see cols. 2, 4, 6). The economic burden on households with children is evident. Compared to households without children, the dummy coefficient for married couples with children showed a deficit of ¥3–4 million, and that for three-generation families was ¥6.2–7.2 million.

The effect of age: In the 2002 estimation, too, all cases showed statistical significance at the 1% level, with primary values negative, square values positive and cube values negative. Net financial assets declined until age 32–33 and increased until age 73–74. We draw from this that net financial assets tend to decline around the time in life when families are being formed through marriage and childbirth, and that net financial assets once again go into decline as the householder approaches the onset of late old age.

Differentials between budgets of ordinary households

In the samples used in this chapter, there are no cases with net financial assets in excess of ¥500 million. As I mentioned, the billionaire types who get into *Forbes* magazine are not represented. In that sense you could say that this chapter is about fairly regular households – the kind you might find in almost any neighborhood. I have looked at differentials in net financial assets among these households with special reference to inheritance, pensions and childrearing.

Inheritance was a cause of differentials in both years; not only was the scale of the impact large, but it increased from ¥4–5 million in 1996 to ¥8.2–10.2 million in 2002. By 2002 the gap had widened to the point where families without inheritance would find it exceedingly difficult to catch up. On top of that, the public pension system and family childrearing patterns, which were not clearly identifiable causes of differentials in 1996, had acquired that status by 2002. The pension system had created a deficit of ¥2–2.2 million for households not enrolled, while childrearing was generating deficits of ¥3–4 million for married couples and ¥6.2–7.2 million for three-generation families: differentials too large to be overlooked.

From 1996 to 2002 the Japanese economy went through a severe recession that included the Asian financial crisis of 1997. We may easily imagine that the impact was more severe on families with limited reserves. In these hard times, a situation has arisen where individuals are faced with differentials so wide that they cannot realistically hope to catch up in their own lifetime, caused by a phenomenon – inheritance – over which they have no control. In a recession-bound economy, inequality of outcome in the parental generation has come to translate into inequality of opportunity in the children's generation, and the gaps are so unbridgeable that the situation cannot possibly be considered fair. Clearly, we need some new thinking about the use of taxation policy as a tool for wealth redistribution.

I believe that by 2002 the pension system and childrearing patterns had clearly become a cause of differentials, on a scale so large that they presented a challenge to Japanese society that was even tougher than that of tax reform. The era when each generation could expect to do better than the one before is already over (see Figure 6.1). The declining birthrate, coupled with a pension system that functions as a form of taxation, has created severe doubts as to whether the pension system itself is sustainable. In times like these, the fact that bearing and raising children has become a major factor pulling households towards the lower end of an increasingly unequal system of economic differentials is a problem that simply has to be addressed. The decision to have children and raise a family is a private choice, made by parents, and should bring them happiness. At the same time children are a human resource that will support society in the future. Yet, social support for the project of bearing and raising the generation that will in turn support the future remains inadequate.

The employment market for public officials should be the most open labor market of all, yet even there we find that most women seeking to rejoin the workforce after childbirth are not even allowed to take the civil service exam because of age discrimination. This is just one symbolic illustration of the hard fact that for most women, giving birth to a child marks the end of their career (Ōi and Matsuura 2003; Matsuura and Shigeno 2005). We cannot believe that all those women are happy about abandoning their careers.

One aspect of Japanese society has been a tendency to force people into a trade-off where wider differentials between households and the abandonment of women's careers have been the price paid for the happiness of having children. As the inexorable processes of declining birthrate and dwindling population grind on, this society foists most of the burden of childbirth and childrearing on to the parents, while skimming off the proceeds via the pension system to transfer income to older, wealthier generations. That is the state of affairs, and it is not one that is sustainable. We cannot hope for younger cohorts to carry on subsidizing older cohorts indefinitely. Unless and until we construct social systems that stop making marriage and family-building such a huge economic demerit, I do not believe we will ever solve the problems of the declining birthrate and aging society.

7 The Consequences of Applying Individual Accounting to Social Security: Public Pensions as a Form of Risk-Sharing

Naomi Miyazato

Individual accounting for social security: The background and new problems

The twin trends of the falling birthrate and aging population are all too well known in Japan today. These trends are expected to bring various socioeconomic impacts, but they will impose a particularly heavy burden on the social security system. As it stands, Japan's social security system works on the premise that payments to the retired generation are financed from contributions paid by the generation in employment: in other words, it is a tax-and-spend system (*fuka-hōshiki*). This structure is especially apparent in the pension system. It has repeatedly been observed that this approach to social security tends to widen inequalities between generations, and Hatta and Oguchi (1999) have produced a highly detailed quantitative analysis showing just how Japan's pension system produces that effect. Asō and Yoshida (1996) have applied a similarly refined quantitative analysis to intergenerational differentials created by the social security system as a whole, not just the pension system.

Here in Japan the birthrate is falling faster, and the population is aging faster, than in other industrialized countries. Consequently, the intergenerational differentials caused by the pension and social security systems are particularly acute in Japan. That in turn has prompted calls for reforms of the entire social security system, including pensions and medical insurance etc., on the principle of 'individual accounting' (*kojin kanjō*). We therefore should ask how much effect 'changing to individual accounting' (*kojin kanjōka*) would actually have on today's younger generation and on future generations. Answering that question is no easy matter.

People face various risks in their daily lives. They may fall ill – or not. They may die young – or live longer than expected. They may be fortunate enough to acquire a lot of assets – or not. A social security system is supposed to share out the various risks of life – relating to illness, unemployment, lifespan, changes in income and assets, etc. – among its contributing members. Switching social security to individual accounting means that each individual accepts responsibility for dealing with those everyday risks on their own account. If people are not overly worried about those risks, then switching to individual accounting to erase intergenerational differentials is an extremely attractive proposition. But if many people are hoping to avoid those risks as far as possible, then it becomes necessary to take a long, hard look at whether individual accounting really will bring happiness to the present working generation and to future generations.

Incidentally, individual social security accounting is already starting to be applied to public pension systems in a number of industrialized countries. The traditional approach to public pensions in industrialized countries has been to define the amount of money to be paid out to pensioners after they retire. This is called a 'Defined Benefit' (DB) pension. In Sweden, however, great changes have been made to the pension system. In the new Swedish system, the amount that people pay in to the system is defined, but the amount they will receive after retirement may vary according to economic circumstances, etc. This is called a 'Defined Contribution' (DC) pension. DC pensions have been around for a long time in many countries in the private pension market. To put it bluntly, it is a kind of pension that holds the individual fully responsible for controlling the rise or fall of his or her pension assets. In the Swedish case, the defined contribution approach has now been applied to public pensions in an attempt to make it clear that a one-on-one relationship exists between an individual's contribution payments and his subsequent pension receipts. The shift to individual accounting is proceeding apace in Sweden. In the US too, there is a very lively debate in progress on the possibility of switching part of the public pension system from the DB to the DC model.[1] There is growing interest in applying the DC approach to public pensions in industrialized countries around the world, and moves in that direction are visibly accelerating.[2] The reason why the DC approach is attracting so much attention is that DC pensions are thought to be neutral in their effect on population structure, and people therefore see them as a possible trump card in the battle to separate public pensions from the issue of intergenerational wealth disparities caused by the falling birthrate, aging population, etc. However, DC pensions do entail individual members of society taking on their own shoulders the risk of changes in the profitability of pension fund management and the risk that they may outlive their pension assets, among others. In this chapter I will take a close look at the concept of individual accounting in social security, concentrating my analysis on a comparison between traditional DB pension systems and some of those with DC elements to them that have already been introduced in various industrialized countries. My objective is to get some idea of to what degree it is necessary to retain the traditional DB-type pension system with its risk-sharing function, and to what extent we need to accept the need for DC-type pensions to get rid of economic differentials between generations.

Japan's pension reform

Before commencing my analysis I should give a brief overview of the Japanese pension system as it currently stands. On 5 June 2004, a new Public Pension Law was passed by the Japanese Diet.[3] The name given to the new system was the 'fixed contribution formula' (*hokenryō kotei hōshiki*). The old system entailed making a grand accounting of the public pension fund every five years, on the basis of which the rate of increase of contributions payable would be calculated to make sure that contribution income would duly reflect the state of the public pension fund. Many other countries have taken a similar approach, adjusting contributions at intervals in light of the financial situation of the public pension fund. In 1999, however, Sweden adopted the DC system for its public pension fund, and this pioneering move prompted various other countries to move towards fixing the contributions payable to their public pension systems. Japan was following this international trend when fixed contributions were introduced in the 2004 reform.

The contribution was fixed at 18.30%, but unlike the Swedish model, Japan did not fix the contribution rate *immediately*. In 2003 the employee pension (*kōsei nenkin*) contribution was set at 13.58% of overall income. From October 2004, the rate was set to rise by 0.345 percentage points per year, to reach 18.30% by 2017.

Another notable feature was that the government also made a public pledge that the income replacement rate (one's pension payments expressed as a percentage of wages earned during employment career) would not fall below 50%. Since Japan's public pension system, like those of most countries, is based on the pay-as-you-go system, guaranteeing a minimum level of payout while fixing the level of contributions means that the possibility remains that disbursements may exceed revenue, which is the very problem that had been plaguing Japan under the old system. Or to put it another way, if the government really will not change the rate of the contributions under any socioeconomic conditions whatsoever, the possibility remains that it will reduce pension payments below the 50% level.

Another important feature of Japan's new public pension system[4] is the introduction of a payment adjustment system called the 'macro-economy slide' (*makuro-suraido*). Japan's public pension system includes a component that reflects the level of wages received in the past. The way this component is calculated is called 'wage reappraisal' (*chingin saihyōka*), and hitherto the index used to make the calculation has been the wage growth rate. Under the new system, however, wage reappraisal will be calculated thus:

> Wage reappraisal rate = wage growth rate − change attributable to demographic factors

Whereas the old system simply used the wage growth rate to calculate the wage reappraisal rate, the new system subtracts changes attributable to demographic factors from that figure. These 'changes attributable to demographic factors' include the number of people enrolled in the pension program and their average remaining life expectancy, calculated as follows:

> Change attributable to demographic factors = percentage decline in enrollment + rate of increase in average remaining life expectancy

These factors were not reflected in the old pension system, and they *are* reflected in the new one. The term used to describe the new approach, 'macro-economic slide,' is similar to the 'self-balancing function,' the term used to describe the system of adjusting pension payments in the Swedish system. Both in Sweden and in Japan, the new system adjusts pension payments in accordance with life expectancy, among other factors, which means that as the probability of people living long lives increases, the amount paid out in pensions decreases. In that sense one of the functions of a public pension system – to reduce the risks attendant on living a long life – is now maintained at a lower level than before.

We have seen that there are a number of similarities between the new Japanese pension system and its Swedish counterpart, but there is one major difference. In Sweden, public pensions are calculated on the basis of Notional Defined Contribution (NDC), meaning that the contributions each individual makes to the system really are added to that individual's account and serve to increase his or her assets. Hence contributions and benefits are basically balanced in a one-to-one relationship. However, the Japanese pension reform of 2004 did not go so far as to create a direct link between individual contributions and benefits.

Pension systems that use a concept such as notional defined contributions to create a link between individual contributions and benefits are thought to be effective in erasing economic differentials between generations. Because of that, moves to include DC elements in public pension systems are afoot in many countries. However, as we shall see in the next section, DC pension systems oblige the individual to shoulder the burden of risk associated with fluctuations in income and above-average longevity, raising serious questions as to whether they really are better than the traditional DB pension systems when viewed as instruments of social welfare. In the following sections I will compare the merits and demerits of these two types of public pension system, and use statistical simulations to address the question of how much of a DB element Japan needs to retain in the public pension system.

Two types of pension system

As we have seen, it is possible to divide pension systems into two broad types: those with defined benefits (DB systems), and those with defined contributions (DC systems). The former is the traditional approach employed in most public pension systems, but recently we have seen some countries, notably Sweden, start to move towards the DC approach. I now propose to look at the pros and cons of both systems.

Pros and cons of defined benefit pension systems

In Table 7.1 I have briefly summarized the pros and cons of DB and DC pension systems. Let us look first at the DB system, the mainstay of public pension systems around the world. Now an important function of public pensions is to guarantee security of income in old age. A DB system does that. Compared with the DC system, where one's income in old age depends on how profitably the pension fund is managed, the DB system greatly lessens the risk of changes in income during old age. The DB system also reduces the risks attendant on living longer than expected. Let us hypothetically assume a situation in which we can accurately predict when people will die. In such a situation we could predict roughly what scale of assets people would need to see them through their old age, and there would be little risk of people finding themselves with insufficient assets to pay for their living expenses between retirement and death. In the real world, however, we cannot accurately predict when people are going to die. Nor can we predict how long any particular person might live. Supposing somebody lives longer than expected, that person will also need more money than expected to cover post-retirement living expenses, and therefore risks suffering a shortage of assets. A DB pension system reduces that risk, since a person who lives longer than expected can still carry on drawing a pension at roughly the same level for however many years he or she may live.[5] These are the advantages of the DB model.

On the other side of the coin, the DB model is vulnerable to changes in the demographic profile. Public pensions are usually run on a pay-as-you-go system, with contributions paid by the working generation being spent on benefits allotted to the retired generation. Since a pension fund using the DB system fixes the benefits paid to the latter, any increase in the relative size of the retired population necessitates extra income for the fund, which means raising the level of contributions paid by the working generation. Under a DB system, if the birthrate carries on falling and the population carries on aging, then the burden on the working generation will steadily rise, creating an unfair relationship between generations. If there is also an increase in life expectancy, then the period during which the average retiree receives his pension payments will lengthen, and this too will put upward pressure on contributions. These problems of widening intergenerational differentials and upward pressure

Public Pensions as a Form of Risk-Sharing

Table 7.1: *Pros and cons of Defined Benefit (DB) and Defined Contribution (DC) pensions*

	Merits	**Demerits**
Defined Benefit	Can depend on a certain level of income after retirement.	Falling birthrate and aging society forces up contributions.
	That level of income will continue even if one lives longer than expected.	Increase in life expectancy also forces up contributions.
Defined Contribution	No need to raise contributions even if birthrate falls, society ages and life expectancy increases.	Risks of fluctuation in operating income of system shouldered by individual.

on contributions have been identified by numerous observers as demerits of the DB model.

Pros and cons of Defined Contribution pension systems

It has long been considered very difficult to apply the DC model to public pension systems, but in Sweden they have succeeded in doing it by using the concept of Notional Defined Contribution (NDC).[6] Several other countries are also starting to introduce the Swedish model, and the number of countries using DC systems is gradually increasing. This model essentially entails an individual building up assets over his or her working career and then spending them to pay for retirement. Consequently, it is more like a form of personal savings than a pay-as-you-go system, and there is no need to raise contributions paid by the working generation even if the birthrate falls, the population ages and life expectancy increases. In other words, the merit of the DC system is that it is not affected by demographic changes and is neutral in its effect on intergenerational differentials.

Conversely, the DC model has the demerit that it forces the individual to shoulder the burden of risk from changes in pension fund operating profits. In the DB model a certain level of post-retirement earnings is guaranteed, but in the DC model the amount paid out will change with fluctuations in operating profit. People who are successful in managing their pension fund will be rewarded with higher pension payments after retirement, while those who have failed to manage their pension well will see their pension payments fall correspondingly. Also, the DC model offers no way of avoiding the risk of above-average longevity, since, in principle at least, no-one can get more out of the fund than they put in. So long as the accumulated assets are sufficient to cover post-retirement living expenses all will be well, but if the individual lives longer than expected, he will be unable to cover his living expenses and will run short of assets. To sum up, the DC model has the advantage that it is not influenced by changes in demographic structure, but also has the disadvantages that it forces the individual to shoulder the risk of changing pension-fund profitability and unexpected longevity – disadvantages that need to be very carefully considered.

Changes in the socioeconomic environment and their impact on public pensions

Population of elderly people

A few years ago the National Institute for Research on Social Welfare and Population Problems predicted that the population of Japan would start to decline in 2007. The decline of the population will no doubt have various impacts on the economy, but when studying pension systems and population problems, a more important figure than the size of the overall population is the balance between the working and retired populations. Since Japan has a DB system of public pensions, funded by taxing the working generation to pay pensions to the retired generation, any increase in the proportion of retirees in the population will lead to higher pension contributions for the working generation. Here I define that proportion as the number of people aged 65 and over, divided by that of people aged from 15–64 (see Figure 7.1).

In the year 1930, there were 3.062 million people in Japan aged 65 and over (1.318 million men and 1.744 million women), while there were 37.804 million people aged between 15 and 64 (19.178 million men and 18.626 million women). The elderly population index stood at just 8.1%. It remained under 10% through the 1950s and 1960s, but climbed above 10% in the 1970s, registering 10.2% in the year 1970. It continued to rise after that, reaching 15.2% in 1985, the year before the basic pension (*kiso nenkin*) was introduced.

Figure 7.1: Trends in the elderly population index

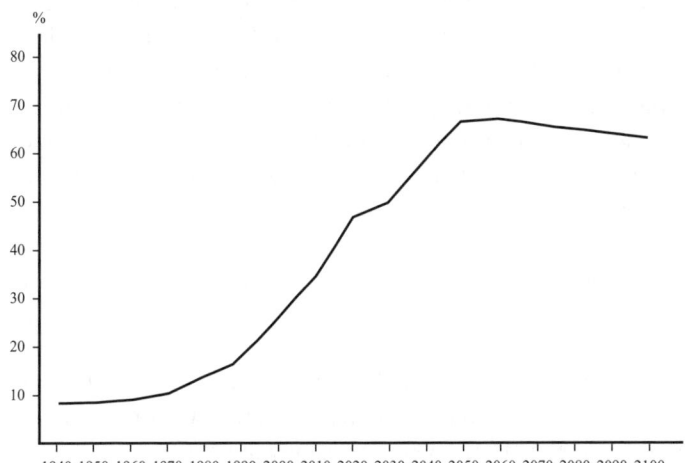

By 1995 it had reached 20.9%, and by 2000 it stood at 25.5% (22.003 million elderly people against 86.223 million working-age people).[7] Estimates for future population trends suggest that the elderly index will reach 35% in 2010, 50% in 2030 and 67% in 2060.[8] Sometime around 2050, the population aging process should finally have run its course, but forecasts for subsequent decades are still in excess of 60%.

I now propose to briefly sum up the relationship between insurance contributions and population trends in a case where a DB-model pension system is being funded on a pay-as-you-go system. Before doing that, however, I must first point out that the following mathematical relationship is among the preliminary assumptions of a pension system based on a pure pay-as-you-go system of financing:

Total disbursement of pension payments = Total income from pension contributions   (Formula 1)

Formula 1 signifies that all the money required to cover disbursements to pensioners, usually older people, must come from contributions paid by the generation still in employment, usually younger people. In other words, this formula encapsulates the pay-as-you-go approach to pension financing, with its characteristic pattern wherein wealth is transferred from younger to older generations. Formula 1 is the theoretical support for the description of public pensions as a system redistributing wealth between generations.

Looking now at the relationship between contributions and population, the 'total income from pension contributions' specified in Formula 1 is the product obtained by multiplying the number of workers by their average wage and then by the rate at which pension contributions are levied, that is:

Total income from pension contributions = Pension contribution rate (θ) x Wages (w) x Number of workers in labor force (L)   (Formula 2)

The other side of Formula 1, 'total disbursement of pension payments,' is the product obtained by multiplying the number of retirees by the average level of pension payments:

Total disbursement of pension payments = Income replacement rate (κ) x Wages (w) x Number of retirees (R)   (Formula 3)

By combining Formulas 2 and 3, we can define the relationship between pension contributions and population thus:

Pension contribution rate (θ) = Income replacement rate (κ) x (Number of retirees (R)/Number of workers in labor force (L))   (Formula 4)

It is clear from the above that if the value of R/L increases (meaning that the number of retirees increases relative to that of workers), which is what happens in an aging society with a falling birthrate, then a pension system predicated on a pay-as-you-go system will have to adjust either the income-replacement rate (κ) or the pension contribution rate (θ). In the traditional DB systems, the income-replacement rate (κ) is fixed; consequently if the number of retirees rises relative to that of workers, the only option is to raise contributions. Let us see how that might work in practice, substituting the elderly population index figures introduced above for R/L, and defining the income-replacement rate as 50% of the wages of the currently working generation. Using the formulae above, the contribution rates θ for 1970, 2000 and 2060 work out thus:

$\theta_{1970} = 0.5 \times 10.2\% = 5.1\%$

$\theta_{2000} = 0.5 \times 25.5\% = 12.75\%$
$\theta_{2060} = 0.5 \times 66.9\% = 33.45\%$

We can see very clearly how the DB system exerts upward pressure on contributions when the proportion of retirees in the population increases. Since that proportion is expected to rise very substantially in Japan over the coming decades, the problems associated with the DB system are only too evident.

Changes in operating profit rate

Let us consider whether the DC model might be more suitable for the Japanese situation. With the proportion of retirees set to rise so sharply, the attractions of a pension system that is neutral in relation to population structure are undeniable. Conversely, as we saw above, the DC model exposes individual pensioners to the risks associated with changes in pension fund profitability. At this point we should add another important element to the picture: the relative profitability of safe versus risky assets in Japan. Here I will use newly issued ten-year government bonds to represent the former and the return on investment in stocks on Section 1 of the Tokyo Stock Exchange to represent the latter.[9] Figure 7.2 shows how the return on these two instruments has varied since 1970.

In the 1970s, even a rock-solid investment like the 10-year government bond brought a return of 6% to 8%. That was maintained for the first half of the 1980s, but the return drifted down to around 5% in the second half of that decade. The return on the 10-year bond declined further in the 1990s and slipped below 1% in 1998, when it hit a low of 0.972%. Since then the return has continued to fluctuate below the 2% level. Now let us look at the return on stock investment, assuming the case where the investor sells stocks 10 years after buying them. An investor buying in the first half of the 1970s and selling 10 years after would have realized an average profit of between 9.8% and 16.4%. Buying in the second half of the 1970s would have produced even better profits 10 years on, between 16% and 22.8%. After that, however, we enter the time zone when investors would be selling following the collapse of the bubble economy, and returns plummet. From the second half of the 1980s, we enter negative territory. For instance, buying in 1987 and selling in 1997 would have generated a loss of 3.5%. Table 7.2

Figure 7.2: Trends in profitability for high-risk and low-risk investments

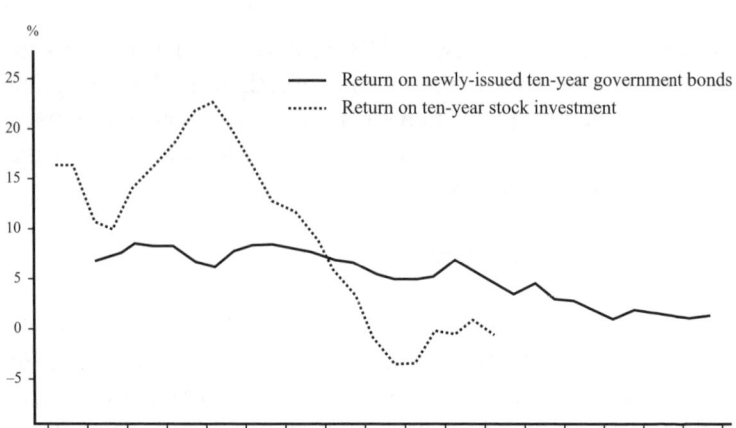

displays the mean return and standard deviation for both investment instruments. The government bond shows a mean return of 5.22% over the period 1972–2003, with a standard deviation of 2.53 points, while the stock investment shows a mean return of 9.40% over the period 1970–1992, but, as one would expect with a riskier investment, it also has a much higher standard deviation, at 8.62 points. The big picture: holding a higher proportion of risky assets will tend to increase return, but will also generate higher risk of fluctuation.

I stated earlier that one of the demerits of the DC model is that the individual has to shoulder the risk of fluctuating returns. Let us now look at a simple numerical example to show the differing effect on the individual of returns that do and do not fluctuate.

Let us suppose that an individual invests in a non-fluctuating instrument, such that he can definitely have ¥1 million to consume at the end of the investment period. Let us compare that with the case of a similar scale of initial investment in an instrument that fluctuates such that there is a 50% chance that the investor will have ¥0.5 million and a 50% chance that he will have ¥1.5 million at the end of the investment period. If we define the utility function as $u=\log(c)$, then the expected utility (EU) of the non-fluctuating investment will be $E[u]=\log(c)$, and that of the fluctuating investment will be

Table 7.2: *Mean return and standard deviation for safe and risky assets*

	Safe investment	Risky investment
Mean return	5.22%	9.4%
Standard deviation	2.53 point	8.62 point

Notes.
'Safe investment' is represented by purchase of newly-issued 10-year government bonds.
'Risky investment' is represented by the purchase of stocks on Section 1 of the Tokyo Stock Exchange and reselling them 10 years later.
Data for bond investment calculated for the period 1972–2003; data for stock investment calculated for the period 1970–1992.

$E[u]=0.5\times\log(c-\alpha)+0.5\times\log(c+\alpha)$. Here, c represents consumption of ¥1 million and the value of α is ¥0.5 million. Substituting these values into the equations produces EU values of six for the non-fluctuating investment, higher than the 5.9375 generated by the fluctuating investment. Measuring the two investments in terms of equivalent variation, the non-fluctuating investment comes out 15.5% higher. The DB-type pension guarantees a certain level of pension receipt after retirement, whereas the benefit received from a DC-type pension is influenced by individual asset management outcomes. Assuming that the desired level of post-retirement income is the same in both cases, people will tend to choose the DB type over the DC type.[10] It follows that in order for the DC type to become more advantageous than the DB type, the merit of not having to raise contributions in an era of falling birthrate and aging population will have to outweigh the demerits of risk attendant on fluctuating returns.

Lengthening life expectancy, increasing survival probability

Let us next consider trends in life expectancy. In 1947 the average Japanese man could expect to live to the age of 50.06, and the average Japanese woman, 53.96. In the period 1950–1955, life expectancy averaged 61.6 for men and 65.6 for women, and international comparisons showed Japan ranking 29th in the world for male life expectancy and 35th in the world for female life expectancy. After that there was a spectacular improvement, to the point where life

Figure 7.3: Trends in Japanese life expectancy

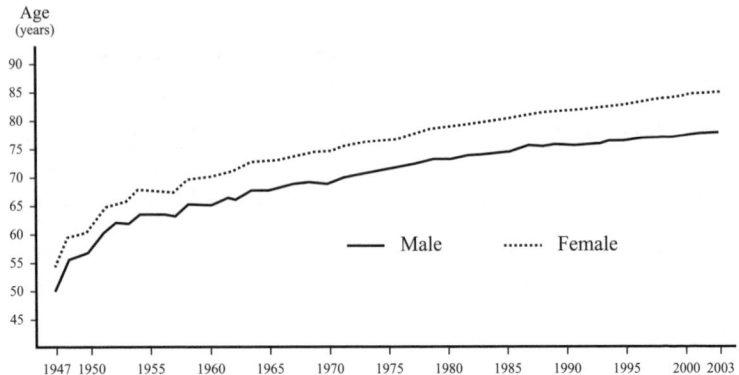

expectancy in Japan was 78.36 for men and 85.33 for women in 2003 (see Figure 7.3). In the period 1995–2000, Japanese life expectancy averaged 77.1 for men and 83.8 for women, putting Japan at Number One in the world for both sexes. Authoritative estimates predict that in this field at least, Japan will still be Number One in the period 2045–2050. It is predicted that by that time male life expectancy will have reached 80.95 and female life expectancy 89.22.[11]

Increasing life expectancy means that people have a higher probability of surviving as they get older. That in turn means that the length of time they live after retirement will tend to increase.[12] As I explained above, a DB-model public pension guarantees a certain level of pension income even if the retiree lives longer than expected. Conversely, the DC model works on the principle that the individual cannot receive more from the pension fund than he or she contributes, and as such faces the risk of running out of money to pay for living expenses if he or she lives longer than expected. As we have seen, in the case of Japan life expectancy has greatly increased in the last 50 years and is expected to increase further still. Figure 7.4 plots projected survival probabilities for Japanese people (the average for men and women) born in 2000 and those born in 2050. This figure graphically illustrates the fact that longevity risk is going to increase in the coming decades. It follows that any discussion on pension reform will have to take particularly careful account of the merit of the DB system that it reduces the risk attendant on long life.

Figure 7.4: Survival probability by age group for Japanese people born in 2000 and 2050

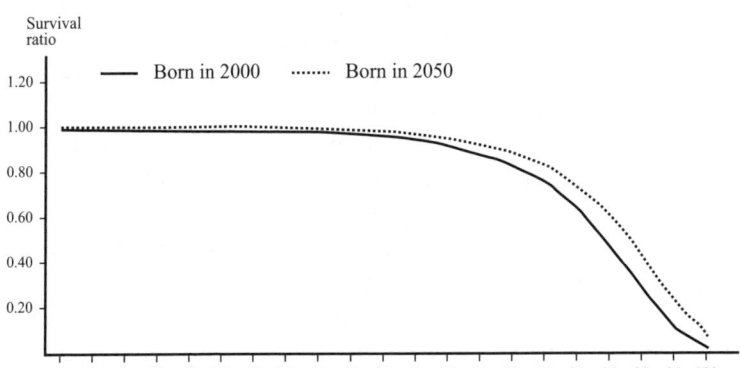

A simple simulation analysis

Since the DB and DC pensions both have merits and demerits, it follows that using one or the other of the two systems will carry the possibility of lowering the level of utility to those covered by it. In this section I will consider what kind of public pension system would be most appropriate to an aging society with a falling birthrate, using a simplified version of a simulation model I devised for an earlier study (Miyazato 2004). I will leave a detailed account of the underlying assumptions of this model to an analytical appendix at the end of this chapter, but for now let me give a brief account of the essence of the model. Its main features are as follows:

1. Assuming that expected values are of the same amount, people will prefer stable income and consumption to fluctuating income and consumption.
2. People's income is generated by one or more of the following three sources: labor income, profits on asset management and pension receipts.
3. The return on asset investment is variable and will fluctuate from one period to the next. Labor income, however, will tend to rise at a certain rate but will not show fluctuations in rates of growth from one period to the next.
4. People face the risk of survival (or the risk of death).

These are the four main features of the simulation model. Item (1) relates to utility for people, and signifies that where people have the same expectations for the value of consumption they will be able to engage in after retirement, then a stable level of consumption will offer a higher level of utility than a fluctuating level of consumption. This is a hypothesis often used in simulation analysis. Item (2) relates to people's budgets. In this paper I have opted to avoid analytical complexity by assuming that people have only three kinds of income source: income earned by their labor; interest (or operating profit such as dividends, etc.) earned on savings and other assets; and pension payments received after retirement. Item (3) is included to account for fluctuations in pension fund operating income, which we have seen is a feature of the DC-type system. Item (4) factors in the probability of a person living or dying during each of two periods in their lives, in order to evaluate the risk of longevity in the risk simulation.[13] These, then, were the hypothetical premises on which I based my simulation.

The results of the simulation are shown in Figures 7.5 and 7.6. Figure 7.5 displays results when we assume wage growth at 2% p.a., the return on investment income averaging 2% p.a. with a standard deviation of five percentage points, and a survival probability of 100% in the first period and 80% in the second period. With these settings in place, I then added in two different models for population growth: one at the standard rate of 2% p.a., the other with a much lower rate of 0.5% p.a. In this analysis I used equivalent variation rather than direct comparison to calculate utility levels.[14] In Figure 7.5 the horizontal axis shows income replacement rate, so that we may view it as displaying the scale of a DB pension. The vertical axis shows the degree of welfare gain accruing at each level of income replacement. I have carried out the analysis using 0.05 intervals for income replacement rate. Looking at the standard case for population growth, we find that welfare gain continues for some time to rise in a linear relation to income replacement rate. In other words, if we start from a position of zero income replacement and gradually increase the rate, then for quite a long interval increases in the rate will generate corresponding increases in utility. Zero income replacement signifies the complete absence of a DB pension system, leaving people to depend on their own accumulated savings to pay for living expenses in old age. This can also be thought of as a situation where social security in old age is conducted

Figure 7.5: Influence on optimal income-replacement rate of declining population growth

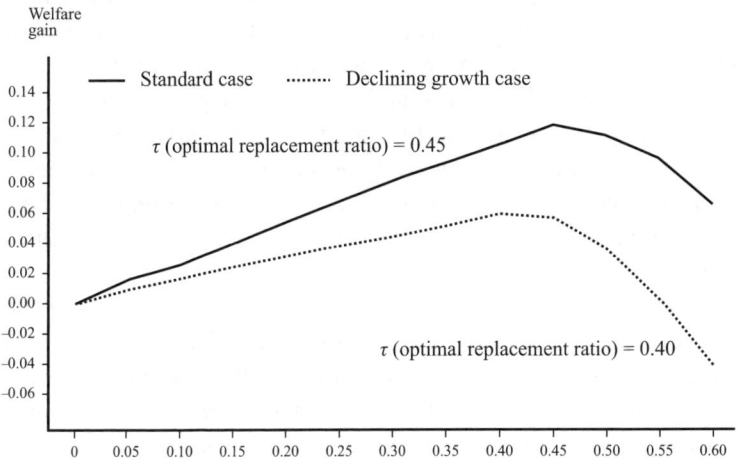

Figure 7.6: Influence on optimal income-replacement rate of increasing survival probability

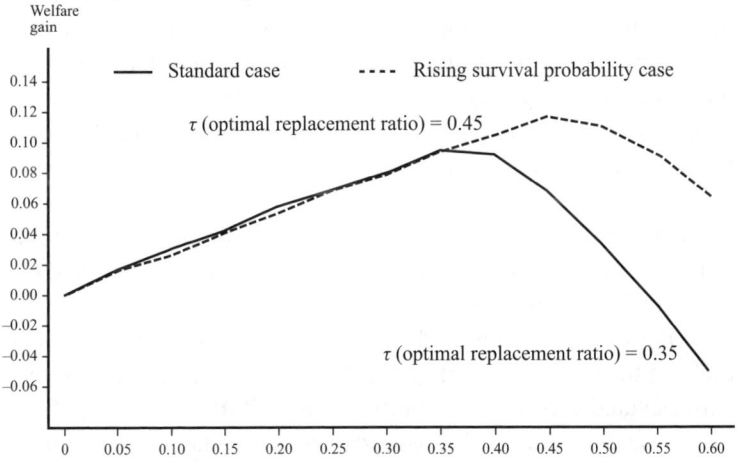

entirely through DC-type pensions. The complete absence of a DB component leaves people fully exposed to the risks of operating income fluctuation and unpredicted longevity. Avoiding those risks has the effect of raising utility for the people, so it is clearly desirable to raise the income replacement rate. Conversely, raising the income replacement rate on a DB-type pension also carries the demerit of raising the level of contributions that working people must pay into the fund. If people are forced to pay excessively high contributions, then lifetime disposable income will fall substantially, and the level of utility will actually fall for most people. The results of the simulation also indicate that raising the income replacement level too high results in lowering the welfare gain. In the standard case, an income replacement rate of 0.45 will generate the highest welfare gain. Raising it beyond that level will actually result in lowering the welfare gain.

In Figure 7.5 I have also displayed results of an analysis for the case of a decline in the population growth rate. The standard model assumes 2% population growth, so that in 30 years the population will grow by about 81% ($1.02^{30} = 1.811$), but if we assume a lower growth rate of 0.5%, then the population will only grow by about 16% in 30 years ($1.005^{30} = 1.161$). In that case, the optimal income replacement rate will come at 0.4, some five points earlier than in the standard case. A decline in population growth forces the smaller working generation to pay higher contributions to finance the pensions of the relatively larger retired generation, and this in turn reduces lifetime disposable income. Maintaining a high level of income replacement at a time of declining population growth forces people to pay very high contributions, exacerbating the main demerit of the DB system. That is why an excessive rate of income replacement in a society with a declining rate of population growth will lower utility for the people.

Next I considered the effect on optimal income replacement rate of an increase in survival probability. The results of this analysis are shown in Figure 7.6.

In Figure 7.6 the standard case assumes survival probability of 100% in the first period, and of 50% in the second period. The case with elevated survival probability assumes 100% in the first period and 80% in the second. The values ascribed to other variables in the two simulations were as follows: wage growth at 2% p.a., the return on investment income averaging 2% p.a. with a standard deviation of five percentage points, and population growth at 2%. In Figure 7.6 the standard case generated an optimal income-replacement rate of 0.35. Here too, an excessive increase in the income-replacement rate results in lowering the welfare gain for the people in general.

Looking now at the case with an elevated survival probability, the optimal level of income replacement comes in at 0.45, considerably higher than in the standard case. One of the merits of the DB-type pension is that it avoids the risk associated with longevity; when survival probability rises, the influence of that merit pushes up the optimal income-replacement rate. Of course, if an increase in survival probability is not matched by an increase in the birthrate, then the proportion of retired people in the overall population will rise and that will apply upward pressure on pension contributions. That will cancel out some of the merit of the DB system; even so, the advantage of avoiding longevity risk is a very considerable merit of the DB system in a society where people's life-spans are lengthening.

To fully draw out the policy implications of these different types of pension, one would have to conduct a more refined simulation. However, even with the rough-and-ready methods used here, it still seems fair to conclude that a hybrid pension scheme, combining elements of defined benefit and defined contribution, would probably be more effective at raising utility for the general public than simply abandoning the former model in favor of the latter. To some degree at least, the people should be given the peace of mind that comes from having a guaranteed minimum level of post-retirement income.

Conclusion

In this chapter we have considered to what degree it remains necessary to maintain the traditional DB model for public pensions, featuring as it does the function of sharing out risk more evenly among members of society. We have asked to what degree it might be better for society if we switched to a DC model, in order to erase differentials between generations. We have seen that in an aging society with a falling birthrate, the DB type of pension forces higher levels of contribution and creates intergenerational disparities. At the same time, the DB system still has the important merit of enabling people to avoid the risks associated with longevity and fluctuations in fund operating income. The simulation analysis used here has shown that totally abolishing the DB system of public pensions in favor of the DC model, in other words switching completely to individual accounting, would reduce utility to the people. The reason for that is simple: totally abolishing the basic guarantee represented by 'defined benefit' would also mean abolishing the risk-sharing function of pensions and the social security system more generally. That said, the intergenerational differentials that have opened up in Japan's aging/low birthrate society are now serious enough to make it a necessity that we sacrifice a degree of risk-sharing by introducing DC elements into social security systems. That naturally leads us to a crucial question: how should we balance the need to keep DB elements with the need to introduce DC elements? I would argue that the simulation analysis discussed here, and similar exercises using values as close as possible to reality, indicate that the optimal rate of income replacement in a public pension system is around 0.4, or 40%.[15] We should therefore retain sufficient elements of the DB system to support public pensions equivalent to about 40% of the employment income for the current working generation. This is significantly lower than the 50% that was pledged by the government at the time of the 2004 pension reform. Simulations like mine entail defining values for a large number of variables, so we cannot place total reliance on the figures generated. Even so, I believe we can safely draw two conclusions: that a complete switch to individual accounting would lower utility for the population as a whole; and that on the other hand, in view of the serious problem of intergenerational disparities now facing Japan, the government will be setting the bar too high if it sticks to its pledge of maintaining public pension payments at 50% of pre-retirement income.

The DB and DC systems that I have analyzed in this chapter represent two extremes on the spectrum of pension systems. Although Sweden has switched its public pension system in the direction of the DC system, the rate of return on fund operation does not vary from one subscriber to another, and in that sense it retains elements of the DB system. Thus, we need to be careful not to over-simplify when we make a straight comparison between the two models. However, it is certainly the case that policymakers will have to take great care to strike a balance between maintaining the risk-sharing function and controlling intergenerational disparities when designing public pension and social security systems from now on.

Analytical appendix

Any attempt at simulation analysis must start by constructing a statistical model. For utility functions I use the following formula for expected utility, one that is used in many analyses:

$$E\left[\sum_{i=1}^{n} \beta^{i-1} P_i u(c_{i,t})\right] \quad \text{(Formula 5)}$$

In this formula P_i represents the survival probability of a person i years old, c_i is consumption at age i, β^i is the discount rate at age i years, t indicates point in time and i represents age in years. I also used the following CRRA to obtain relative risk avoidance levels for each utility function:

$$u(c_{i,t}) = \frac{c_{i,t}^{1-\gamma}}{(1-\gamma)} \quad \text{(Formula 6)}$$

Here, γ is the coefficient indicating level of risk avoidance, and may be described as showing how sensitive individuals are to fluctuations in consumption. Prior to retirement an individual receives labor income of w_i, and after retirement s/he receives public pension benefits of b_i. Return on assets is r, and pension contributions are represented by θ. In that case the individual's budgetary constraint equation for each period will be as follows:

$$c_{i,t} + a_{i,t} = (1+r_t)a_{i-1,t-1} + (1-\theta_t)w_{i,t} + b_{i,t} \quad \text{(Formula 7)}$$

Here, $a_{i,t}$ represents assets held at age i years. Pension benefits $b_{i,t}$ are not receivable while still of employment age ($b_{i,t} = 0$), but are receivable after retirement ($b_{i,t} > 0$). Pensions are assumed to be paid under the DB model, so that the amount received in pension benefits is guaranteed to be equivalent to a certain proportion of wages received prior to retirement – that proportion being the income replacement rate. If we define pre-retirement wages as w_t and the income replacement rate as κ, then the amount received in pension benefits will be obtainable by $b_{it} = k \times w_t$. We assume that the pension system is financed on the pay-as-you-go (*fuka*) system, meaning that contributions will be set at a level such that the sum of all pension benefits received will be equal to that of all pension contributions paid. Hence the pension contribution rate will be determined in accordance with Formula 4 described above. In order to take account of fluctuations in pension fund operating profits, we assume that the mean return on assets and the distribution σ^2 fluctuate in conformity with the normal distribution. Since operating profit varies between each period, in this analysis we use Dynamic Programming to solve the problem of individual optimization. We can find the solution to the problem of individual optimization by resolving the following equation:

$$V_{i,t}(x_{i,t}) = \max_{c_{i,t}} \left\{ u(c_{i,t}) + \beta^{i-1} \frac{P_{i+1,t+1}}{P_{i,t}} E\left[V_{i+1,t+1}(x_{i+1,t+1}) | r_t \right] \right\}$$ (Formula 8)

s.t. Formula 7

$V_{i,t}$ represents the status value function. Here the status variables are assets and rate of operating profit, expressed as $x_{i,t} = (a_{i-1,t-1}, r_t)$. Since it would greatly complicate the calculations if we matched the model to actual population growth rates, this analysis applies exogenous fixed population growth rates to the simulation. To further simplify calculations, the simulation assumes a model in which people's lives can be divided into a maximum of two periods. The value for each parameter is obtained by defining one period as 30 years and then raising the value of the annual rate to the power of 30. For example, if the wage growth rate is 2% then the value for one period will be $(1.02)^{30} = 1.811362...$

Such was the model used to carry out the simulation analysis in this chapter.

Conclusion: The Changing Structure of Social Inequality in Japan

Sawako Shirahase

The present work has attempted to clarify the structures of inequality inherent in the inexorably progressing twin trends toward fewer births and a higher proportion of old people in Japan today. Though much is said about the advent of the aging society, there are many things that are still not understood about it. Obviously there will be fewer children and more elderly, but people do not really know what it will be like to *live* in such a society. There is still not enough research that treats the twin population changes of the falling birthrate and aging society as macro-changes and examines how these quantitative shifts will play out in relation to existing socioeconomic mechanisms. We tend to look at change from the perspective of the present examining the past, saying 'such and such has changed,' but when it comes to the question of future change, the fact of the matter is that we are stuck in the realm of guesswork.

That is not to say, however, that the Japanese proverb 'one step beyond is darkness' (*issun saki wa yami*) necessarily applies to this issue. This is precisely where the value lies in meticulously analyzing data relating to the present or the past to elucidate existing social mechanisms and patterns. The world is not standing still, but neither does it generally make sudden rapid leaps from zero to a hundred. To see things as they are requires a static vantage point. Elucidating the problems of the present will help us prepare a reasoned response to the problems of the future, based at least on *informed* guesswork.

In a society characterized by rapid change, the rationale for focusing on differentials that had not previously been noticed lies not so much in claiming that those differentials had gone unnoticed because they did not previously exist, as in debating *why* exactly those differentials have just now become a problem. If we content ourselves with merely drawing attention to themes that happen to have hitherto been overlooked, then the debate will be over before it has properly begun. It is our task, as the authors of this book, to include in our analysis such questions as why we feel the need to focus on differentials hitherto overlooked, and why differentials thus far concealed have now come to the surface. I will now look through the chapters of the book in order, summarizing each chapter's perspective and seeking pointers toward an understanding of the meaning of the inequalities and differentials that have emerged in the course of the change toward a low birthrate/aging society.

Looking first at Toshiki Satō's chapter on the 'Explosion of Inequality Consciousness,' I read this as an attempt to reinterpret one aspect of macro-level population change – the falling birthrate – at the micro level, as a way of explaining the mechanisms behind the sudden upsurge in debate on inequality during the 1990s. Satō read the macro-phenomenon of the falling birthrate as signifying a weakness in parent-child continuity. This in turn implied a personal consciousness in which all accounts must be settled in one's own lifetime. He argued that the old myth of the all-middle-class society stemmed from a loss of awareness of inequality. With the macro level showing strong economic growth, the micro level of individual consciousness was rendered unaware of inequality because (1) it was possible to believe that one's children would have a better standard of living than one's own, and (2) there were enough children around to maintain the sense of parent-child continuity necessary to make this a comforting thought. However unfair one's own position in life might appear to be, one's children would be able to overcome their disadvantages and achieve a more prosperous lifestyle. Thinking along those lines made it easier to put up with any negatives in one's own situation.

Satō argued that people's ability to think of the settlement of life's accounts in terms of a long time span covering their children's generation expunged their awareness of inequality, or at least dulled it. In recent years, however, people have come to have a much higher probability of ending their lives childless, meaning that life's accounts have to be settled in their own lifetime. This shortening of the time-span over which people have to settle accounts, and its limitation to the individual, has heightened people's awareness of inequality, causing what Satō calls an 'explosion' of inequality consciousness.

However, Shirahase and Takeuchi (2009) suggest that the social group most keenly aware of inequality is not the middle-aged and older generations trying to lead lives without children, but rather the younger generation that has yet to make the big decisions about marriage or childbirth. To put it another way, among the younger generation – the generation yet to decide whether or not to start a family – the sense of inequality is particularly acute. We may conclude that their sense of inequality is being inflamed, not so much by a direct sense of the limited time available to settle accounts in a childless lifetime as from their personal experience of a bad macro-environmental situation – particularly in employment – and that the sense of resentment is no longer softened by the assumption of parent-child continuity.

In short, the explosion of inequality consciousness is triggered by a combination of anticipated and real factors: the anticipation of a single-lifetime settlement of accounts, and the reality of bitter struggle in a recession-bound job market. The mechanism behind that explosion cannot, I think, be explained simply by saying that the factors that made people forget about inequality are now working in the reverse direction. What I take from Satō's chapter is the important perception that the loss of parent-child continuity combines with a deteriorating macro-environment to worsen the general outlook for the individual. The stronger impact of economic trends on a person forced to settle accounts in a single lifetime due to the lack of intergenerational continuity (in which children serve as what Satō calls a *jun-honnin* or 'sub-self') represents a collision of macro- and micro-level factors that suggests an extremely promising approach to explaining the formation of individual consciousness.

Satō also touched on the issue of equality of opportunity, criticizing a tendency he observed to only argue the issue in terms of basic principles. True enough, we can only observe (in)equality of opportunity once the results are in, making it impossible to escape entirely from the realm of speculation. However hard we may struggle to analyze equality of opportunity, the fact is that we cannot hold it in our hands and so our attempts will [tend to] end up being argument for the sake of argument. However, it would be just as fruitless to ignore this fundamental dilemma, turning out extreme arguments that pretend they have discovered the answer. Satō refused to go down that road, closing his chapter by stating his commitment to boldly continue tackling the problem of opportunity inequality. One could perhaps call that the holy grail for sociologists of stratification: to take studies of inequality and unfairness out of the realm of first-principle theorizing, and take on the challenge of clarifying the mechanisms that make them happen, in a way that can lead to concrete policymaking to set the problems straight.

The second chapter, my own work on 'Unequal Japan: Implications for Households and Gender,' addressed the falling birthrate/aging society in terms of economic inequality, looking at changes in household structure in an attempt to study population shifts from the point of view of people's ways of life. My most important finding was that the falling birthrate/aging society implied a move away from the traditional life course characterized by marriage, childbirth and co-residence of old people with their adult offspring, and that this shift is intimately connected with a high level of economic risk. I discussed the steady increase in the proportion of people who never marry, have no children and live on their own even in old age. I also discussed the growing numbers of people who do marry but do not stay with the same partner 'till death us do part,' though they are still a relatively small part of the population in Japan. Thus we saw that the phenomena of the falling birthrate and aging society included a variety of trends diverting people from traditionally prescribed life courses.

Along with the diversification in life courses and household composition has come a clear increase in economic risk associated with divergence from the traditionally prescribed norm. This relates to the question of how social policy should go about incorporating these divergent cases into welfare systems. Such cases, admittedly, are still a minority in simple numerical terms. Still, as the working generation declines relative to the retired generation, the question of how to support these divergent cases, bound as they are to increase steadily over the coming years, not as 'exceptions' but as a genuine social minority, will be an important policy challenge. How can society as a whole support its minorities? That very question represents a major shift away from the existing framework of social policy, which is designed to serve the majority. How can the social disadvantages of the minorities be treated more fairly across society? This, surely, is a policy challenge that demands our urgent attention.

In Chapter 3, 'Young, Japanese, and Not in Education, Employment or Training', Yūji Genda looked at the phenomenon of NEETs – young people 'not in employment, education or training.' Pointing to the dangers of arguing the issue merely from emotion or prejudice, he went in search of empirical data that might show the true state of affairs. NEETs are often held responsible for their own predicament, since they neither look for work nor hope for employment. But where many critics have discussed the attitude or consciousness of NEETs, Genda found a more fundamental problem in the structure of Japan's social system. NEETs tend to have low-level academic credentials that restrict their range of employment opportunities; there is no equality of opportunity in employment. More than a few NEETs have in fact experienced employment, and Genda argued that the bitterness of that experience was a major trigger factor in their present condition. The complex tangle of human relations in the workplace brings a psychological weariness that can lead some young people to fatigue and an inability to work. How should adult society and the government respond to that reality? Genda suggested that a more all-embracing employment policy is called for.

An important insight from Genda's chapter is that the problems of unemployed people need to be tackled not only within the framework of employment policy, but also from the standpoint of welfare policy. The plain fact is that the main reason why most NEETs do not get jobs is illness. Hitherto there has been a big hole in the debate on employment policy when it comes to people whose poor health means they are not even in a position to make the choice between working and not working. Debate on inequality and differentials has tended to center on the labor market and to focus on people who have income. Even when the debate *has* looked at those outside the labor market, it has largely been restricted to elderly retirees and housewives. In other words, where people are unable to work because of psychological or physical illness, they have barely impinged on the analytical field. However, we should not so simply exclude those absent from the labor market from the scope of our analysis. If we are to explicate the distributive structure of society as a whole, it is a pressing research challenge to define the position of those without jobs in that great structure.

Hitherto NEETs have mostly been young people, but with the passing years, growing numbers have entered middle age without exiting the NEET condition. We have to look at non-employment not just as a youth problem, but in the context of the whole lifecourse. Nowadays a growing number of Japanese are entering their 50s still unmarried and living alone. When people talk about the postwar baby-boomers, it is usually in relation to the '2007 problem,' 2007 being the date when this large population segment started to leave the labor market and enter into retirement. However, this generation also deserves attention because of the variation in lifeways that started to emerge among its members when they were in their 50s. As this generation, with its variety of lifeways, enters retirement, how on earth shall we define their systemic position? Any attempt to grasp the nature of differentials and inequality will also have to clarify the position of those out of employment as a matter of urgency.

In Chapter 4, 'Hidden Educational Inequalities in Postwar Japan: Misconceptions and Reconceptions,' Takehiko Kariya demonstrated that although postwar Japanese education was designed to outstrip even the US model in its thoroughgoing egalitarianism, seeking to abolish the competitive principle and get rid of selective education, inequality did in fact remain concealed within the system. The concept was that anyone could score 100% if only they tried hard enough; accordingly, meritocratic ranking systems were avoided, even despised. This became the foundation for Japan's ultra-conformist, one-size-fits-all style of educational culture. Individualism was crushed: pupils were expected to sit quietly in straight lines and listen carefully to what the teacher said. Discipline was emphasized, and there was a serious shortage of sites in the education system where free expression might be positively evaluated. This was one of the evils of education that sought to cram knowledge into young minds without fostering individuality or creativity. At the same time, a more positive outcome of the policy of enforcing standardized education such that a pupil would receive the same product anywhere in the land was to generate cohorts of pupils with high average test scores and a low level of deviation from the mean. Indeed, the ability of Japanese elementary school pupils in arithmetic was found to be impressively high by international standards, showcasing Japan's high standards of compulsory education.

In the 1970s and '80s, educational opportunities expanded to the point where over 90% of the population was going on to senior high school, and complaints that the poor could not afford to send their children to senior high gradually abated. The proportion of students going on to junior college or university also rose, as education increasingly became a part of mass culture. The increasing availability of upper secondary and higher education opportunities appeared to mean that anyone who worked hard enough could acquire high-level educational credentials and thereby elevate their social status. The message was that nowadays anyone could sit university entrance exams and get the chance to be 'reborn' at a higher social stratum. In a limited sense it may be true that anyone in Japan has a chance to grab that ticket to a better future. Ironically, however, educational institutions became so intensely stratified that the notion of equal educational opportunity for all was largely an illusion.

Kariya argued that the mass education society gave the appearance of a credentialist society open to all, while concealing a rigid structure of inequality. Under the banner of egalitarianism, everyone was invited to join in academic competition; competition thus became overheated. But because of the unequal structure hidden within the mechanism of mass educational opportunity, the result was a credentialist society with wide differentials. In pointing to the paradox between the surface and inner meaning of Japan's mass education society, Kariya has performed a valuable service.

Japanese youths have been confronted with examinations at increasingly younger ages, and the massive industry of *juku*, private after-hours schools, has spread even to preschool infants. How is the excessive competition in the credentialist society to be corrected? One answer to that question has been the government's attempt to introduce 'relaxed education' (*yutori kyōiku*) to Japanese schools. Suddenly alive to the evils of force-fed knowledge, the Ministry of Education, Culture, Sports, Science and Technology has tried to lower the amount of knowledge that has to be imparted in schools and grant more space for creativity and individual study. Yet, in another sad irony, this policy has actually served to further widen educational differentials. Specifically, Kariya pointed out that the new approach increased the influence of the household environment on pupils' grades since higher status households would make more effort and spend more money than lower status households to replace the educational content lost from the school curriculum. He concluded that an overtly egalitarian education system had ended up creating a deeply divided credentialist society.

That said, the fact remains that Japan's standardized education system did succeed in raising the nation's educational standards – an achievement not to be lightly discounted. The ruthlessly egalitarian approach that viewed competition – even fair competition – as 'bad equality' and disapproved of selection certainly did some damage. But at least it guaranteed a certain minimum level of standardized education to everyone in Japan, irrespective of location or family circumstances. It contributed to raising the level of compulsory education in Japan. As for individuality and creativity, they are not things that will somehow naturally emerge from 'relaxed education.' Nowadays, with so many people calling for small government and emphasizing the benefits of choice, the question of at what point in the lifecourse equality will be secured will surely become an even more important policy challenge in the years to come. With the number of children falling, the amount of money available for investment in education varies ever more greatly according to household economic circumstances. It would be well nigh impossible to reduce the influence of the household on educational opportunity to zero; nonetheless, it is important to defend equality of opportunity sufficiently to prevent excessive gaps opening up between the starting lines from which children begin the educational race.

Healthcare is another area in which there has been a strong, though unspoken, assumption of equality in Japan. In Chapter 5, 'Health and Differentials: What Lies Behind the Falling Birthrate and Aging Society?' Hiroshi Ishida analyzed healthcare in terms of social stratification theory. The value of this chapter lies in Ishida's determined bid to figure out the status differences observable in people's state of health.

Since the establishment of the National Health Insurance system in 1961, Japanese healthcare has worked on the principle that whoever one might be, and wherever one might live, one would receive the same level of medical services as any other citizen. But under this system of equal access to medical services, is the opportunity to be healthy really being afforded equally to all members of the population? Medical problems have tended to attract attention not in terms of health so much as in relation to the escalating costs of medical care for the elderly. As one gets older, the likelihood of falling ill increases. But that process does not play out the same way for all people. Ishida used the job in which old people were employed the longest before retirement as a dummy variable for social status, and conducted an empirical analysis to see whether differences in status had a significant impact on post-retirement health condition. He found that the incidence of chronic disorders showed no significant variation traceable to social status.

Conclusion

Whether the retiree was from an elite professional/managerial status group or was an unskilled blue-collar worker, the risk of contracting a chronic health disorder seemed to be about the same. However, when Ishida broadened the definition of health to cover the health-related aspects of quality of life, a different picture emerged. When it came to physical fatigue, restricted movement in everyday life, depression and subjective health conditions, status differentials *did* show a statistically significant effect. In other words, status-related differences were not apparent in easily observable health indices where people were either sick or well, but they did emerge in health indices that were harder to observe, like fatigue or depression.

Ishida's most valuable observation came where he stressed the disjuncture between the strong popular belief in social equality of health and the status-based differentials that nevertheless exist. Health issues have tended to be debated simply in terms of age, not least because the aging of society appears to be the main factor causing the rise in Japan's medical costs. But not all people show the same increased susceptibility to illness once they pass the age of 65. It is possible that further status differentials may be observed if we look beyond the easily observable sick/not sick dyad, and consider such intangibles as health consciousness or level of access to medical facilities. We still do not have a solid answer to the question of whether inequality in health has really worsened in recent years, or whether there has simply been a rise in people's concern with the issue. But there can be no doubt that as society continues to age, the question of health as a quality-of-life issue will be an increasingly important challenge to policymakers.

In Chapter 6, 'Inheritance, Pensions, Childbirth, Childrearing and the Inequalities They Bring: The Case of Pure Financial Assets,' Katsumi Matsuura considered the fundamental and unfair fact of life, that one cannot choose one's own parents. Focusing on inheritance, the micro-level intergenerational transference of assets, he attempted an explanation derived from pensions (a macro-level intergenerational transfer), and childbirth/childrearing (micro-level activities). Though children cannot choose their parents, the fact remains that parents play a large part in determining what opportunities the children will have in life, and this chapter's outstanding achievement was to clarify the all too unfair mechanism through which this fact of life translates into inequality of outcome. Matsuura suggested that reforms to taxation and other state systems might make a big contribution to reducing intergenerational continuity/ expansion of differentials by stopping or slowing the process by which inequality of opportunity inherited from the parental generation leads to inequality of outcome in the children's generation.

Another important message we may take from Matsuura's chapter is that society needs to take a bigger role in childrearing. Noting the low quality of social support for child-rearing, he argued that an excessive burden was being placed on the shoulders of mothers as the price for experiencing the joy of childrearing, itself a subjective concept dependent on personal evaluation. By defining childrearing as a strictly private matter between mother and child, society has evaded its responsibility to assist in this process. Behind the phenomenon of the falling birthrate lies the subtlety with which society has defined childrearing as a purely private activity. But there has always been an irony concealed here, for in fact childrearing is and always has been dependent on contact between parents, the local region and society in general. Nevertheless, society has continued to define childrearing as a closed private space between mother and child, and is now paying the price for that evasion of responsibility in the form of the rapidly falling birthrate.

In Chapter 7, 'The Consequences of Applying Individual Accounting to Social Security: Public Pensions as a Form of Risk-Sharing,' Naomi Miyazato looked at the public pension system and used the results of a simulation analysis to discuss whether a shift to individual accounting, a move advocated by some theorists as a way to reduce intergenerational imbalances, would really result in a significant improvement to people's welfare. It has been observed that the fixed-benefit public pensions used in Japan assume a 'taxation model,' whereby the working generation is taxed to pay the retired generation's pensions. With the working population getting smaller while the retired population expands, this is putting a heavy burden on the former and causing a widening and increasingly problematic differential between generations. But the taxation formula for pensions also has the important function of pooling the risks of illness, unemployment and aging, etc., among all members of society. Conversely, the fixed contribution model obliges the individual to shoulder these various risks, while being unaffected by macro-level population shifts. At a time like the present, when the birthrate is collapsing and the population is rapidly aging, one can understand the appeal of individual accounting. At the same time, however, Miyazato stressed that switching to a complete individual accounting system would not necessarily enhance the welfare of the individual.

Another important observation of Miyazato's concerned public consciousness. He pointed out that even while rapid change in population structure is disrupting the balance between the working and retired generations, opinion in Japanese society does not undervalue the merits of a social security system that shares out future risks within society. The choice between a fixed contribution system entailing individual accounting and the existing fixed benefit system is not an all-or-nothing choice: Miyazato stresses the importance of establishing a system that combines the merits of both systems to the ideal degree. The next big question is how to identify the ideal balance between the two. We do not yet have an answer to that one, but further research on the appropriate scale of social security, and the best balance between public and private responsibility for pensions, is an urgent necessity.

The inequality concealed in the world around us

The aging society is one with relatively few young people and many old people, and the intergenerational balance is becoming worse: the working-age generation is burdened with the increasing number of those in the retired generation to support. At the same time, the youth labor market has taken a downturn. The needs that must be met by social welfare services are accordingly becoming more numerous and various than before. The question of how to distribute the cost of meeting those needs, and how to provide multifaceted support for them, poses the most important policy challenge of all as we learn to live with the aging society. When I say 'multifaceted,' I mean that as well as the traditional suppliers of services to meet people's needs – the family, local authorities and the state – we need to include new participants such as NPOs, NGOs and the non-profit sector generally. However, accepting new participants to the enterprise of meeting needs does not automatically mean lightening the responsibility of the state, local authorities or the public sector as a whole. As well as demonstrating the existence of differentials in various aspects of Japanese society, the papers collected in this book have also shown a shared perception that government needs to do more. But a big role for government does not necessarily imply big government. The great role we envisage for government can probably be realized through a delicate division of labor with families, regions, markets, non-profit organizations and other actors.

This book has focused on the changes accompanying the falling birthrate and aging society, seeking to unravel the complex mechanisms creating inequality and differentials. One important point that has emerged is that inequality, though a seemingly simple word, contains a great variety of meanings, and is not susceptible to simplistic explanations. Inequality has been found to exist in places where it was hard to see, or at least did not receive sufficient attention. Also, the aging society has generated changes in people's lifeways and in the nature of the family. Despite this fact, the socioeconomic risks attendant on deviation from the 'typical' lifestyle remain high, and society has not yet sufficiently developed the function of distributing that level of risk through society. It is clear enough from reading this book as a whole that Japanese society is not yet fully prepared to systemically support the various non-typical lifeways that are a feature of the aging society.

As has always been the case, the socioeconomic status of a child's parents still plays an undeniable role in determining the kind of life that child will lead. As Satō says in Chapter 1, that does not mean that we must totally reject the continuity between parent and child, although we would deplore a society where inherited wealth created great gaps between the starting positions of children in life, and where those gaps persisted and did not narrow later in life. But a starting line that is not entirely straight, or some individual obstacles on the track, need not be cause for serious alarm so long as the social environment provides a number of chances later in the lifecourse to correct those starting-line inequalities. The aging society is bringing with it greater variety in individual lifeways, and cases that do not fit traditional stereotypes are increasing. The point is that choosing a way of life different from traditional norms should not in itself determine all the various risks awaiting the individual in the course of life.

Faced with the rapid onset of massive social change, what should we social scientists be doing? It is our duty to coolly assess the changes all around us, neither exaggerating nor understating them but maintaining a certain distance from which we can achieve a degree of objectivity. Being trained as a social scientist means seeing the world, and the changes coming over it, from a certain distance and with a steady gaze. To sensitively respond to changing events and emerging problems in the world around us: that, I believe, is what people expect of researchers like us. That is not to say that I have the slightest intention of dismissing the intuitions of the people as mere amateurish complaints – far from it. Rather, I believe it is our mission to elucidate with due detachment the social, economic and political mechanisms underlying those intuitions. At a time when people are feeling flustered and panicky about social change, I cannot accept that it is right for researchers to casually inflame those feelings further. Behind the visible changes affecting society, how is the distributive mechanism changing, or not changing? That is what we have to ascertain. As I approach the end of the final chapter, I cannot help feeling that we have only partially succeed in that mission. Even so, as I stated in the Introduction, I hope we can maintain a willingness to face up to change and continuity alike with a professional sensitivity. If the arguments presented in this book have served to clarify the workings of the world even a little, nothing could please me more. And to close on a personal note, I hope to further sharpen my own awareness of the complex mechanisms underlying the social world in the years to come.

Notes

Chapter 1

1 To be precise, this applies only to the Massachusetts Bay colony, based in Boston and deriving its legal status from a license issued by the Massachusetts Bay Company. In contrast, the Plymouth colony, based in Plymouth, Massachusetts, licensed by the Virginia Company, and often referred to as the Pilgrim Fathers, allowed the children of church members to become members without any tests having to be passed. This was related to differences in the two colonies' relationship to the Anglican Church: the Boston group was non-separatist, whereas the Plymouth group was separatist (see Morgan 1965). Since Morgan published *Visible Saints* in 1965, a colossal amount of research has been published on the religious conflicts in early colonial America and their political background. However, we have yet to see any convincing refutation of Morgan's powerful analysis.

2 Hence the use of terms like 'cultural capital,' which carry the implicit assumption that something as ineffable as culture can in fact be counted like cash.

3 It follows that in considering inequality of opportunity, the starting point of parental occupational status and the end point of children's occupational status do not need to have the same number of categories.

4 As such, it may be somewhat of an overstatement to posit parental occupational status as that for children until they enter into occupations of their own. In reality the status of a person before they acquire an occupation is probably much more nebulous than that, and parental status is used as a makeshift proxy for want of anything better.

5 A particularly vivid example of the Japanese obsession with appearing to give everyone a totally equal chance to access higher education would be the introduction of the English-language listening test to the National Centre University Entrance Examination, sat each year by over 500,000 candidates. To avoid the slightest possible unfairness resulting from seating position relative to the source of the tape-recorded questions, every single candidate was issued with a miniature IC audio player. The inevitable malfunctions created yet more stress over how to give affected candidates a second chance without creating fresh kinds of inequality.

6 If we can identify differentials in a system resulting from variables that cannot be ascribed to the individual, we may legitimately describe that system as 'unequal' (see Satō 2000b).

7 Needless to say, this is not to say that the postwar family system was a just institution – I merely observe that it had this effect in connection with the specific issue of opportunity inequality.

Chapter 2

1 The study was supported by a Grant-in-Aid for Scientific Research (S) (#20223004) from the Japan Society for the Promotion of Science.
2 The Gini coefficient is the most widely recognized indicator of the degree of income inequality in use today. Graphing cumulative population against cumulative income, with the total of each defined as one, produces the Lorenz curve. In a hypothetical society with absolute income equality, the Lorenz curve would be a straight diagonal line at 45 degrees to both axes. Two times the area of the space between the actual Lorenz curve and that diagonal generates the Gini coefficient. The nearer the coefficient is to zero, the more equal is the distribution of income in the economy being studied; conversely, the nearer the figure is to one, the more unequal is the distribution of income.

$$Gini = \left(\frac{2}{\mu n^2}\cdot\sum_{k}^{n} kW_k\right) - \frac{n+1}{n} = \frac{2\operatorname{cov}\left(W_k, \frac{k}{n}\right)}{\mu} = \frac{\frac{2}{n}\sum_{k=1}^{n}(W_k - \mu)\cdot\left(\frac{k}{n} - \frac{1}{n^2}\sum_{k=1}^{n}k\right)}{\mu}$$

In the formula, W_k is the equivalent disposable income of household k, and we can show that $W_k = D_k/S_k^{\varepsilon}$, where D_k indicates the disposable income of household k and S_k is the number of members of household k. ε is called the equivalent elasticity value, and here is set at 0.5. n is the total number of households, and μ denotes mean disposable income.
3 The Gini coefficients used in this chapter are calculated on the basis of household disposable income, meaning the income remaining after mandatory social contributions such as taxation and social insurance have been subtracted from total household income. In order to take into account the household size, I have divided disposable income by the square root of the number of household members. In this chapter I use this equivalent disposable income to measure economic inequalities unless otherwise stated.
4 In this chapter the term 'childless couple' refers to households with a married couple but no children – including cases where children have grown up and started their own households, as well as those where no children have been born.
5 Iwata (2004) uses public assistance criteria as her standard for measuring poverty.
6 This survey was conducted by the Ministry of Welfare (MOW) until 2001, when the ministry was merged with the Ministry of Labor (MOL) to form the Ministry of Health, Labor and Welfare (MHLW). The analysis was carried out as part of a MHLW research project (2004–6) entitled 'International comparative research on socioeconomic differentials in aging/low birthrate societies.'
7 The absolute unemployment rate for those aged 15–24 (men and women combined) stood at 9.6% in 2001, 3.5 points up from the 6.1% registered in 1995 (Sōmushō Tōkeikyoku, 2005).
8 The '2007 problem' refers to the fact that the postwar baby-boom generation will start reaching retirement age that year. It also used to be estimated

that Japan's population would make the shift from expansion to decline in 2007, although as it happened the moment came earlier, in 2005.
9 'Other households' show a high level of inequality for all age groups. This residual category by its very nature covers a wide variety of households, so it is in a sense only natural that it shows wide economic differentials. I will not attempt detailed analysis of this category here.
10 Note in particular that elderly women in Japan are exposed to a higher level of risk than their counterparts in the industrialized countries of Europe and North America (Seike and Yamada 2004; Shirahase 2006).
11 This study takes the percentage of men who have never married at the age of 50 as a rough guide to the lifetime male non-marriage ratio.
12 The present data does not permit detailed analysis that might explain the gender gap in the proportion of never-married people.
13 The word '*dankai*' was first applied to the baby-boom generation by novelist Tai'ichi Sakaiya, when he used it in the title of his 1976 novel *Dankai no Sedai* (The Dankai Generation). It most frequently refers to the approximately eight million people born in the three years from 1947–1949, although some writers use the term more roughly to refer to people born in the first decade after the war.
14 The data here covers both sexes, but it is a fact that a great majority of the wealthy singletons in their 30s and 40s are men.
15 In trying to explain why male single-parent families have suffered this widening of economic differentials vis-à-vis two-parent families, we may guess that having to bring up children alone has had a greater negative economic impact on these men than in the past; or that a higher proportion of low wage-earners are appearing in the population of men bringing up children on their own. As of 2001, about 70% of men bringing up children without a wife live with their parents, presumably to assist with childrearing.
16 Male single-parent families are not eligible for the same welfare support as female single-parent families. However they became eligible to receive the child support allowance in 2010.
17 These issues naturally raise questions of cause and effect. Does divorce increase the risk of falling into the low-income group, or is it that people highly at risk of falling into the low-income group are also more likely to get divorced? I make no attempt to address this question here. Doing so would require an entirely new research project, ideally a large-scale panel survey that would track family fortunes dynamically. For now, I merely wish to emphasize the close connection between divorce/separation and a higher risk of experiencing low income.

Chapter 4

1 See Kariya (1995) for a more detailed version of the analysis in this section.
2 By 'model I,' Galtung means a conservative society.
3 Sixteen elementary schools in the Kansai area were chosen in both the 1989 and 2001 surveys, with 2227 (1989) and 921 (2001) fifth grade students as the respondents. For more details about the surveys, see Kariya and Shimizu (2004).

4 *Dōwa* district refers to areas with high populations of *Burakumin*, the descendents of Edo-era outcastes still subject to discrimination today. These areas were named *dōwa* ('peaceful assimilation') districts under government policies to improve Burakumin standards of living by providing subsidized housing, educational scholarships, etc. in designated areas.
5 In 2010, the Ministry of Education revised the national curricula again, indicating their policy changes, by increasing contents of curricula and teaching hours. A part of these changes are led by social recognition of expanding inequality in education under the *Yutori* reforms. Recent research, including that conducted by the Ministry itself, reveals that inequality in academic achievements among school children is expanding.

Chapter 5

1 An earlier version of this paper was presented at the meeting of the International Sociological Association's Research Committee on Social Stratification (RC28), at Radboud University Nijmegen, the Netherlands, on May 11–14, 2006.
2 *Nihon Keizai Shinbun*, 3 July 2005, morning edition. The survey was carried out from mid-May to early June 2005 by the paper's research affiliate, Nikkei Risaachi. It sampled 1,000 men and 1,000 women, all of them living within a 30-km radius of Tokyo, Osaka or Nagoya. The response rate was 67.3%.
3 Healthy life expectancy is computed from life expectancy, but includes an adjustment for time spent in poor health. Healthy life expectancy measures the equivalent number of years in full health that a newborn child is expected to live based on the present level of mortality rates and the distribution of health states in the population (World Health Organization 2004).
4 People who are receiving pubic assistance (low income families) are exempt from the payment of premium for the national health insurance scheme. It is reported that about 10% of people do not pay the premium (Kokumin Kenkō Hoken Chūōkai 2002).
5 Ishida (2009) reports the results of health conditions among the Japanese youth (aged 20–34) and middle-aged (aged 35–40) using the Japanese Life Course Panel Survey (JLPS). The younger generation indeed has much better health conditions (self-reported health and activity restriction), except for mental health (depression). The JLPS was conducted using grants from the Japan Society for the Promotion of Science (number 18103003 and 22223005).
6 This study used data from the Nihon University Japanese Longitudinal Study of Aging (NUJLSOA). The survey was conducted by the Nihon University Center for Information Networking as one of their research projects. I am grateful to the Nihon University Center for Information Networking and the researchers who conducted the survey for giving me permission to use the data set. In particular, I thank Professor Yasuhiko Saito for his kind assistance and comments on the earlier version of this paper.

7 Our analysis is based on the weighted sample (n=4997). The sample size in each analysis is smaller than this total usable sample because there were missing cases in some of the variables included in the analysis.
8 There were 12 items measuring the CES-D scale, and the reliability (Cronbach's alpha) among them is .877.
9 The entire distribution of the self-reported health question is as follows: poor (2%), not good (12.6%), fair (33%), good (33.5%) and very good (18.8%). The three-category version (bad, fair and good) was also experimented, but there was very little difference between the 'fair' and 'good' groups. Therefore, the paper employs the dichotomous version of the self-reported health variable.
10 The entire distribution of self-reported change in health conditions is as follows: got better (6%), about the same (67%) and got worse (27%).

Chapter 6

1 Another route by which parental economic power is transmitted to children is of course through education. Chapter 3 of an earlier work (Matsuura and Shigeno 1996) demonstrates that parental income influences choice of private elementary and junior high schools that are thought to provide good educational conditions. However, the question of education is beyond the scope of the present chapter.
2 On inequality of opportunity, see Satō in Chapter 1 of the present volume.
3 Ideally one would hope to focus on net assets, including housing and land (cf. Matsuura 2002). However, since data on net assets cannot be obtained from the 2002 survey, here I will narrow the focus to net financial assets.
4 The Ministry of Posts and Telecommunications (Yūseishō) was merged with several other bodies to form the Ministry of Internal Affairs and Communications (Sōmushō) in the bureaucratic restructuring of 2001. Japan Post (Nippon Yūsei Kōsha) was created in 2003 as a public corporation in charge of the postal service.
5 Using the Japanese government's definition of 'total unemployment,' excluding job-seekers working part-time, married women with husbands in employment, anyone considered not to be seeking work, etc.
6 In this chapter I include *inter vivos* gifts, i.e. intergenerational transfers of wealth made while the parent is still alive, in the category of inheritance.
7 For an empirical survey on inheritance in Japan see Campbell (2004). For a debate on the importance of inheritance in overall household assets, see Kotolikoff and Summers (1981), Kotolikoff (1988) and Modigliani (1988). Kotolikoff and Summers define wealth accumulated during the life-cycle as the sum of savings from earnings + interest on those savings, and the residue [at death] as inherited wealth. They find that inheritance accounts for 80% of household assets. In contrast, Modigliani defines wealth accumulated during the life-cycle as the sum of earnings during each phase in the cycle, plus interest, minus consumption, with the residue of that being inherited wealth. Under his formulation, inheritance accounts for just 20% of household assets. For a broadly inclusive survey of these issues, see Ishikawa (1991), chapter 7 ('Tomi no Keisei to Bunpai'; The formation and distribution of wealth).

Notes

8 This figure comes from materials on inheritance and gift taxes distributed at a meeting of the Government Tax Advisory Commission (Zeisei Chōsakai) held on 23 May 2006.
9 In March 2005, Japan's biggest bank, Mizuho, announced that it had developed a private bank specifically for people with financial assets in excess of ¥500 million. People in this bracket are not covered in the samples used for this chapter.
10 The influence of inheritance and gift taxes on inheritance strategies will tend to vary according to the parental motivation in making a bequest (Kunieda 2002). Page (2003) uses differences in inheritance tax between states to demonstrate the effect of taxation levels on *inter vivos* gift-giving in the US case.
11 Such at least is the theory. In practice, however, some 40% of people supposed to be covered by the national pension scheme are not paying their contributions. This very high level of delinquency – despite the fact that enrollment in the scheme is supposed to be compulsory – is often ascribed to two reasons. First, some of the people supposed to enroll in the scheme know about its financial weakness and are suspicious that they may not actually get the pensions they are supposed to be paying for; and second, some people are simply too poor to pay the contributions.
12 On the pension system, see for example Takayama (2004).
13 In the context of the 2004 pension reform, the Ministry of Health, Labor and Welfare stated that pension payments would exceed contributions, narrowly defined as the premiums paid by the employee, excluding the employer's premium. However, a better comparison to assess the value to the household of future receipts from a public employee pension would be not the cost of employee contributions to that pension, but the amount of pension payments that might be expected if s/he did not enroll in the employee pension scheme, instead taking the money saved in premiums by employee and employer alike and putting them into a personal pension scheme in the private sector. See also Hashimoto and Yamaguchi (2005).
14 In a study I participated in (Matsuura and Shigeno 2005), we studied the career patterns of women in the greater Tokyo region who quit work for marriage and/or childbirth, and found that the success rate at subsequently getting employed as a public official or regular employee at a major corporation was a rather depressing 0.0%.
15 If we consider marriage as a preliminary to childbirth, differences in asset ownership between single and married women become another important research focus here. In a panel survey on consumer life covering the period 1993–1995 (Matsuura and Shigeno 2000), it was found that single women held financial assets worth on average ¥2.75 million, and that 91.3% of single women had at least some financial assets. By contrast, the value of financial assets held by married women averaged ¥0.99 million, and only 70.5% reported having some financial assets. This was a statistically significant difference.
16 In 2004 the Cabinet Office conducted a special opinion poll to help draft policy on the falling birthrate (Naikaku fu 2004). Some 71.9% of respondents said that 'influence on social security, such as pensions and medical costs' was particularly important.

17 The results are for the combined total for adult men and women, and the issue of whether or not respondents actually have children is not addressed. Multiple responses were allowed. The survey question was as follows: 'What do you think are the things making it tough to bring up children? Choose as many as you like from the following.'
18 For detailed data from these two surveys, see the Report on the Fifth Survey Regarding Financial Asset Choice Etc. in Household Budgets (Yūsei Kenkyū-jo 1996) and the Report on the Eighth Survey Regarding Financial Asset Choice Etc. in Household Budgets (Yūsei Sōgō Kenkyū-jo 2003).
19 One could more directly extrapolate the effect of childbirth and childrearing on household budgets if only one could include households with no children at all. However, this was not always possible with the data at my disposal and so I was obliged to adopt the approach used here.
20 The maximum effect on net financial assets of any explanatory variable is the cash amount of the explained variable and the explanatory variable, divided by 1,000. If we call that parameter β, then we can obtain the maximum effect by the formula $1,000 \times \beta$.
21 For the specific contents of the instrumental variable, see the notes on tables 6.3 and 6.4.

Chapter 7

1 Feldstein and Ranguelova (2001) argue that the introduction of Individual Retirement Accounts (IRAs) would be relatively unlikely to lead to lower pension payments compared with the traditional public pension system.
2 Takayama (2004) offers a detailed comparison between the Japanese public pension reform of 2004 and pension reforms in various other countries.
3 See Takayama (2004) for a detailed account of the Japanese public pension reform of 2004 and international comparative analysis.
4 I am talking here about employee pensions (*kōsei nenkin*). See Matsuura in Chapter 6 of the present volume for a discussion of this and the other two public pension systems, national pensions (*kokumin nenkin*) and mutual-aid pensions (*kyōsai nenkin*).
5 Diamond (1977) argues that it is difficult to offset the risk of longevity other than through the social security system.
6 The Swedish model of pensions based on notional defined contribution retains a pay-as-you-go system in which one generation's contributions pay for the previous generation's pensions. However, each individual's pension entitlement is limited to the amount s/he has contributed. The amount received by pensioners also varies with fluctuations in wage growth rate, economic growth rate and demographic variables such as size of labor force, average life expectancy, etc. In that sense the Swedish system is thought of as using the DC model. For a detailed explanation of the new Swedish system, see National Social Insurance Board in Sweden (2002).
7 Data for years up to and including 2000 comes from the *Kokusei Chōsa Hōkoku* (National Census Report) compiled by Sōmushō (the Ministry of Internal Affairs and Communications 2005).

8 Future estimates are taken from *Nihon no Shōrai Suikei Jinkō* (Future Population Projection for Japan) published by Kokuritsu Shakai Hoshō/ Jinkō Mondai Kenkyūjo (National Institute of Population and Social Security Research 2002a).
9 My data for interest on ten-year government bonds comes from the Bank of Japan's Financial and Economic Statistics (*Kin'yū Keizai Tōkei*), and the data on returns on investment in stocks on Section 1 of the TSE comes from the 'Stock Investment Returns' (*Kabushiki Tōshi Shū'eki-ritsu*) published by the Japan Securities Economic Research Institute (*Nihon Shōken Keizai Kenkyūjo* 2003).
10 See Matsuura and Shiraishi (2004) for a detailed empirical analysis of asset selection by Japanese households and corporations.
11 These estimates are taken from the lifespan tables in 'Future Population Estimates for Japan' (*Nihon Shōrai Suikei Jinkō*), published by Kokuritsu Shakai Hoshō/Jinkō Mondai Kenkyūjo (National Institute of Population and Social Security Research). I have used estimates made in January 2002.
12 Of course, if the retirement age is raised in pace with increases in average life expectancy, then longer life expectancy need not necessarily lead to a lengthening of the post-retirement period. As things stand in the real world today, however, actual retirement ages are not directly linked to mean life expectancy.
13 Oshio (2000) also carries out a simulation analysis of public pensions that accounts for uncertainty, but the risk of longevity is not accounted for in that model.
14 For example, if we are comparing an income replacement rate of 0.2 with one of 0.0, then the equivalent variable (*tōka henbun*) is the amount of money we would have to add to the 0.0 case in order to generate the same level of utility as the 0.2 case. The figure for equivalent variation can then be used to calculate welfare gain (*kōsei ritoku*).
15 In my earlier study (Miyazato 2010), I carried out a more complex simulation, using data based on the actual population profile of Japan. That also generated an optimal income-replacement rate of around 40%.

Bibliography

Abe, Aya and Akiko Ōishi. 2005. 'Boshi setai no keizai jōkyō to shakai hoshō' (Single-mother families and social security). In Kokuritsu Shakai Hoshō/Jinkō Mondai Kenkyūjo (National Institute of Population and Social Security Research) (ed.), *Kosodate Setai no Shakai Hoshō* (Social security for households raising children). Tokyo: University of Tokyo Press.

Acker, Joan. 1973. 'Women and social stratification: A case of intellectual sexism.' *American Journal of Sociology*, 78: 936–945.

Acker, Joan. 1980. 'Women and stratification: A review of recent literature.' *Contemporary Sociology*, 9(1): 25–35.

Asō, Makoto. 1991. *Nihon no Gakureki Erīto* (Japan's educational elite). Tokyo: Tamagawa University Press.

Asō, Yoshifumi and Hiroshi Yoshida. 1996. 'Sedai kaikei kara mita sedai-betsu no jueki to futan' (Generational benefits and burdens seen in terms of generational accounting). *Fainansharu Rebyū* (Financial review), 39: 1–31.

Campbell, David W. 2004. 'Explaining Japan's saving rate.' *Journal of Asian Economics*, 15: 41–58.

Cole, Robert. 1979. *Work, Mobility, and Participation: A Comparative Study of American and Japanese Industry*. Berkeley: University of California Press.

Cummings, William K. 1980. *Education and Equality in Japan*. Princeton: Princeton University Press.

Diamond, Peter. 1977. 'A framework for social security analysis.' *Journal of Public Economics*, 8(3): 275–298.

Dore, Ronald. 1973. *British Factory, Japanese Factory: The Origins of National Diversity in Industrial Relations*. Berkeley: University of California Press.

Dore, Ronald. 1976. *The Diploma Disease: Education, Qualification and Development*. Berkeley: University of California Press.

Erikson, Robert and John H. Goldthorpe. 1992. *The Constant Flux: A Study of Class Mobility in Industrial Nations*. Oxford: Clarendon Press.

Erikson, Robert, John H. Goldthorpe and Lucien Portocarero. 1979. 'Inter-generational class mobility in three Western European societies.' *British Journal of Sociology*, 30: 415–41.

Ezawa, Aya and Chisa Fujiwara. 2005. 'Lone mothers and welfare-to-work policies in Japan and the United States: Towards an alternative perspective.' *Journal of Sociology and Social Welfare*, XXXII(4): 41–63.

Feldstein, Martin and Elena Ranguelova. 2001. 'Individual risk in an investment-based social security system.' NBER Working Paper No. 8074.

Fujiwara, Chisa. 2003. 'Boshi katei no shūgyō jōkyō: Chōsa kekka kara erareru chiken' (Employment circumstances of single-mother households:

What we can learn from survey findings). *Nihon Rōdō Kenkyū Kikō Chōsa Kenkyū Hōkokusho, 'Boshi Katei no Haha e no Shūgyō Shien ni kan-suru Kenkyū'* (Japan Institute of Labor Survey Research Report, 'Research on employment support for mothers of single-parent families'), 177–211.

Galtung, Johan. 1971. 'Social structure, education structure and life long education: The case of Japan.' In OECD (eds.), *Reviews of National Policies for Education: Japan.* OECD.

Ganzeboom, Harry B.G., Ruud Luijkx and Donald Treiman. 1989. 'Intergenerational class mobility in comparative perspective.' *Research in Social Stratification and Mobility,* 8: 3–84.

Genda, Yūji. 1994. 'Kōgakureki-ka, chūkō nenrei-ka to chingin kōzō' (Higher levels of education, more middle-aged and elderly people and wage structures). In Tsuneo Ishikawa (ed.), *Nihon no Shotoku to Tomi no Bunpai* (Income and wealth distribution in Japan), 141–168. Tokyo: University of Tokyo Press.

Genda, Yūji. 2001. *Shigoto no Naka no Aimai-na Fuan* (That vague feeling of anxiety in the workplace). Tokyo: Chūō Kōron Shin-sha.

Genda, Yūji. 2002. 'Misugosareta shotoku kakusa: Jakunen sedai vs. intai sedai, ji'eigyō vs. koyōsha' (Overlooked income differentials: Young generation vs. retired generation, self-employed vs. employed). *Kikan Shakai Hoshō Kenkyū* (The quarterly of social security research), 38(3): 199–211.

Genda, Yūji. 2005. *A Nagging Sense of Job Insecurity: The New Reality Facing Japanese Youth.* Tokyo: International House of Japan.

Genda, Yūji. 2005. *Hataraku Kajō* (Over-commitment to work). Tokyo: NTT Publishing.

Genda, Yūji. 2006. 'Chūnen mugyō no jittai' (Social differential problems in middle-aged nonemployed). In Sawako Shirahase (ed.), *Henka suru Shakai no Fubyōdō* (Inequality in a changing society). Tokyo: University of Tokyo Press.

Genda, Yūji. 2007. 'Jobless youths and the NEET problem in Japan.' *Social Science Japan Journal,* 10(1): 23–40.

Genda, Yūji and Mie Maganuma. 2004. *Nīto: Furītā demo Naku, Shitsugyōsha demo Naku* (NEET: Neither freeters nor unemployed). Tokyo: Gentō-sha.

Genda, Yūji, Reiko Kosugi and the Japan Institute for Labor Policy and Training. 2005. *Kodomo ga Nīto ni Natta nara* (If your child becomes a NEET). Tokyo: NHK Publishing.

Goldthorpe, John H. 1983. 'Women and class analysis: In defense of the conventional view.' *Sociology,* 17(4): 465–488.

Goldthorpe, John H. 1984. 'Women and class analysis: A reply to the replies.' *Sociology,* 18(4): 491–499.

Hara, Junsuke and Kazuo Seiyama. 1999. *Shakai Kaisō: Yutakasa no Naka no Fubyōdō* (Social strata: Inequality amid prosperity). Tokyo: University of Tokyo Press.

Hara, Junsuke and Kazuo Seiyama. 2005. *Inequality amid Affluence.* Melbourne: Trans Pacific Press.

Hashimoto, Kyōji and Kōji Yamaguchi. 2005. 'Kōteki nenkin no shimyurēshon bunseki: Setai ruikei-betsu no eikyō' (Simulation analysis of public pensions: The effect of public pensions by different household types). PRIDP 4: A–27.

Hatta, Tatsuo and Noriyoshi Oguchi. 1999. *Nenkin Kaikaku-ron: Tsumitate Hōshiki e Ikō Seyo* (Pension reform theory: Shift to an accumulation model). Tokyo: Nihon Keizai Shinbun-sha.
Higuchi, Yoshio. 1991. *Nihon Keizai to Shūgyō Kōdō* (The Japanese economy and employment activities). Tokyo: Tōyō Keizai Shinpōsha.
Higuchi, Yoshio. 2004. 'Defure ga kaeta josei no sentaku' (How deflation has changed women's choices). In Yoshio Higuchi, Kiyoshi Ohta and Kakei Keizai Kenkyūjo (The Institute for Research on Household Economics) (eds.), *Joseitachi no Heisei Fukyō* (Women in the Heisei recession), 9–28. Tokyo: Nihon Keizai Shinbun-sha.
Inoki, Takenori. 2003. 'Naze shotoku kakusa ga mondai ka? Kongo no risāchi no hōkō ni tsuite no shiron' (Why are income differentials a problem? Notes on the direction of future research). In Yoshio Higuchi and Zaimushō Zaimu Sōgō Seisaku Kenkyūjo (Ministry of Finance, Policy Research Institute), *Nihon no Shotoku Kakusa to Shakai Kaisō* (Japan's income differentials and social stratification), 245–263. Tokyo: Nihon Hyōron-sha.
Ishida, Hiroshi. 1993. *Social Mobility in Contemporary Japan: Educational Credentials, Class and the Labour Market in a Cross-National Perspective*. Stanford: Stanford University Press.
Ishida, Hiroshi. 2000. 'Sangyō shakai no naka no Nihon' (Japan among industrial societies). In Junsuke Hara (ed.), *Nihon no Kaisō Shisutemu 1: Kindaika to Shakai Kaisō* (Japan's stratification system, volume 1: Modernization and social stratification), 219–248. Tokyo: University of Tokyo Press.
Ishida, Hiroshi. 2002. 'Shakai idō kara mita kakusa no jittai' (The reality of differentials seen from social transition). In Hiroshi Miyajima and Rengō Sōgō Seikatsu Kaihatsu Kenkyūjo (Research Institute for the Advancement of Living Standards) (eds.), *Nihon no Shotoku Bunpai to Kakusa* (Income distribution and differentials in Japan), 65–98. Tokyo: Tōyō Keizai Shinpō-sha.
Ishida, Hiroshi. 2003. 'Shakai ido kara mita kakusa no jittai' (The degree of inequality based on trends in social mobility). In Yoshio Higuchi and Zaimushō Zaimu Sōgō Seisaku Kenkyūjo (Ministry of Finance, Policy Research Institute), *Nihon no Shotoku Kakusa to Shakai Kaisō* (Japan's income differentials and social stratification), 65–98. Tokyo: Nihon Hyōron-sha.
Ishida, Hiroshi. 2004. 'Socio-economic differentials in health in Japan.' Paper presented at the meeting of the International Sociological Association's Research Committee on Social Stratification (RC28), August 7–9, Rio de Janeiro.
Ishida, Hiroshi. 2009. 'Social inequality in health in Japan.' Panel Survey Project Discussion Paper Series No.27, Institute of Social Science, University of Tokyo.
Ishikawa, Tsuneo. 1991. *Shotoku to Tomi* (Income and wealth). Tokyo: Iwanami Shoten.
Iwamoto, Yasushi. 2000. 'Raifusaikuru kara mita fubyōdō-do' (Degrees of inequality seen in terms of the life-cycle). In Kokuritsu Shakai Hoshō/Jinkō Mondai Kenkyūjo (National Institute of Population and Social Security Research) (ed.), *Kazoku/Setai no Hen'yō to Seikatsu Hoshō Kinō* (Changes in families and households and livelihood security functions), 75–94. Tokyo: University of Tokyo Press.

Iwata, Masami. 2004. 'Defure fukyō-ka no "hinkon no keiken"' ('Experience of poverty' in the deflationary recession). In Yoshio Higuchi, Kiyoshi Ohta and Kakei Keizai Kenkyūjo (The Institute for Research on Household Economics) (eds.), *Joseitachi no Heisei Fukyō* (Women in the Heisei recession), 203–233. Tokyo: Nihon Keizai Shinbun-sha.

Kariya, Takehiko. 1995. *Taishū Kyō'iku Shakai no Yukue: Gakurekishugi to Byōdō Shinwa no Sengo-shi* (The direction of the mass education society: A postwar history of credentialism and the myth of equality). Tokyo: Chūō Kōron-sha.

Kariya, Takehiko. 2001. *Kaisōka Nihon to Kyō'iku Kiki: Fubyōdō Saiseisan Kara Iyoku Kakusa Shakai e* (Stratifying Japan and the educational crisis: From reproduction of inequality toward a society of differentials in aspiration). Tokyo: Yūshindō Kōbun-sha.

Kariya, Takehiko and Kōkichi Shimizu. 2004. *Gakuryoku no Shakaigaku: Chōsa ga Shimesu Gakuryoku no Henka to Gakushū no Kadai* (A sociology of academic ability: Changes in academic ability and issues in learning, as revealed by surveys). Tokyo: Iwanami Shoten.

Katase, Kazuo. 2008a. 'Gakureki kaiso to kenkō risuku kanren kōdō' (Education and health-risk-related behavior). In Takeshi Sugano (ed.), *Kaisō to Seikatsu Kakusa* (Social stratification and disparities in quality of life), 29–41. Sendai: The 2005 SSM Research Committee.

Katase, Kazuo. 2008b. 'Jyakunen rōdōsha no desutoresu' (Distress of young workers). In Takeshi Sugano (ed.), *Kaisō to Seikatsu Kakusa* (Social stratification and disparities in quality of life), 43–57. Sendai: The 2005 SSM Research Committee.

Katase, Kazuo. 2008c. 'Shigoto no jyōken to shokugyōsei sutoresu' (Work conditions and occupational stress). In Takeshi Sugano (ed.), *Kaisō to Seikatsu Kakusa* (Social statification and disparities in quality of life), 79–92. Sendai: The 2005 SSM Research Committee.

Kawachi, Ichiro and Bruce Kennedy. 2002. *The Health of Nations*. New York: New Press.

Kawakami, Norito, Yasuki Kobayashi and Hideki Hashimoto (eds.). 2006. *Shakai Kaisō to Kenkō* (Social disparity and health). Tokyo: University of Tokyo Press. English version published in 2009 as *Health and Social Disparity: Japan and Beyond*. Melbourne: Trans Pacific Press.

Kenkō/Eiyō Jōhō Kenkyūkai. 2004. *Kokumin Eiyō no Genjyō* (The present state of nutrition: The results of the 2002 national nutrition survey). Tokyo: Daiichi Hōki.

Kikkawa, Tōru. 2006. *Gakureki to Kakusa, Fubyōdō: Seijuku suru Nihon-gata Gakureki Shakai* (Academic credentials and differentials/inequality: The maturing Japanese-style credentialist society). Tokyo: University of Tokyo Press.

Kojima, Katsuhisa. 2003. 'Kōreisha no kenkō jyōtai to shotoku kakusa' (Health conditions and income gaps among the elderly). *Jinkōgaku Kenkyū* (The Journal of Population Studies), 33: 85–95.

Kokumin Kenkō Hoken Chūōkai (All-Japan Federation of National Health Insurance Organizations). 2002. *Kokumin Kenkō Hokenryō (zei) Shūnōritsu Kōjō Notameno Teigen* (Proposal for increasing payment of insurance premiums). Tokyo: Kokumin Kenkō Hoken Chūōkai.

Kokuritsu Shakai Hoshō/Jinkō Mondai Kenkyūjo (National Institute of Population and Social Security Research). 2002a. *Nihon no Shōrai Suikei Jinkō* (Population Projection for Japan), estimates for January 2002.
Kokuritsu Shakai Hoshō/Jinkō Mondai Kenkyūjo (National Institute of Population and Social Security Research). 2002b. *Josei to Nenkin* (Women and pensions). Tokyo: University of Tokyo Press.
Kokuritsu Shakai Hoshō/Jinkō Mondai Kenkyūjo (National Institute of Population and Social Security Research) (ed.). 2005. *Jinkō Tōkei Shiryōshū 2005* (Latest Demographic Statistics, 2005).
Kondō, Katsunori. 2005. *Kenkō Kakusa Shakai* (Health unequal society). Tokyo: Igaku Shoin. English version published in 2010 as *Health Inequalities in Japan: An Empirial Study of Older People*. Melbourne: Trans Pacific Press.
Konishi, Hideki. 2002. 'Shotoku kakusa to Jini keisū' (Income differentials and Gini coefficients). In Hiroshi Miyajima and Rengō Sōgō Seikatsu Kaihatsu Kenkyūjo (Research Institute for the Advancement of Living Standards) (eds.), *Nihon no Shotoku Bunpai to Kakusa* (Income distribution and differentials in Japan), 209–240. Tokyo: Tōyō Keizai Shinpō-sha.
Kōsaka, Kenji (ed.). 1995. *Social Stratification in Contemporary Japan*. London: Kegan Paul International.
Kōsei Tōkei Kyōkai (Health, Labor and Welfare Statistics Association). 2000. *Jinkō no Dōkō: Nihon to Sekai: Jinkō Tōkei Shiryō 2000* (Population trends: Japan and the world; statistical resources for 2000). Tokyo: Kōsei Tōkei Kyōkai.
Kōsei Rōdō Shō (Ministry of Health, Labor and Welfare). 2004. *2002-nen Hoken Fukushi Dōkō Chōsa* (2002 Survey on Trends in Healthcare and Welfare).
Kōsei Rōdō Shō (Ministry of Health, Labor and Welfare). 2005. *2004-nen Kokumin Seikatsu Kiso Chōsa* (The MHLW 2004 Comprehensive Survey of People's Living Conditions).
Kosugi, Reiko. 2003. *Furītā to iu Ikikata* (The freeter way of life). Tokyo: Keisō Shobō.
Kotolikoff, Laurence J. 1988. 'Intergenerational transfers and savings.' *Journal of Economic Perspectives*, 2: 41–58.
Kotolikoff, Laurence J. and Lawrence H. Summers. 1981. 'The role of intergenerational transfers in aggregate capital accumulation.' *Journal of Political Economy*, 89: 706–732.
Kunieda, Shigeki. 2002. 'Sōzokuzei/zōyozei no riron' (A theory of inheritance tax and gift tax). *Fainansharu Rebyū* (Financial review), 95: 108–125.
Kyō'iku Seido Kentō I'inkai (Committee to re-examine the education system). 1974. *Nihon no Kyō'iku Kaikaku o Motomete* (Calling for educational reform in Japan). Tokyo: Keisō Shobō.
Lee, Yean-Ju, Yasuhiko Saito and Yi-Li Chuang. 2005. 'Gender, lifetime socioeconomic environments, and health among the elderly: The cases of Taiwan and Japan.' *Population and Society*, 1(1): 99–125.
Luhmann, Niklas. 1973. *Zweckbegriff und Systemrationalität* (The concept of purpose and system rationality). Frankfurt: Suhrkamp Insel.
Marmot, Michael G. and George D. Smith. 1989. 'Why are Japanese living longer?' *British Medical Journal*, 299: 23–30.
Matsuura, Katsumi. 2002. 'Nihon ni okeru bunpai mondai no gaikan' (An over-

view of the distribution problem in Japan). In Hiroshi Miyajima and Rengō Sōgō Seikatsu Kaihatsu Kenkyūjo (Research Institute for the Advancement of Living Standards) (eds.), *Nihon no Shotoku Bunpai to Kakusa* (Japan's income distribution and differentials), 25–48. Tokyo: Tōyō Keizai Shinpō-sha.

Matsuura, Katsumi and Sawako Shirahase. 2002. 'Kikon josei no shūgyō kettei to kosodate' (Employment decisions and child-rearing by married women). *Kikan Shakai Hoshō Kenkyū* (The quarterly of social security research), 38(3): 188–198.

Matsuura, Katsumi and Sayuri Shiraishi. 2004. *Shisan Sentaku to Nihon Keizai* (Asset selection and the Japanese economy). Tokyo: Tōyō Keizai Shinpō-sha.

Matsuura, Katsumi and Toshiaki Tachibanaki. 1993. 'Nihon no shisan no fubyōdō no yō'in bunseki: Tochi hoyū no ari-nashi ni yoru futatsu no kaisō bunka' (Analyzing the causes of asset inequality in Japan: Division into two status groups according to ownership/non-ownership of land). Yūsei Kenkyūjo (Postal Services Institute), Discussion Paper, 1993–23.

Matsuura, Katsumi and Yukiko Shigeno. 1996. *Josei no Shūgyō to Tomi no Bunpai* (Women's employment and the distribution of wealth). Tokyo: Nihon Hyōron-sha.

Matsuura, Katsumi and Yukiko Shigeno. 2000. 'The cost of marriage: Inhibiting factors.' *Yokohama Shiritsu Daigaku Ronsō* (Bulletin of Yokohama City University), 53(1): 95–125.

Matsuura, Katsumi and Yukiko Shigeno. 2005. 'Daitoshi-ken ni okeru ikuji to josei no shūgyō' (Child-rearing and women's employment in metropolitan areas). *Kaikei Kensa Kenkyū* (Accounting and auditing research), 32: 181–213.

Miura, Atsushi. 2005. *Karyū Shakai: Arata-na Kaisō Shūdan no Shutsugen* (Lower-class society: The emergence of a new status group). Tokyo: Kōbun-sha.

Miyazato, Naomi. 2010. 'The optimal size of Japan's public pensions: An analysis considering the risks of longevity and volatility of return on assets.' *Japan and the World Economy*, 22(1): 31–39.

Modigliani, Franco. 1988. 'The role of intergenerational transfers and life cycle saving in the accumulation of wealth.' *Journal of Economic Perspectives*, 2: 15–40.

Monbukagakushō Shōgai Gakushū Seisaku-kyoku (Ministry of Education, Culture, Sports, Science and Technology, Lifetime Learning Policy Bureau). 2004. *Monbu Kagaku Tōkei Yōran* (Statistical abstract of education and science).

Monbushō (Ministry of Education). 1969. *Wagakuni no Kyō'iku no Ayumi to Kongo no Kadai* (A history of Japanese education and the challenges ahead). Tokyo: Ōkurasho Insatsukyoku.

Monbushō Chūō Kyō'iku Shingikai (Ministry of Education, Central Education Council). 1996. '21-seiki o tenbō shita wagakuni no kyōiku no arikata ni tsuite' (On the state of Japan's education, with a view to the 21st century). First report, http://www.mext.go.jp/b_menu/shingi/12/chuuou/toushin/960701.htm.

Monbushō Chūō Kyō'iku Shingikai (Ministry of Education, Central Education Council). 1997. '21-seiki o tenbō shita wagakuni no kyōiku no arikata ni tsuite' (On the state of Japan's education, with a view to the 21st cen-

tury). Second report, http://www.mext.go.jp/b_menu/shingi/12/chuuou/toushin/970606.htm.
Morgan, Edmund. 1965. *Visible Saints: The History of a Puritan Idea*. New York: Cornell University Press.
Morgan, Edmund. 1966. *The Puritan Family: Religion and Domestic Relations in Seventeenth-Century New England*. New York: Harper & Row.
Murakami, Yasusuke. 1977. 'Shin-chūkan kaikyūsō no genjitsusei' (The reality of the new middle class). *Asahi Shinbun*, May 20.
Murakami, Yasusuke. 1984. *Shin-Chūkan Taishū no Jidai: Sengo Nihon no Kaibōgaku* (The era of the new middle-class masses: An anatomy of postwar Japan). Tokyo: Chūō Kōron-sha.
Nagase, Nobuko. 1997. 'Josei no shūgyō sentaku' (Women's employment choices). In Hiroyuki Chūma and Terukazu Suruga (eds.), *Koyō Kankō no Henka to Josei Rōdō* (Changes in employment practices and female labor), 279–312. Tokyo: University of Tokyo Press.
Nagase, Nobuko. 2003. 'Boshi setai no haha no kyaria keisei, sono kanōsei' (Career formation for single mothers: The possibilities). In *Nihon Rōdō Kenkyū Kikō Chōsa Kenkyū Hōkokusho, 'Boshi Katei no Haha e no Shugyō Shien ni kan-suru Kenkyū'* (Japan Institute of Labor Survey Research Report, 'Research on employment support for mothers of single-parent families'), 239–289.
Naikakufu (Cabinet Office, Government of Japan). 2004. *Shōshika Taisaku ni kan-suru Tokubetsu Yoron Chōsa* (Special survey of attitudes towards policies related to declining birthrates).
Nakata, Tomoo. 1999. 'Shakaikaisō, kenkō, karei' (Social stratification, health and aging). *Hokusei Ronshū*, 36: 15–46.
Nakata, Tomoo. 2001. 'Kenkō akka no purosesu to shakai kaisō' (The process of health deterioration and social stratification). *Hokusei Ronshū*, 38: 1–10.
National Social Insurance Board in Sweden. 2002. *The Swedish Pension System: Annual Report 2001*.
NHK Hōsō Bunka Kenkyūjo (NHK Broadcasting Culture Research Institute). 1973–2000. *Gendai Nihonjin no Ishiki Kōzō* (The structure of Japanese attitudes today), 2nd–5th editions. Tokyo: Nihon Hōsō Shuppan Kyoukai.
Nihon Kyōshoku'in Kumiai (Japan Teachers Union). 1952–1964. *Nihon no Kyō'iku* (Education in Japan), volumes 1–13. Tokyo: Kokudo-sha.
Nihon Shōken Keizai Kenkyūjo (Japan Securities Economic Research Institute). 2003. *Kabushiki Tōshi Shū'eki-ritsu* (Stock investment returns).
Nippon Ginkō (Bank of Japan). 2004. *Kin'yū Keizai Tōkei* (Financial and economic statistics).
Nitta, Michio. 2003. 'Mondai no shozai to hon-chōsa kenkyū no igi' (Location of the problem and the significance of this research). In *Nihon Rōdō Kenkyū Kikō Chōsa Kenkyū Hōkokusho, 'Boshi Katei no Haha e no Shūgyō Shien ni kan-suru Kenkyū'* (Japan Institute of Labor Survey Research Report, 'Research on employment support for mothers of single-parent families'), 10–21.
Ohta, Kiyoshi. 2005. 'Nihon no Keizai Kakusa wa Hirogatte-iru ka?' (Are Japan's economic differentials widening?). *Keizai Seminā* (Economics seminar), 607: 14–17.
Ohtake, Fumio. 1994. '1980-nendai no shotoku/shisan bunpai' (Income and

asset distribution in the 1980s). *Kikan Riron Keizaigaku* (The economic studies quarterly), 45(5): 385–402.

Ohtake, Fumio. 2005. *Nihon no Fubyōdō: Kakusa Shakai no Gensō to Mirai* (Inequality in Japan: The fantasy and future of a differential society). Tokyo: Nihon Keizai Shinbun-sha.

Ohtake, Fumio and Makoto Saitō. 1999. 'Shotoku fubyōdōka no haikei to sono seisakuteki gan'i: Nenrei kaisō-nai kōka, nenrei kaisō-kan kōka, jinkō kōreika kōka' (The background to widening income inequality and its policy implications: Effects within and between age groups, and the effect of population aging). *Kikan Shakai Hoshō Kenkyū* (The quarterly of social security research), 35(1): 65–76.

Ōi, Masako and Katsumi Matsuura. 2003. 'Josei no shūgyō sentaku ni eikyō suru mono to shinai mono' (Things that do and do not influence women's employment choices). *Kaikei Kensa Kenkyū* (Accounting and auditing research), 27: 213–226.

Ōkouchi, Kazuo, Bernard Karsh and Solomon B. Levine (eds.). 1973. *Workers and Employment in Japan: The Japanese Employment Relations System*. Tokyo: University of Tokyo Press.

Ōsawa, Machiko. 1993. *Keizai Henka to Joshi Rōdō* (Economic change and women's labor). Tokyo: Nihon Keizai Hyōron-sha.

Ōsawa, Mari. 2002. *Danjo Kyōdō Sankaku Shakai o Tsukuru* (Creating a gender-free society). Tokyo: NHK Books.

Oshio, Takashi. 2000. 'Fukakujitusei to kōteki nenkin no saiteki kibo' (Uncertainty and the optimum scale of public pensions). *Keizai Kenkyū* (Economic review), 51(4): 311–320.

Page, Benjamin R. 2003. 'Testing for a bequest motive using cross-state variation in bequest taxes.' *Congressional Budget Office Technical Paper Series*, 2003–1.

Peterson, Mark A. 1997. *The Price of Redemption: The Spiritual Economy of Puritan New England*. Stanford: Stanford University Press.

Radloff, Lenore S. 1977. 'The CES-D scale: A self-report depression scale for research in the general population.' *Applied Psychological Measurement*, 1: 385–401.

Robert, Stephanie A. and James S. House. 2000. 'Socioeconomic inequalities in health: Integrating individual-, community-, and societal-level theory and research.' In Gary L. Albrecht, Ray Fitzpatrick and Susan C. Scrimshaw (ed.), *The Handbook of Social Studies in Health and Medicine*, 115–135. London: Sage Publications.

Saitō, Osamu. 1996. 'Population.' In Shunsaku Nishikawa, Kōnosuke Odaka and Osamu Saitō (eds.), *Nihon Keizai no Ni-hyaku Nen* (Two hundred years of the Japanese economy). Tokyo: Nihon Hyōron-sha.

Sakai, Junko. 2003. *Make'inu no Tōboe* (The distant howling of beaten dogs). Tokyo: Kodan-sha.

Satō, Toshiki. 1998. 'Kindai o kataru shisen to buntai' (The gaze and literary style that speaks of modernity). In Kenji Kōsaka and Yōsuke Kōtō (eds.), *Kōza Shakaigaku 1: Riron to Hōhō* (A course in sociology, volume 1: Theory and method). Tokyo: University of Tokyo Press.

Satō, Toshiki. 2000a. *Fubyōdō Shakai Nihon: Sayonara Sōchūryū* (Japan as an unequal society: Farewell to the mass middle class). Tokyo: Chūō Kōron Shin-sha.

Satō, Toshiki. 2000b. 'Sore demo susumu: Fubyōdō shakai' (Even so it continues: The unequal society). In Chūō Kōron (ed.), *Ronsō: Chūryū Hōkai* (Debate: The collapse of the middle class). Tokyo: Chūō Kōron Shin-sha.

Satō, Toshiki. 2001. *Kikai no Byōdō Shakai e no Michi: Byōdō Genri no Tenkan ga Imi Suru Koto* (The road to a society of equal opportunity: What the change in the equality principle means). *Hōshakaigaku* (Legal sociology), 55: 7–21.

Satō, Toshiki. 2003. 'Fubyōdō shakai no yukue to kyōdō no ronri: "Jakusha" kara "haisha" e' (The direction of the unequal society and the logic of community: From 'the weak' to 'the losers'). *Seikatsu Kei'ei-gaku Kenkyū* (Journal of family resource management of Japan), 38: 3–7.

Satō, Toshiki. 2005a. '"Kachi-make" no yokubō ni toritsukareta Nihon' (Japan possessed by the desire for 'winners and losers'). *Ronza*, 121: 87–93.

Satō, Toshiki. 2005b. 'Jakunensō to "me de mieru" Kakusa' (The younger age group and 'visible' differentials). *Keizai Seminā* (Economics seminar), 607: 28–31.

Sawyer, Malcolm. 1976. 'Income distribution in OECD countries.' *OECD*.

Seike, Atsushi and Atsuhiro Yamada. 2004. *Kōreisha Shūgyō no Keizaigaku* (The economics of elderly employment). Tokyo: Nihon Keizai Shinbun-sha.

Seiyama, Kazuo. 1994. 'Intergenerational occupational mobility.' In Kenji Kōsaka (ed.), *Social Stratification in Contemporary Japan*. London: Kegan Paul International.

Seiyama, Kazuo. 2000. 'Kaisō saiseisan no shinwa' (The myths of status reproduction). In Yoshio Higuchi and Zaimushō Zaimu Sōgō Seisaku Kenkyūjo (Ministry of Finance, Policy Research Institute), *Nihon no Shotoku Kakusa to Shakai Kaisō* (Japan's income differentials and social stratification), 85–103. Tokyo: Nihon Hyōron-sha.

Shakai Hoken Kenkyūjo (Social Insurance Research Institute). 2002. *Josei to Nenkin* (Women and pensions).

Shakai Hoshō Kenkyūjo (Social Security Research) (ed.). 2005b. *Kosodate Setai no Shakai Hoshō* (Social security for households raising children). Tokyo: University of Tokyo Press.

Shibuya, Kenji, Hideki Hashimoto and Eiji Yano. 2002. 'Individual income, income distribution, and self rated health in Japan: Cross sectional analysis of nationally representative sample.' *British Medical Journal*, 324: 1–5.

Shimoebisu, Miyuki. 1993. 'Boshi katei e no shakaiteki shien' (Social support for single mothers). In Kokuritsu Shakai Hoshō/Jinkō Mondai Kenkyūjo (National Institute of Population and Social Security Research) (ed.), *Josei to Shakai Hoshō* (Women and social security), 247–266. Tokyo: University of Tokyo Press.

Shinbori, Michiya (ed.). 1967. *Gakureki Ishiki ni kan-suru Chōsa Kenkyū* (Survey research on awareness of academic credentials). Hiroshima: Hiroshima University.

Shinotsuka, Eiko. 1982. *Nihon no Joshi Rōdō* (Female labor in Japan). Tokyo: Tōyō Keizai Shinpō-sha.

Shinotsuka, Eiko. 1992. 'Boshi setai no hinkon o meguru mondai' (Problems concerning poverty among single-mother households). *Nihon Keizai Kenkyū* (Japan Economic Review), 22: 77–118.

Shirahase, Sawako. 2002. 'Nihon no shotoku kakusa to kōreisha setai: Kokusai hikaku no kanten kara' (Income inequalities and elderly households in Japan: From an international comparative perspective). *Nihon Rōdō Kenkyū Zasshi* (Japanese Journal of Labor Studies), 500: 72–85.

Shirahase, Sawako. 2004. 'Shakai kaisō to setai/kojin: "Kojinka" ron no kenshō' (The household and the individual in social stratification: Examining the argument of individualization). *Shakaigaku Hyōron* (Japan Sociological Review), 54(4): 370–385.

Shirahase, Sawako. 2005a. 'Seifu e no kitai to jendā kōzō: Seifu e no sekinin kitai, katei-nai seibetsu yakuwari bungyō-kan to hitori-oya setai ni chakumoku shite' (Expectations of government and gender structure: Focusing on expectations of government responsibility, gender role division within the household and single-parent families). In *Kōsei Rōdō Kagaku Kenkyū Kenkyū-hi Hojokin Seisaku Kagaku Suishin Kenkyū Jigyō 'Kazoku Kōzō ya Shūrō Keitai Nado no Henka ni Taiō Shita Shakai Hoshō no Arikata ni kan-suru Sōgōteki Kenkyū'* (Health and Labor Science Research Grant, Final Report: Comprehensive study on how social security should respond to changes in household type, styles of employment, etc.), 287–311.

Shirahase, Sawako. 2005b. *Shōshikōrei Shakai no Mienai Kakusa: Jendaa/Sedai/Kaisō no Yukue* (The unseen gaps in an aging society: Locating gender, generation and class in Japan). Tokyo: University of Tokyo Press.

Shirahase, Sawako. 2005c. 'Kōrei shakai ni miru kakusa: Kōreisō ni okeru shotoku kakusa to shien nettowāku ni chakumoku shite' (Socioeconomic inequality in the aging society: Inequality in income and support networks among the elderly). *Shakaigaku Hyōron* (Japan sociological review), 56(1): 74–92.

Shirahase, Sawako. 2006. 'Kōreiki o hitori de kurasu to iu koto: Kore kara no shakai hoshō seido o saguru' (Living alone in old age: Looking for a new social security system). *Kikan Shakai Hoshō Kenkyū* (The quarterly of social security research), 41(2): 111–121.

Shirahase, Sawako and Toshiko Takeuchi. 2009. 'Jinkō kōreika to keizai-kakusa kakudai saikō' (Ageing population and increase in the degree of income inequality, reconsidered). *Shakaigaku Hyoron* (Japan sociological review), 60(2): 259–277.

Sōmushō (Ministry of Internal Affairs and Communications). 2005. *Kokusei Chōsa Hōkoku* (Japan census report).

Sōmushō Tōkeikyoku (Ministry of Internal Affairs and Communications, Bureau of Statistics). 2005. *Rōdōryoku Chōsa Hōkokusho* (Labor force survey report).

SSM 1995 Research Group. 1997. *The report of basic calculation.*

Stevenson, Harold W. and James W. Stigler. 1992. *The Learning Gap: Why Our Schools are Failing and What We Can Learn from Japanese and Chinese Education.* New York: Summit Books.

Suthers, Kristen, Yasuhiko Saito and Eileen Crimmens. 2003. 'Emotional well-being among older persons: A comparative analysis of the 70+ population in Japan and the United States.' In M. Joseph Sirgy, Don Rahtz and A. Coskun Samli (ed.), *Advances in Quality-of-Life Theory and Research*, 41–50. Dordrecht: Kluwer Academic Publishers.

Tachibanaki, Toshiaki. 1998. *Nihon no Keizai Kakusa* (Japan's economic differentials). Tokyo: Iwanami Shoten.

Tachibanaki, Toshiaki and Seiji Takada. 1994. 'Bequest and asset distribution:

Human capital investment and intergenerational wealth transfer.' In Toshiaki Tachibanaki (ed.), *Savings and Bequests*, 197–229. Ann Arbor: University of Michigan Press.

Tajika, Eiji, Yoshihiro Kaneko and Fumiko Hayashi. 1996. *Nenkin no Keizai Bunseki: Hoken Shiten* (Economic analysis of pensions: An insurance perspective). Tokyo: Tōyō Keizai Shinpō-sha.

Takayama, Noriyuki. 2004. *Shinrai to Anshin no Nenkin Kaikaku* (Pension reform with trust and peace of mind). Tokyo: Tōyō Keizai Shinpō-sha.

Takeuchi, Yō. 1995. *Nihon no Meritokurashī* (Japan's meritocracy). Tokyo: University of Tokyo Press.

Takeuchi, Yō. 1999. *Gakureki Kizoku no Eikō to Zasetsu* (The glories and mishaps of the Japanese academic aristocracy). Tokyo: Chūō Kōron Shin-sha.

Tateiwa, Shinya. 2004. *Jiyū no Byōdō* (Equality of freedom). Tokyo: Iwanami Shoten.

Townsend, Peter and Nick Davidson. 1982. *Inequalities in Health*. New York: Penguin Books.

Tsumura, Atsuko. 2002. 'Kazoku seisaku no kokusai hikaku' (International comparison of family policies). In Kokuritsu Shakai Hoshō/Jinkō Mondai Kenkyūjo (National Institute of Population and Social Security Research) (ed.), *Shōshi Shakai no Kosodate Shien* (Support for child-rearing in a society with a low birthrate), 19–46. Tokyo: University of Tokyo Press.

Tsutsumi, Akizumi. 2006. 'Shokugyō kaisō to kenkō' (Occupational strata and health). In Norito Kawakami, Yasuki Kobayashi and Hideki Hashimoto (ed.), *Shakai Kaisō to Kenkō* (Social disparity and health), 81–101. Tokyo: University of Tokyo Press.

Tsutsumi, Akizumi, K. Kayaba, K. Tsutsumi and M. Igarashi. 2001. 'Association between job strain and prevalence of hypertension: A cross-sectional analysis in a Japanese working population with a wide range of occupations.' *Occupational and Environmental Medicine*, 58: 367–373.

Umino, Michio. 2000. 'Yutakasa no tsuikyū kara kōhei shakai no kikyū e' (From seeking affluence to hoping for a just society). In Michio Umino (ed.), *Nihon no Kaisō Shisutemu 2: Kōheikan to Seiji Ishiki* (Social stratification system in Japan 2: A sense of fairness and political consciousness). Tokyo: University of Tokyo Press.

Vogel, Ezra. 1979. *Japan as Number One: Lessons for America*. Cambridge: Harvard University Press.

Working Group on Inequalities in Health. 1980. *Inequalities in Health: Report of a Research Working Group*. London: Department of Health and Social Security.

World Health Organization. 2002. *World Health Report 2001*. World Health Organization.

World Health Organization. 2004. *Core Health Indicators 2004*. World Health Organization.

Yamada, Masahiro. 2004. *Kibō Kakusa Shakai* (Disparity in hope). Tokyo: Chikuba Shōbō.

Yamazaki, Yosihiko (ed.). 1989. *Toshi-ka to Jumyō no Kankei ni kan-suru Kenkyū: Tokyo-to to Osaka-fu no Hikaku o Chūshin ni* (A study on the relationship between urbanization and longevity: A comparison of Tokyo and Osaka). Tokyo: Chiiki Shakai Kenkyū-sho.

Yashiro, Naohiro. 1983. *Josei Rōdō no Keizai Bunseki* (Economic analysis of female labor). Tokyo: Nihon Keizai Shinbun-sha.

Yashiro, Naohiro. 1999. *Shōshi-Kōreika no Keizaigaku: Shijō Jūshi no Kōzō Kaikaku* (The economics of the falling birthrate and aging society: Market-oriented structural reform). Tokyo: Tōyō Keizai Shinpō-sha.

Yūsei Kenkyū-jo (Japan Post Research Institute). 1996. *Dai 5-kai Kakei to Chochiku ni kan-suru Chōsa* (The Fifth Survey on Household Economy and Savings).

Yūsei Sōgō Kenkyū-jo (Japan Post Research Institute). 2003. *Dai 8-kai Kakei to Chochiku ni kan-suru Chōsa* (The Eighth Survey on Household Economy and Savings).

Index

1.57 shock 3, 46

access to medical information 130–1, 134, 142–7, 149
aging population 6, 14, 48–9, 53, 57–8, 74, 181, 183, 193
aging society 1, 4–5, 9–12, 14–15, 73–5, 125, 152, 180, 187, 190, 195, 199, 203–4, 206, 210, 213–4
aging/low birthrate society *see* low birthrate/aging society
alcohol consumption 145
all middle-class society 1
average lifespan 125, 127
awareness of health issues 126

baby-boom generation 66, 217–8
birthrate 1, 3–4, 6, 9–12, 15, 32, 53, 55, 58, 73–5, 117, 125, 152,–3, 158, 160, 180–1, 183, 186–7, 190, 193, 195, 199–200, 203–4, 206, 210, 212, 214, 217, 221
 low 1, 4, 9, 74–5, 152
Black Report 126
Bridging the Gap 77

childbirth 46, 151–5, 159–61, 168, 174–5, 179–80, 205–6, 211, 221–2
 and childrearing 46, 151–4, 159, 161, 174, 180, 211, 222

childrearing 6, 14, 23, 35, 46, 151–5, 159–61, 169, 174, 179–80, 211–12, 218, 222
 see also childbirth
chronic medical conditions 130–1, 133, 135–6, 138, 140–1, 143, 145, 147–8, 150

defined benefit pension system 182–3, 185–91, 193–200
 see also pension system
defined contribution pension system 182–3, 185–8, 191–200 *see also* pension system
depression 84, 127, 131–2, 134, 140–2, 146–50, 211, 219
differentials and inequality 6, 8, 208
differentials in consumption levels 163
diploma disease 99, 116
discrimination 13, 33, 40, 100–2, 104–6, 109, 113–14, 116, 122–4, 159, 180, 219
discriminatory education 102, 104, 106, 108–9
distributive principle 6, 8, 9
drinking 127, 130–1, 133–4, 143–6, 149

economic burden of raising children 161 *see also* childrearing

Index 237

educational attainment 51, 87–9, 93, 96, 123, 130
egalitarianism 13, 98–9, 108–10, 208–9
employment 11, 13, 18, 40, 49–52, 60, 62, 69, 76–9, 82, 84–5, 89, 92–3, 97, 103, 110, 126, 132, 153, 157, 159, 180–1, 184, 189, 200–1, 205–7, 220
enrollment/non-enrollment in a pension program 154 *see also* pension system
equal educational opportunity 209
equality of opportunity 18–19, 21–2, 24–6, 28–9, 32, 35–6, 38, 40, 42–5, 99, 102, 152, 179, 205, 207, 210, 212, 216, 220
equality 1, 3, 17, 20–2, 24–9, 31–2, 35, 37–8, 40, 42, 44–5, 48, 99, 102, 108, 123–4, 163, 205, 207, 210–11, 217
erasure of inequality consciousness 19–20, 36 *see also* inequality consciousness
expectations of negative return 158
express no desire to work 79–81, 87–93, 96

freeters 13, 49, 76–8, 84
full-time career jobs 84

Genda, Yuji 11, 13, 4–9, 59, 76–7, 80, 93, 96, 206–7
GMM (Generalized Method of Moments) 154, 169

Gross National Income 153

Hara, Junsuke 30, 50, 128
Health and Differentials 210
Higuchi, Yoshio 49, 51, 59
household 10–13, 15, 44, 46–77, 89, 91–4, 96, 117, 131, 133–5, 142, 153–62, 167–71, 173–5, 177–80, 206, 209–10, 217–18, 220–3
  changes in structure 206
  income 91–3, 133–5, 142, 217
  saving rate 153–4
  type 50–3, 55, 56, 60, 63, 65, 70, 72, 161

illness or injury 82
individual accounting 14, 181–3, 199–200, 212–13
  social security accounting 182
inequality/inequalities
  between generations 181
  consciousness 12, 16–20, 36–8, 204–5
  income 11–12, 48–9, 57–8, 60, 62–3, 65, 73, 127, 217
  of opportunity 18–19, 21, 25–6, 36, 38, 40, 42–5, 152, 179, 212, 216, 220
  of outcome 152, 179, 211–12
inheritance tax 43, 155–6, 221
inheriting wealth 154, 167, 175
intergenerational transference of assets 211
Ishida, Hiroshi 3–4, 9, 11, 14, 20, 39, 111–12, 125, 128–9, 210–11, 219
Ishikawa, Tsuneo 155, 220
Iwata, Masami 51, 72, 217

Japanese demographic change 5
Japanese pension reform 185
jobseekers 78–82, 84–96
justice 8, 35, 48

Kariya, Takehiko 2, 13, 98, 102, 119, 208–9, 218

life expectancy 39, 71, 127, 184–7, 193–4, 219, 222–3
  lengthening of 193
lost decade 76
low birthrate/aging society 1, 74, 200, 204, 217 *see also* aging population, aging society, and birthrate
Luhmann, Niklas 45

mass education society 100, 108–9, 114–16, 209
Matsuura, Katsumi 3, 14, 151, 153, 155, 160–1, 180, 211–12, 220–3
mechanism of policy failures 37
medical information 130–1, 133–4, 142–7, 149
meritocracy 14, 22, 100–2, 109–10, 122, 124
middle-aged NEETs 96–7
middle class 1, 20, 30, 46, 92, 204
Miyazato, Naomi 14–15, 181, 195, 212–13, 223
Murakami, Yasusuke 1, 46

NEETs 13, 49, 76–7, 79, 80–2, 84–7, 89–97, 206–7

net financial assets 151, 153–5, 157, 159, 161–2, 167, 169–70, 174–5, 178–9, 220, 222
nonemployed 77–81, 87–95
non-jobseekers 78–82, 85, 87–96
non-labor 79–80

Ohtake, Fumio 3–4, 47–9, 57–8
opportunity cost 87
opportunity inequality 9, 18, 28–9, 36, 38–9, 41, 156, 205, 216
outcome inequality 9, 156

parent-child bond 27
parent-child continuity 14, 30, 36, 42, 204–5
participatory ability of the individual 39
pension program *see* pension system
pension system 3, 14, 152–5, 157–8, 160, 163, 168, 178–91, 184, 195–6, 200–1, 212, 222
  and cohorts 157
physical ability 131
physical discomfort 131, 134–6, 138–40, 142, 144–9
population decline 11
postwar-type family 20, 32
preventive health measures 125
principle for distribution 74

qualitative change 5–6, 10
quality of life 6, 125, 149–50, 211
quantitative change 6, 10, 12

redistribution 27–8, 41, 180
risk-sharing 181, 183, 199–200, 212

Satō, Toshiki 2, 7, 12, 16, 19, 21, 26, 29, 40, 42, 47–8, 128, 204–5, 214, 216, 220
Seiyama, Kazuo 2, 4, 9, 20, 30, 50, 128
self-reported health 128–9, 132, 134–5, 140–3, 146–7, 219–20
self-responsibility 15, 23–5, 36, 38
Shirahase, Sawako 1, 4, 9, 29, 46, 49–52, 56, 58, 60, 160, 203–4, 218
simulation analysis 195–6, 199–200, 202, 212, 223
single-mother households 51
single-person households 12, 15, 51–3, 55–6, 60, 62–3, 65–9, 74, 168, 178
social inequality of health 128
social minorities 74
spoiled children 92
standard model 74–5, 198
sub-self 27–30, 32, 36–7, 40, 205

Tachibanaki, Toshiaki 2, 47, 155
Takeuchi, Yo 40, 112, 115, 204
tax-and-spend model 152
total fertility rate 3, 46, 52

unemployed 2, 13, 15, 49, 77, 79–81, 88, 92–3, 95–6, 129, 207

unemployment 1, 2, 6, 10, 14, 46–7, 49, 55, 59, 69, 76, 80–1, 90, 96, 153–4, 182, 212, 217, 220
rate 80, 153–4
unfairness 2, 7–9, 12, 26, 32, 47–8, 114, 206, 216

vicious circle of disadvantage breeding disadvantage 94
visits to a doctor's office 131, 136, 142, 148

widening inequality 12, 16–19, 21, 37, 124
work experience 82, 89–91
working class 30, 130, 132, 138, 140–1, 143, 148